D0564018

AFTER FURTHER REVIEW

My Life Including the Infamous,
Controversial, and Unforgettable
Calls That Changed the NFL

Mike Pereira with Rick Jaffe

Copyright © 2016 by Mike Pereira and Rick Jaffe

No part of this publication may be reproduced, stored in a retrieval system, or transmitted in any form by any means, electronic, mechanical, photo-copying, or otherwise, without the prior written permission of the publisher, Triumph Books LLC, 814 North Franklin Street, Chicago, Illinois 60610.

Names: Pereira, Mike, 1950- author.
Title: After further review : my life including the infamous, controversial, and unforgettable calls that changed the NFL / Mike Pereira with Rick Jaffe.
Description: Chicago, Illinois : Triumph Books, 2016.
Identifiers: LCCN 2016011620 | ISBN 9781629371610 (hardback)
Subjects: LCSH: Pereira, Mike, 1950- | Football referees—United States—Biography. | National Football League. | Football—Rules. | Football—Officiating—United States. | BISAC: SPORTS & RECREATION / Football. | BIOGRAPHY & AUTOBIOGRAPHY / Sports.
Classification: LCC GV939.P46 A3 2016 | DDC 796.332092 [B] —dc23 LC record available at https://lccn.loc.gov/2016011620

This book is available in quantity at special discounts for your group or organization. For further information, contact:

Triumph Books LLC
814 North Franklin Street
Chicago, Illinois 60610
(312) 337–0747
www.triumphbooks.com

Printed in U.S.A.
ISBN: 978-1-62937-161-0
Design by Amy Carter
Page production by Meghan Grammer
Photos courtesy of Mike Pereira unless otherwise indicated.

*To my sister, Linda, for her strength and courage
as she cared for Mom, Dad, and her husband,
Mark, in their last days and months on this earth.
My greatest gift is having her as my sister.*

CONTENTS

Foreword *by Joe Buck and Troy Aikman*   vii

1 The Value of a Quarter   1

2 The Scare of My Life   17

3 This College Experience Was an Education   35

4 The Process of Reaching the Pinnacle   51

5 Leaving the Field for Greener Pastures   71

6 Breaking It Down: Finances and the CBA   91

7 As Good as It Gets...or Is It?   103

8 The Blame Game   123

9 Plays That Changed NFL History   151

10 Finally, "Instant" Gratification   179

11 The Golden Rules...and How to Change Them   191

12 A New Sheriff—and New Rules—in Town   197

13 The NFL's Cast of Characters   233

14 The Lockouts and Impact of 9/11   255

15 Pressures of the NFL and Why I Almost Left...Twice   273

16 The Move to TV: Lights, Camera, Satisfaction   283

17 The Future of Officiating   297

18 The Brotherhood and the Battle with My Old Nemesis   313

FOREWORD

JOE BUCK: FOR TROY AND ME, AND THE OTHER BROADCASTERS and producers with whom we work, having Mike at FOX has been a great security blanket. We do games with a lot of odd calls, a lot of opinions, a lot of stress, and a lot of scrutiny. To know that he's in our back pocket—and in the biggest games, in our booth—is a great feeling.

Because the rules are so difficult to grasp, before Mike came on board, people kind of took what we said and ran with it. In the end, it really wasn't 100 percent correct. That's not a good feeling. And it's not just the rules that confuse everybody. It's a lot of subjective things, and when Mike is in the booth to help guide Troy and me, it gives us the authority and the confidence to go out and then stick our chin out on the national broadcast with a big audience and say it's a good call.

But having Mike on our team is beyond a security blanket, really; it's a weapon. The other networks have tried to find it, but the others can't bring what Mike does—which is the knowledge, having been an official in the NFL and having run the officiating program for 12 years. The knowledge combined with the personality, and the ability to deliver the information in a digestible way—that's a skill.

Troy Aikman: Joe's right; that's an amazing skill. When Mike joined FOX we didn't know exactly how things would turn out, but we knew he had the knowledge and a personality.

I guess you could say that FOX and [FOX executive] David Hill, in particular, along with Mike, became pioneers in 2010 because nobody really had rules analysts back then. Now, almost every sport has a guy like Mike. Of course, nobody's as good as our guy.

Mike started something that has become part of the fabric of the game and I think it will be forever now. But just having that expertise and knowing the rules, as we've found out from the other guys who do the same role, doesn't necessarily translate to being good on television. That's why Mike's unique. He's got great credibility to go along with a great style. He's got the ability to take something complicated and, in 20 seconds, make people understand it.

Buck: Troy's got a good point. I've been surprised at the audience's thirst for this kind of information. But what I love most about Mike is that he's got the skill to stand there, removed from the game, and put it all together in his mind and deliver it succinctly into the camera, which is really hard to do.

More importantly, Mike is not scared to say that somebody made the wrong call. That's what the other networks don't have. We have the guy.

Aikman: It's a great asset for us, and I speak for Joe and everyone else at FOX who does this job in the booth. A lot of times you feel exposed and a bit naked up there when something like that happens in a game. To have Mike there to succinctly explain it and get it right is of great comfort. But the biggest beneficiary of all this has been the viewer at home.

—Joe Buck and Troy Aikman

1　THE VALUE OF A QUARTER

"YOU'RE NOT WORTH THE QUARTER IT TAKES TO BUY A COKE."

Remember those words, folks. Because while it might sound like the lyrics to a country song, that phrase became the driving, motivational force in my life and just might be the key reason for many of the successes I've had. However, you might be a little surprised to find out that the source of those words came from a most unlikely place—my dad.

Before you judge, you have to know a little about my dad, one Amaro Louis (Al) Pereira.

I doubt that there has ever been a father that has had more influence on a son than my dad. Why? Maybe it was because he was never afforded the opportunities that he was able to provide me with when I was growing up. He came to America on a boat from the Azores Islands off the coast of Portugal at the age of two. He grew up on a real dairy farm, where he would milk cows both in the morning before school and in the evening when he got home.

But my dad was quite an athlete, too. He could really play,

but because of his daily chores, he never really had time to pursue playing high school sports.

He and his family went through the Great Depression, and they lost everything. I mean everything. All they ended up with was their car, their belongings, and $10,000 in debt. It was interesting in those days; my dad's father had to work off all the debt. There was no way this immigrant from Portugal was going to declare bankruptcy, so he learned valuable lessons from his father when he was young.

I truly believe that he wanted to give me the chances that he'd never had. But my dad did get to go away to college, to California Polytechnic State University in San Luis Obispo, better known as Cal Poly SLO. There, he played baseball, and I remember people saying he was a very good player. He continued playing baseball and softball afterward in Stockton, California. That's where I grew up as a child, and I recall watching his every move as a third baseman in fast-pitch softball. To this day, he might have been the biggest jock I've ever seen.

Not only was he a big fan of mine, he was a big fan of just about anything to do with sports. We always used to laugh and say if there wasn't a baseball game, a basketball game, or a football game to watch, my dad would find out where the nearest tiddlywinks match was just so he could watch somebody playing something. I'm joking, but it gives you an idea of how big a sports fan he was.

— —

HE RELISHED WATCHING ME GET INTO SPORTS, BUT MY ENTRY INTO the sports world was not all that spectacular. Ironically, my athletic career had nothing to do with football, though I did give it a shot.

As a high school sophomore, I was a lanky 140 pounds—and that was with weights in both hands. *Lanky* was one of those unflattering words they used back in the '70s for *tall* and *skinny*. The first day of football tryouts, some kid who was about 30 pounds heavier than I was gave me a vicious shot—at least in my mind it was vicious—to the hip. I think I was trying out as a wide receiver, and after catching a pass, the hit was one of those bone-crushing kind of hits that you see in those car commercials where they use crash dummies. I was one and done, as in one day and I'm finished with football and ready to move on.

Hello, basketball.

The next day I was in the gym shooting free throws. While I never played football, which makes where I ended up rather amazing, I did play basketball and baseball, and that piqued much of my dad's interest in me. He was always in the stands when I played, whether it was in Little League in the Hoover Tyler Youth Baseball program in Stockton or my games at Amos Alonzo Stagg High School.

Then in 1968, it was off to college at the University of Santa Clara. Believe it or not, I actually received a scholarship to play both basketball and baseball there. I'm still not sure what my dad had to do with it exactly, but I suspect it was something, because the basketball coach, Dick Garibaldi, and he were good friends. Of course, it could have been that Santa Clara sent a football coach, Bill McPherson, to scout me to play *baseball*.

Or maybe it was really Dusty Baker who was responsible

for me getting that scholarship. Yes, *that* Dusty Baker, the very successful 19-year major leaguer and 20-year manager Dusty Baker who is now managing the Washington Nationals.

Baker was a great high school baseball player at Del Campo High School in Sacramento and he was highly recruited by a lot of schools, including Santa Clara. Baker even signed a letter of intent to attend Santa Clara on a full scholarship. Fortunately for me, Baker also happened to be drafted by the Atlanta Braves and he eventually chose professional baseball over college.

As the saying goes…when one door closes, another one opens. Who cares if it was the back door I was walking through now that Santa Clara had one last scholarship available? I think they divided up Baker's scholarship eight ways and I got one-eighth. All I cared about was that I was in.

I took a shot at basketball first. But I was still a runt, the skinniest guy on the team, and I quickly saw that my future in basketball was going to be very limited. Let me put it in perspective for you: Larry Bird and Magic Johnson would not have been threatened by my basketball prowess. At the time, Santa Clara had a pretty good freshman team. We had a 15-man team, and my toughest job each game was finding where the 15th chair was going to be located on the floor because that's where I'd be sitting.

That was a pretty good indication that my future was not in basketball, either. I was such a perceptive young man. So I turned to baseball and actually did pretty well. So much so that I thought I might have a shot at a career in professional baseball.

— —

BEFORE I CONTINUE, I MUST TELL YOU THE "QUARTER STORY."

In any relationship between a father and son, certain things are said or done that shape you as an individual. Before going to Santa Clara, I played American Legion baseball. I was 15 years old and played for the Karl Ross team in Stockton. I remember one game against a team from Lodi, California, like it was yesterday.

Picture this: Lawrence Stadium in Lodi, in June, just the beginning of summer. Yet it was unbelievably hot: 104 degrees in the shade. It was the kind of hot that would have burned the back of your legs when they hit the leather seats in your car.

The heat was so stifling, you could barely breathe when you walked, let alone run. In fact, I think the devil actually vacations in Lodi during the summer, but I digress. I was a first baseman at the time, and I probably had one of my worst games ever that day: I went 0-for 4 and made two errors, and we lost.

I was dehydrated, parched, and simply wiped out at the end of the game; it was a real day to forget. Afterward, I remember walking up to my dad and telling him I was really thirsty. I asked if he would buy me a Coke. He looked at me and, without hesitation, said those fateful words: "You're not worth the quarter it takes to buy a Coke."

That's what my father, my No. 1 fan, said to me. *"You're not worth the quarter it takes to buy a Coke."*

Suddenly, a day to forget became one I'd always remember. I don't think he really understood how much that hurt me. My mother, Lydia, who was also there, knew. She wanted to whack him, because she could see the look on my face and how much it stung. Make no mistake, the words cut through me like a sharp knife slides through butter.

Those words truly would become a big part of what defined my life.

They made me want to be good at something—to be great at something, to stand out at something—just to prove my dad wrong. I was going to show him that I was worth more than a quarter it took to buy a Coke. I didn't know what it was going to be at the time, but I knew I needed to find it. So I concentrated on baseball.

But I didn't get off to such a great start my freshman year at Santa Clara. I was a weak-hitting first baseman, with a nickname of Chicks.

Why Chicks? Because my teammates said I had bird legs. I used to tell them that my legs were built for speed, not strength. My batting average was around .200 my first season, not something Hall of Fame careers are built on. But Santa Clara would send guys to play summer baseball in semipro leagues and I got sent to Springfield, Oregon, in the summer of 1969. I was assigned to play for the Pitchford Mac Bulldogs. Thank heavens Eugene was close by, because the big hangout in Springfield might have been the Dairy Queen.

Jim Dietz was the coach of the Bulldogs and also coached the Oregon JV team. Dietz would go on to become a very successful head coach at San Diego State from 1972 to 2002.

Coach Dietz wasn't one of those "players' coaches" you hear so much about today. In fact, I can't recall any player that actually liked him. He was the kind of coach that would check our garbage cans to make sure he didn't find any beer containers.

I know we were underage, but it was summertime, for gosh

sakes. For all I know, the beer might have made me a better hitter. I can tell you that it couldn't have hurt, because I didn't seem to be much better at summer baseball.

The sad part is, I could run, I could bunt, I could throw, and I could chase down pop-ups like you wouldn't believe. But a left-handed hitter who can't hit? That's like saying you have a 280-pound fullback who can't score from the 1-yard line. And if you're not a pitcher, you don't need to be a Rhodes Scholar to know that not being able to hit is not good.

Then came the miracle. I went back to Santa Clara and all of a sudden, I started to develop. I was 19, and I don't know why, but I gained weight. I didn't lift weights, mind you, but there was a proposal at one point for me to be part of a weight program.

One day, a guy from Lodi came by to talk to my dad and told him that I had great natural ability and he wanted to work me out and give me Dianabol. That's right; he said "great natural ability." Was he at the right address?

His name was Lee Allerdice and he was a fitness instructor at the YMCA. And I didn't know it at the time, but I learned later that Dianabol was a steroid. My dad told Allerdice no dice, and that was a good thing because I certainly had no desire to take steroids or get involved with a weight regimen.

When you've got a body like Adonis, why bother? In all seriousness, I'm not sure why I started putting the pounds on and gaining strength, but I did.

In my sophomore year at Santa Clara, they moved me to center field because our center fielder was slow. But on the flip side, he could hit the ball a mile and he was also a left-handed hitter. His name was Bruce Bochte, and he ended up playing for 12 years in the majors with four teams—the Angels, Indians, Mariners, and A's.

So with that switch, I ended up playing center field the rest of my career, and I think I played pretty decently. My teammates played pretty well, too. In 1970 we went down to the University of Southern California to play in the District 8 finals. We were playing powerhouse USC in a best-of-three showdown for the right to go to Omaha and the College World Series. However, we got blown out in the first two games, and that was it.

The very next season, we ended up playing USC again in the District 8 finals. We actually won the first game, but then USC beat us like a drum in the final two. You know, drums were always a staple of those great Southern California marching bands.

After we lost to USC the first time during my sophomore year, a guy by the name of Paul Deese, who was the summer coach of the Anchorage Glacier Pilots, came up to me and offered me an opportunity to play in Alaska. I bet you didn't even know they played baseball in Alaska. Why in God's name would they?

Somebody up there must have thought it was a good idea, because they've been playing baseball there since the 19th century.

But I knew guys from Santa Clara who had gone there, and when I told them I had gotten an offer, they told me I'd be nuts if I didn't go. I had been up there before because we had a great road trip to Alaska when I played for the Pitchford Mac Bulldogs.

The Bulldogs played four games in Fairbanks against a team called the Gold Panners and four games against the Glacier Pilots. I still remember a funny thing that happened when we played Anchorage.

The catcher for the Pilots was a guy by the name of Jim Caviglia. He also played for Santa Clara and was from Stockton as well. I've already spoken about my prowess in the batter's box, so you can only imagine what's coming next.

I was facing off against Craig Swan, who ended up having a 12-year major-league career with the New York Mets and California Angels. He was a great pitcher who had a fastball that clocked in around 95 miles per hour. That was faster than most of the cars in Anchorage.

So I was choking up on the bat and trying to concentrate because I already knew I had no chance in hell of getting a hit. Right before each pitch, Caviglia would flash the signals to Swan and then lean in and whisper to me, "fastball" or "curveball." He literally called every pitch for me the entire game. I knew what was coming but still never touched the ball. In fact, I'm pretty sure I was Oh-for-Alaska on that trip.

While that visit was disastrous, I eventually played well in Alaska, enjoying my four seasons up there (1970–73). A few of you might drop this book after reading the next paragraph, but it's absolutely true.

I was one of the first players inducted into the Anchorage Glacier Pilots Hall of Fame. And, I still hold five records (most career walks, most career games played, most career hits, most career runs scored, most career stolen bases) and I'm second in another category (most career at-bats).

In reality, it probably had less to do with my ability and more to do with my longevity. Everybody who played up there was so good that they usually signed a professional contract after one year—or two at the most.

Longevity is usually a good thing in just about any other thing in life, just not so much for playing baseball in Anchorage. And even though I thought I had a shot at doing something at which I could be great, I soon realized that nothing great was going to happen for me in baseball.

No, baseball would not be the answer for how I was going to prove my dad wrong.

So how did I get interested in officiating? Let's go back to my junior year at Santa Clara. Ready for the great epiphany? It had to do with two things—money and beer—and while I'm not saying those things were the only reasons, let's just say they were motivating factors at the time.

My family wasn't hurting for money, but they certainly weren't going to give me any dough to buy beer. My buddies would go out, yet I didn't have any money to join the party.

But one day in 1971, Tommy Ichishita, who was a high school football official, told me that I could officiate Pop Warner football games in East Palo Alto on Sundays. He assigned officials for games and told me that I would get three games at $10 apiece for a grand total of $30 in cold, hard cash. Done and done. That would certainly be more than enough beer money for the week.

I can't lie; I was intrigued, and not just because of the beer money. It's because the guy who told me I wasn't worth the quarter it took to buy a Coke was also an official. I thought maybe I could beat him at his own game.

Remember, I told you that my dad always came to my games, watching every depressing swing of the bat and every awful free-throw attempt. Well, in return, I used to go watch him officiate during the football season. It wasn't like I was very busy during that time of year. I learned the game of football without really playing the sport to any degree.

I learned it through the eyes of an official. I learned it through the eyes of my father.

He was good, really good. He officiated for 34 years and made it to major college football in a league that was called the Pacific Coast Athletic Association (PCAA). At the time, it included schools such as San Jose State, Fresno State, Long Beach State, and the University of Pacific to name a few. He also got a sniff of officiating in the Pac-8 conference, but he only got to work some scrimmages and never actually made it. He had a good career and worked a couple bowl games.

So I knew when Ichishita asked me to officiate those games in East Palo Alto at Ravenswood High School, it didn't bother me that it was in a very tough neighborhood; I was all-in. And even though I never had any desire to follow in my dad's footsteps, I ended up doing just that.

I remember putting on my uniform to go to work in my first Pop Warner game and looking in the mirror. I thought I looked ridiculous. Before I left, I studied the rules and learned the basic concepts of the game and of officiating. However, these were just 10- to 12-year-olds playing in these games. I didn't think you had to be a master of where to spot the football after a penalty. I thought I would learn the basics to get by, and for $30, why not?

That was until I stepped onto the field for the first time, because as I did, a sudden feeling swept over me.

I had finally found it. I found the thing I'd been looking for, the thing that I felt I could be great at, the thing that could help me overcome the stigma that I wasn't worth a quarter it took to buy a Coke.

That uniform suddenly didn't feel so ridiculous. If fact, it felt like I was wearing a tuxedo and I had just met the love of my life. I had never felt that way before and I was ready to drop to a knee and propose. I had found my passion.

Baseball didn't do it for me any longer. Even getting a hit with the bases loaded never gave me the feeling I got while officiating. I knew, at that very moment, that I had found something that was going to be with me for the rest of my life. So every Sunday for that season, I trotted out there for my three games and my $30. I still had beer to buy.

But if there was any doubt of what I was feeling, it crystallized the next year when I signed up to officiate with the Fermar High School Officiating Association in San Jose. I started working freshman and JV games and I volunteered to work games where they had only three officials because, in the early '70s, there wasn't enough money to have four officials. They would ask for unpaid volunteers so they could at least have a full crew.

While this started over the money, I no longer cared about getting paid. I would have worked games for free at that point. I continued doing it because it gave me such a thrill. And while I quickly got hooked on officiating, obviously, I still had school to deal with at Santa Clara as well as going up to play summer baseball in Alaska.

I loved the fans in Alaska and I loved being there. After my senior year in 1972, I decided I wasn't going to sign the free-agent professional contract that was offered to me, because I knew I wasn't going to make it despite my record-breaking, Hall of Fame career in Anchorage. But I did want to go back there to play one more season of semipro ball with the Glacier Pilots.

I played that season and then decided to stay and become the director of sales and promotions for the Pilots. I worked there through the winter, and then in June 1973, I returned home to marry my girlfriend of three years, Carin, who I had met during my junior year at Santa Clara.

I loved the outdoors and I loved to fish. Alaska fit my lifestyle and I wanted to go back as soon as possible. I had already convinced Carin to move to Alaska with me, so just one day after we got married, we left for Anchorage. I know, quite the romantic. But hey, tell me who wouldn't want to honeymoon in Alaska?

Never mind, don't tell me; honeymooning and living there are two different things.

Carin was from Los Gatos, where the weather is mild 365 days a year. She was actually a pretty good sport about it that first year. She even came to watch me officiate high school football games in the freezer-like temperatures in August and September. Yes, I continued my passion with officiating in Alaska. But when you're talking about living in Alaska, where the weather is mild about 65 days a year, you don't really talk in terms of years, but rather, in winters.

Carin made it through that first winter, but there would not be a second. We came home to her parents' house in Los Gatos at Christmas, and I remember we were lying in bed with the windows open and it was 63 degrees. The temperature in Anchorage at the time: 3 degrees—and that didn't include the wind chill.

As we were lying there, Carin looked at me and shook her head no. Being in bed, it's not the kind of no that those of you with dirty minds are thinking about. It was much worse. She shook her head and said she wasn't going back—to Alaska.

I pleaded that she had to go back because we had jobs; we had an apartment and a car that we had left at the airport. But she wanted no part of it. And she was true to her word. I went back to pack up the apartment, to give notice for both our jobs, and to sell the car, among other things, before moving back to California.

It wasn't the end of my association with Alaska and the baseball program, because after my baseball career, I went back up there for a couple summers and did the play-by-play on the team's radio station. Anchorage had a 50,000-watt station, KYAK, that broadcasted the Glacier Pilots' games, and they hired me. I use the word "hired" in the loosest sense of the word, because as I think back now, I'm not really sure I got paid. But people that know me know I like to talk. So I had a blast for a couple summers, being in Anchorage…and talking.

Hmmm, that was my first taste of being in the media. Who knew that 35 years later I'd end up coming full circle with FOX?

However, before I could go down that road, I'd have to complete the circle of life. And that meant that I would eventually have to face the inevitable. Because what turned out to be even harsher than the Alaskan winters was the reality that I'd be back in California without any real plan of what next to do with my life, other than cling to my obsession with officiating.

2   THE SCARE OF MY LIFE

My wife, Carin, dragged me back to California. I wasn't kicking and screaming, but I was close, still not knowing exactly what I was going to do when I got back. I had a degree in finance, but I already knew that degree wasn't going to do me any favors because, as I've mentioned, I already had a monster crush on officiating. However, officiating wasn't going to pay the bills, either.

Carin started working at a travel agency specializing in trips to Hawaii, while I went back to Santa Clara and did some work in the athletic department. I did a bit of marketing, but more importantly, I became an assistant baseball coach, one of Sal Taormina's coaches. Sal's nickname was The Hog, because, well, he kind of looked like one. But he was a guy who was universally loved. He was a former pro who played for the San Francisco Seals in the old Pacific Coast League. And I was as happy as a pig in slop, coaching for the Hog.

I thought it might be interesting to see if I wanted to get

involved with coaching, but my real motivation and excitement remained in officiating. Remember, my father was an official and a catalyst for me wanting to be one, too.

And that comment he made in Lodi about the quarter would prove to be one of the most pivotal moments in my life. Ever since that day, I've never been able to look at George Washington quite the same way.

That moment certainly shaped my life, but I was about to face another life-altering juncture that would give the quarter a run for its money.

I was coaching at Santa Clara early in 1975, having the time of my life, working with kids who were barely younger than I was. I really didn't have a care in the world, but that quickly changed.

I was 25 years old and we were playing in a tournament at the University of California, Riverside. Something started happening to my body, and it wasn't good. I didn't feel that bad overall, but I had an incredible amount of pain and sensitivity in my nipples. Just a T-shirt rubbing against them hurt like hell. I had no idea what was happening to me.

That night, in my dorm room on UC Riverside's campus, I was in bed and scratching my testicles. Okay—before you say anything, I was scratching and nothing else. Give me a break; it's what guys do. While scratching, though, I felt a lump, a firm spot. It was not that big, but big enough to really scare me— the kind of scared where you have trouble breathing. I just sat there in bed, staring at nothing, thinking the worst possible things. I didn't have the courage to call Carin or my parents at that point. I had never felt more alone in my life.

So when the tournament ended, I went back home to Los Gatos, which is where Carin and I lived in her grandmother's house. Once I told Carin, who was equally as shocked, we both felt that I shouldn't wait any longer, so I decided to get it checked out the next morning. I was fearful, but my fortitude overcame the fear and got me to go to the doctor.

I made an appointment with a local internist, Dr. Jacob Belogorsky, who was the first doctor I would see. I told him that my nipples were sore and I had a lump on my testicle. His response? "I can't help you." No lie, that's what he said. The man's a doctor and he tells me he can't help me? But the not-so-good doctor wasn't finished. He explained to me that I likely had testicular cancer and it was beyond his area of expertise. Belogorsky then told me that I needed to go to O'Connor Hospital in San Jose.

When I walked out of there, you can imagine what I was feeling. I quickly went from scared to petrified. As if it couldn't get any worse, later that evening I walked out to the mailbox at our house. Someone from Dr. Belogorsky's office had brought a bill from the appointment that very afternoon and stuck it in my mailbox.

I opened it as I was walking back into the house, and it was almost as if the bill inside the envelope suddenly came to life and began speaking to me: "Don't take this too hard, Mike, but the doctor felt like you might not be around much longer and since we already know that you don't have any insurance, we just thought if you had any money…"

Thanks for the pick-me-up, Doc.

I got up the next day and made an appointment to go to

O'Connor Hospital. Two days later, I went there and explained the same thing to those doctors. I told them the exact same thing I had said to Belogorsky.

Unfortunately, they told me the very same thing Belogorsky did. They said it was probably testicular cancer, but it was beyond their capabilities to treat me. Folks, we're talking about a hospital, one of San Jose's main hospitals.

— —

IF YOU THOUGHT I WAS SCARED AFTER MY VISIT WITH BELOGORSKY, I now had to deal with shocked, startled, and stunned. I didn't know where to turn. But the doctors at O'Connor did tell me if it was in any way possible, I should try and get to Stanford Medical Center. That's great—I was a guy with testicular cancer and no insurance. I'm sure I was just the guy that Stanford's doctors were looking to treat. It didn't seem fair to me, at that young age, that nobody was willing to help me. I didn't think about this until afterward, but my guess is that neither of the first two places I went wanted to help me because I didn't have insurance.

I felt like I was dying.

I was devastated, to say the least. So was my dad. Because after I began officiating, we had developed a special kind of kinship. Obviously, my family was frightened as well. Not knowing where to go or what was going to happen next, I got a call from my dad a day later. He told me that I was going to Stanford. I could barely speak. I was able to get out one word: "What?"

My dad said it had been arranged for me to go to Stanford

Medical Center to get checked out. He said he was going to drive with me and that we were going to meet with the doctors in the Urology Department. I managed to get out a few more words as I asked my father who this was "arranged by."

When he said "Dean," I was somewhat surprised. Dean Wendt was my dad's boss at Eagal Leasing, a place that leased cars and trucks, and he had a lot of connections. Golfing legend Johnny Miller was one of his friends, and he also happened to be one of his partners at the Ford dealership in Stockton. Dean had arranged for me to go to Stanford Medical Center.

As you'll soon find out, Dean Wendt became the second-most-influential man in my life. In fact, he would save my life... in more ways than one.

In early April 1975, my dad and I made the journey to Stanford and sat down with the doctors in the Urology Department. I basically told them the same story I told Belogorsky and the doctors at O'Connor Hospital. Instead of saying, "We can't help you," the doctors at Stanford said the one word that would suddenly, drastically change my outlook and attitude on life.

"Welcome," they said.

I thought they were kidding at first, but after being checked out, the doctors told me they were going to get that tumor out of me. They described the process, telling me they were going to take the testicle out and test the tubing around it. It would then be a couple of weeks to see if the cancer had spread and if so, by how much. That's when we'd know whether the news would be good, bad, or in the middle. What in the world is the middle? I'll get to that. But the surgery would take place in the next two days, and then we'd go from there.

Now I had hope. We found this wonderful hospital that was willing to take me in, knowing I didn't have insurance—willing to attack this thing I had inside me. Two days later I was on the operating table and the testicle was out. To say it hurt would be an embarrassment to the word *pain*. It was excruciating. They pulled my muscles out of a big incision in my groin and then pulled them apart to pull the testicle out, up through the incision. I think it's done differently these days. At least I hope to God it is.

Ironically, it wasn't the first time I had dealt with testicles being removed. My mother's parents were Basque and they emigrated to the United States from the Pyrenees. Her father was a sheepherder and he first landed in Bakersfield, California. My mom's brother, Peter, followed in the family tradition and raised sheep as well. His flocks were located in the Altamont Hills outside Tracy, California.

— —

I HAVE TO TELL YOU A QUICK ASIDE ABOUT MY UNCLE PETER. I WAS named after him.

Peter Michael Pereira. That's my given name.

So why do I go by my middle name? My mother's mom and dad were killed in an auto accident three years before I was born. My Uncle Peter had moved in with my family, and then I showed up in 1950.

According to my dad, almost immediately everyone started calling my uncle Big Peter. You can just imagine what they started calling me. Yep, I was Little Peter.

At age two, my father made a great decision. The older I got, my old man realized it could be a real problem for me to go by Little Peter. That's when I became Michael, forevermore.

Let's go back to the silence, or rather, the screaming of the lambs.

Well, the lambs had to be castrated. And my dad recruited me at 16 years old to join his buddies to help perform the duties. Each lamb had to have its testicles removed, followed by having their tails cut off. Then tar was used to stop the bleeding on the tail, and finally the lambs were branded. I was the guy with the tar. There was nothing worse than cold winter mornings castrating lambs.

That was until I had my testicle removed. It was no fun for the lambs…and it was definitely no fun for me.

— —

THE WAIT AFTER SURGERY BEGAN, AND I REMEMBER THE DOCTORS explaining to me what my three options were. I'm no doctor, but I recall they said that if what I had was the worst kind of cancer then it would be really bad for me. You think?

And here's where the "middle" comes in. Option No. 2 was a bit more positive—a three-year wait before we'd actually know for sure if I would be cancer-free.

Option No. 3 would be the good kind. That's the one that everyone hopes for at that point, the kind where I would be all right and be able to go on with my life immediately.

I have to tell you, the two weeks of waiting were torture. I'm pretty sure this is where the expression "Those two weeks felt like two years" comes from. At least I think it came from that moment. Seriously, though, I didn't know whether I was going to live or die, and it was a very strange feeling.

It was so strange, in fact, that while I was definitely scared, I also had the feeling that I really didn't care one way or the other. By that, I mean I just wanted the process to be over.

D-day finally arrived. The two weeks were up, and Carin and my family joined me on the trip back to Stanford. I was nervous, but I wasn't freaked-out-of-my-mind nervous. I sat down with these wonderful doctors, who informed me that I had the "middle" kind—which meant if I could survive three years without a recurrence, the odds of me getting cancer again would be the same as anybody else who had never had cancer before.

The doctors praised me for having the courage to come and get it checked out right away because they didn't see any spreading. It was no thanks to Belogorsky or O'Connor Hospital. I'm not bitter; I'm just saying.

The tubes they removed around the testicles showed that the lymph nodes were clear and that my chances were good. But they also told me I needed to do radiation. Back in those days, that was the preferred form of treatment. I took 23 radiation hits to the gut four to five times a week over a five-week span.

They weren't good, but they weren't that bad either, compared to what some others were going through in that hospital. Throughout the whole process, the thing I found most interesting was the way people treated me when I went back to coaching baseball.

The feeling I got was really weird, almost in a demeaning kind of way.

The people who knew I had testicular cancer didn't really

know what to say to me. I might have had a successful surgery, but I still had a "disease." That was the disease of making people feel uncomfortable around me. The forlorn look on their faces said it all. I didn't need to hear the obligatory, "Oh, we feel so sorry for you. Are you okay?" platitudes.

I just wanted to be treated like a normal human being, but like I said, that was nothing compared to what I experienced when I returned to Stanford for the treatments. I'd see these little kids getting their radiation treatments. It was so disturbing...and so sad.

During my recovery, while I was going through the radiation treatments, my dad's boss, Saint Dean—the guy who got me into Stanford Medical Center, the guy who helped save my life—was up to his old ways again doing more good deeds. He, along with others, would have food sent to our house almost on a nightly basis to make sure we were eating. He would call a restaurant in Los Gatos and then have the food delivered to our house. Unbelievable.

But he wasn't finished yet. Unbeknownst to me, the man put together a group of people who raised money to help pay for my medical bills. And all my dad's buddies got involved, too, to offset what I was going to have to pay Stanford for my surgery and treatment.

I'll never forget that. I'll also never forget when I was finally well enough to play golf again. I got a call from my dad telling me to come to the Stockton Golf and Country Club.

As I was driving there, thoughts were racing through my head like it was the Daytona 500. I was trying to figure out what was in store for me when I got there.

I couldn't have guessed what happened next, but it blew me away. I met with all the people that contributed the money to pay my bills. To have people take it upon themselves to help pay my medical bills left the guy who liked to talk...speechless.

It was incredible. Without question, it was the most emotional day I had ever experienced in my life. And it's quite possible that I may never again feel the kind emotion I felt on that day.

As we were finishing up lunch, I was looking forward to getting back out on the course that I played as a kid growing up. What could be better than that?

You're about to find out.

As we walked up to the first tee, I got out my driver and I noticed something strange on the tee box. I was about to tee it up when I saw something new had been added.

Normally there were two sets of tees—the men's tees, which were farther back and white, and the women's tees, which were red.

But there they were, new gold tees, placed right in between the two. I had never seen them before.

I remember turning around to the group and asking them what the story was with the gold tees. They all just stood there laughing. They told me that the gold tees were for me because after my surgery where I lost a testicle, they weren't sure if I was a man or a woman, so they put the gold tees halfway in between. And they had put them on every hole.

How cool was that? I laughed during the entire 18 holes. I was back to normal for the moment. But if it wasn't for Dean Wendt, I probably wouldn't be here telling you this story. I will always be indebted to him.

Just after I finished my treatments, I had this overwhelming urge to escape. I didn't look very healthy, and like one of those Southwest Airlines commercials, I just wanted to get away. I was tired of the questions, so I went back to Alaska in June 1975 and spent my summer up there doing baseball broadcasts. Nobody in Alaska knew about the cancer, and that was just great. It kind of cleared my head a little bit.

There was actually one person who knew, Jack Brushert, who was the general manager of the team. He also had a new title when I got there. He was Jack Brushert, The Man Who Watched Over Me. But in that role, he was sworn to secrecy.

"You were going through some emotional times," Brushert recalled when I asked him about my return to Alaska.

"You came back and you had a great summer as well as being able to get away from the people in California. That was a great escape for you, and then you just fell right into what you had been doing prior up in Alaska, and it changed your whole attitude."

That it did. When I tell you it was a great summer, it was a really *great* summer. The normalcy, at least as normal as you can get when you've had cancer at 25, returned. But I knew I had to go back home.

When the season was over, I headed back to Los Gatos. But I had gotten back to such a comfort level in Alaska that I wanted to keep that feeling going. I don't have to tell you what would make me feel most comfortable. Yes, I'd turn to my old friend, officiating.

I never missed a season of officiating, even though I was

going through all this. I came back in August 1975 and I immediately put on the striped shirt and knickers. I was getting the feeling back, both my health and that feeling I got when I stepped on the field to officiate—euphoria. When I was on the field, I had no problems whatsoever.

Off the field, however, I still had a little problem with money coming in. That's because it wasn't. I was married and had responsibilities, but I had no real job; therefore, I got paid no real money. My wife, Carin, was the breadwinner, but when you are talking about a travel agent's salary, it was more like we were trying to get by on crumbs.

I had lost every ounce of drive to do anything, and I basically considered myself a dropout. All that motivation I had from the quarter story seemed to be gone, except for officiating. I didn't care what I did.

That was pretty obvious from what I did next. I went to work for J & J Sports Productions, owned by Joe Gagliardi, and he put me to work doing a collection of odd jobs, which included doing sales and promotion for the San Jose Missions, a Triple A baseball team, as well as being the general manager of the Stockton Ports, a Single A baseball team. But it was in the third job Joe had me do that I would encounter yet another brush with fame and the media.

Joe promoted live boxing matches as well as fights that used to be shown on closed-circuit television in local theaters around the country. He would send me to small towns around the western US to collect money from these little theaters and bring it back.

Here's where the story gets interesting. Joe also got me

involved in ring announcing. Yeah, I could have been Michael Buffer before Michael Buffer, but I must not have been ready to rumble.

But I did have a run-in with promoter Don King. Yes, the same Don King whose hair even looked like it was shocked to be associated with him. The same Don King who promoted one of the most famous fights in boxing history, the Rumble in the Jungle, between Muhammad Ali and George Foreman in Zaire.

— —

HOWEVER, MY EXPERIENCE WITH KING TURNED OUT TO BE MORE like the Bumble in the Jungle.

Here's what happened: I had just gotten my license to be a ring announcer and Joe assigned me to the Jimmy Young–Ron Lyle fight in 1976 at the Civic Auditorium in San Francisco that would be televised live on ABC's *The Wide World of Sports.*

My instructions were simple: give the vital statistics and introduce the fighters. Nothing else. That included not announcing any of the dignitaries that were in the audience.

But just before I was about to climb into the ring, Don King told me to introduce him. I told him I couldn't do it. He told me I had no choice.

So here I am, this 26-year-old punk, trying to stand up to the legendary blowhard with the big hair. That was a lot to stand up to, because I think with his hair straight up, he was about 8'0".

The bell rang, which was my cue to get into the ring for the introductions. Now this was a big stage for me because it was my first opportunity to be on national television. As I climbed through the ropes, another legendary boxing personality happened to be sitting ringside, right where I was getting into the ring. It was none other than Howard Cosell, who was calling the fight for ABC.

As I was climbing up, I heard him say to the live TV audience, "Let's get the tale of tape from ring announcer Mike Pee-area."

He totally botched the pronunciation of my name. There I was, standing in the middle of the ring in my three-piece rust-colored suit, humiliated that my name got so badly mispronounced. To make matters worse, Don King had followed me into the ring.

I did my job, just as I was told to do. I introduced the fighters and ignored Don King. If looks could kill, I'd have been dead before the bell rang for the first round to begin.

But there would be one more insult before I would go. As I was leaving the ring, I again heard Cosell speaking to the live audience. "You just heard the tale of the tape from ring announcer Mike Pee-area."

It was obvious that ring announcing wasn't going to be my calling. But I recently caught up with Gagliardi and asked him what in the world he was thinking by putting me on national TV like that. Foreshadowing, maybe?

"One thing I always recognized about you was that you had a lot of charisma. You talked a good game." Gagliardi said.

"You had the personality. You also had the desire in sports and you had the makeup for it."

What I didn't have was the initiative when it came to working, and those jobs with J & J didn't do much to inspire me. Money didn't mean anything to me, and the thought of having a professional career was the furthest thing from my mind. I was just happy to be a survivor of cancer, and I wanted to live each day like it would be my last. That was until my dad called one day and said Dean wanted to see me.

Saint Dean would be back to the rescue to save my life yet again. I asked my dad why Dean wanted to see me and he said he didn't know.

While I was working for J & J, Gagliardi had lent me his old, beat-up Volkswagen bus to drive. That VW barely made it up the hill of my driveway, let alone the huge hill of the Altamont Pass on the way to Stockton to meet with Dean Wendt. The little bus chugged and chugged like the little engine that could, but I as I got to the top of the hill, I took my foot off the gas and just coasted all the way down to the San Joaquin Valley.

It was kind of like that feeling you get when you're riding your bike down a very steep hill and you have to take your feet off the pedals because they can't keep up. But I didn't mind driving that VW bus. I thought it was kind of cool.

I finally got there, but since I didn't really know what the meeting was about, I saw no need to dress up. I got to the office and I was wearing my grungy jeans. My dad took me right to Dean's office and I sat down. Dean told my dad to leave the room and then proceeded to tell me that he had a plan for me.

Picture my eyes rolling at this point, because Dean told me his plan was to send me to each of the offices he owned for a week. Such fine places included Reno, Orange County, Fresno, Sacramento, Stockton, Mountain View, and Newport Beach.

And when I was finished with my visits, I would then have to decide where I wanted to work.

I then explained to the fine Mr. Wendt that I had no intention of working in any of those offices...or working, period, for that matter.

He asked if I was hard of hearing and then repeated what I was going to do. He wasn't going to listen to any of my BS and said that I really had no choice but to do his plan.

As I said, it was a private vehicle-leasing company. It was a very reputable organization and a very good company that Dean had founded. If what he had just told me wasn't shocking enough, what he said next hit me like a stun gun.

Dean then told me to get rid of that ratty, old VW bus and to go pick out any new car I wanted. He told me to leave that instant and go pick it out, and I could take my dad with me. We're talking about a brand-new car. I remember laughing, thinking he was joking, but he wasn't.

Son of a gun if that didn't do the trick. Dean's plan had totally worked. Finally, I was ready to work. Dean Wendt had found a way to get me off my duff.

I took my dad, and off we went to Hansel and Ortman, a Cadillac dealership in Stockton. Gagliardi got his VW bus back. That's because I suddenly was living large in my new Cadillac Coup Deville.

I went home and drove up the driveway right underneath the window of the kitchen, so my wife, who had become a grammar school teacher by then, could get a good look at my new baby. Of course, I hadn't listened to the advice she gave me. She told me to get something economical, something that got good gas mileage. But there I was, with my white Cadillac Coup Deville with the tan cabriolet vinyl top and a big smile. That's because I'm a man. We get fancy cars, even when we shouldn't. Go big or go home.

I was finally out of my funk, and the man most responsible for that was Dean Wendt. He passed away a few years ago, but I'm sure he's on some cloud up in heaven, somewhere next to God, trying to convince him that leasing is a good thing. I will never forget Dean and all that he did for me and my family.

By this time, the three years had passed and I returned to Stanford in 1978 for my last checkup—and my last test results. The doctors told me I was clean. It was heaven to my ears. They said they didn't need to see me ever again. While I loved those doctors because they saved my life, their words were something I longed to hear.

I had a clear conscience and a clear goal of focusing on my obsession with officiating, along with a job in Mountain View, California, that would support it.

Moving forward, my next task was to figure out how I was going to proceed to the next level, officiating in college.

3 THIS COLLEGE EXPERIENCE WAS AN EDUCATION

I THINK I'VE ESTABLISHED HOW IMPORTANT A ROLE MY FATHER played in my life, from the brutal toughness of the quarter story to the complete support he gave me by always showing up at my games.

Yes, Al Pereira was a tough cookie and he would never be fully satisfied with my life choices. Yet he was eternally there for me, as were my mother and sister, Linda. They were all pillars of strength during my cancer scare and they had the kind of friends who'd do anything for them, which in turn meant they'd do anything for me.

And, fittingly, it would be my dad who would indirectly help me take the next step to becoming a college official.

My father ended his officiating career after the 1981 football season, retiring from the Pacific Coast Athletic Association. I knew I was never going to get to the college level until my dad left the field, and sure enough, under the direction of the late Jack Roberts, I was basically hired to replace my dad in 1982.

The best times I've ever had in officiating were when I was

35

a college official. There was something about college football that made it feel really special. The pomp and circumstance, the atmosphere—it was just pure, unadulterated fun. The officials during those years weren't subjected to the scrutiny like today, and thank heavens not, because if they were, there was one year I would have had an issue passing a physical.

You are going to have a hard time believing this next story. It's definitely one of my fondest memories—and also one of the funniest.

I was working at Eagal Leasing and we specialized in leasing cars to doctors who were members of the Santa Clara and San Francisco medical societies. I remember leasing a car to a doctor who practiced in San Francisco. The timing of this coincided with the need to take my yearly physical to qualify to officiate in the PCAA.

I figured, what the heck—I'd ask this doctor to fill out my medical form, without actually taking the physical, which was a common practice in those days. Some officials even filled them out themselves. After signing his lease for his new Mercedes, the doctor graciously agreed, signed the form, and gave it back to me. I sent it in to the league office the next day.

A week later, while looking through the San Francisco Medical Society roster, I saw a picture of the good doctor and I almost fainted. That was because I saw he was a…gynecologist.

How embarrassing. I figured my days with the PCAA might be over. Luckily for me, nobody in the PCAA ever read the San Francisco Medical Society book.

It all goes back to a lack of scrutiny. Officials went out and did the best job they could on a Saturday, and that was all that was required. It was extremely rare to be called on the carpet to explain something about a decision that you made during a game. It just didn't work that way. You worked with a great bunch of guys who weren't under the type of pressure they might have been associated with if they were trying to scale the mountaintop to the next level.

I joined the PCAA as a line judge and I got to work with a lot of people that my dad worked with, including the late Jack Gatto. If you don't know the name, Google him, because Jack Gatto will go down as one of the greatest college referees in the history of the game. He was also a Stockton resident and certainly a good friend of my dad's.

My first year, I didn't get a postseason game, but I did in my second, and it was truly a Christmas to remember. In fact, I'd say it was one of the best presents I had ever gotten. Do you remember Christmas Day when you were a kid? That was one day that your parents didn't have to wake you up. Just a hint of morning and you were out of your room and next to the tree quicker than the time it takes to rip the bow off a present. The joy and excitement that kids feel on Christmas Day was the same feeling I got when I found out my first bowl game would come gift-wrapped in the form of Penn State and Washington in the 1983 Aloha Bowl in Hawaii. Yes, for me it would be Christmas in Hawaii. The stocking filler was that I could work with Gatto, who was the referee on my first bowl game.

I spent the better part of my college officiating career in the PCAA, later the Big West Conference, as it became known in 1988. I spent nine years in the conference, becoming a referee in 1985. I spent the first three years as a line judge and then was asked to try out for the referee position. There was definitely a whole lot of love going on, because not only did I love the job, the job—or the people who gave me the job—loved me. It was a match made in heaven, and I became a full-time referee in 1985.

The opportunity was truly great and I got the tremendous experience of working postseason bowl games like the Holiday Bowl, the Freedom Bowl, and the Aloha Bowl.

But the league was going through some changes, and that included Fresno State moving to the Western Athletic Conference. The WAC was a step up from the Big West, and, just like Fresno State, I was also ready for a change to a better level of football. I figured that the WAC would also be looking to bring in some officials from Central California, so I sent an application to John Adams, who was the supervisor of officials.

To say I was excited to get the call from Adams offering me a schedule is an understatement. But the joy was quickly tempered when he informed me that I would not be guaranteed a referee position, even though that's what I was doing in the Big West. He hired me as a line judge, and I worked the Cotton Bowl after my first season. Adams made me a referee the next year, and I remained at that position until I went to the NFL in 1996.

I already told you that doing college games was fun, but there were times it was downright crazy. Take the time when I officiated a game between Cal Poly, San Luis Obispo and San Francisco State. I was the back judge in that game and I remember feeling very intense. I also recall Cal Poly, SLO being much better than San Francisco State. So much so that the first time Cal Poly got the ball, it scored a touchdown faster than it takes to microwave popcorn. So when the Mustangs lined up for the extra point, the back judge's job was to stand underneath the goal post to gauge if the ball went through the uprights or not. I did my job and so did the ball. The extra point was good.

You might not believe this, but at that point, I had not even noticed the Cal Poly cheerleaders, who were lined up right behind me. The next time the Mustangs got the ball, they scored again. And it was the same drill—me, the ball, and the extra point were all good. Again, those cheerleaders were right there with me. But I was concentrating so intensely—you just have to trust me on this one—I really paid no attention to them. That, however, would change.

For the Mustangs, scoring touchdowns became easier and quicker than saying "Cal Poly, San Luis Obispo," so by the middle of the second quarter, my concentration began to wane. I became a little less intent on deciding whether the extra point was good or not and more intent on spending a little time with the lovely group of cheerleaders that was right behind me. It was such a one-sided game, by the time the fourth quarter was over, we had all become pretty good friends.

I really didn't think too much about it again until a few weeks later when I had that same Cal Poly team in a game at Fresno State. The legendary Jim Sweeney, who was a real tough guy, was the coach of the Bulldogs. Come to think of it, Sweeney had the personality of a bulldog. Before the game, one of my responsibilities as a line judge was to bring the visiting team from the locker room down the walkway to the field. So there I was, doing my job, and I happened to run into my old pals, the cheerleaders. What did they do? Jumped down on the field, of course, to shake my hand, and in some cases, give me a hug.

It didn't really faze me until I looked back up the runway and there was Sweeney staring at me with his arms crossed. Busted.

But the show—and the game—must go on, so it did. I made a call during the game, a defensive holding penalty on Cal Poly, that really should have been called pass interference instead. I knew it after the fact, but I should have gotten it right the first time. Sweeney, from the other side of the field was yelling at me, calling me an idiot, which really wasn't all that unusual. With Sweeney, I'd say it used to happen as often as the coin toss takes place to start a football game. Meaning it was pretty much automatic.

Nevertheless, Fresno State won the game. Then Monday came. Normally, nothing good happens on a Monday, and this Monday, in particular, was no exception. John Adams, the supervisor of officials for the WAC, called and left me a message asking me to call him back. I was fully prepared for what was about to happen, or at least I thought I was. When I returned Adams' call, I was ready to get my butt chewed out for making the wrong decision on the defensive holding call. That actually would have been much better, if you can believe that.

Instead, the butt-chewing from Adams went more like this: "Pereira, if I ever hear about you screwing around with the cheerleaders before a game, you will never again work another game in this conference."

That was never...as in ever.

Sweeney had called the conference to complain that I was fraternizing with the cheerleaders. Never mind what I said earlier about the lack of scrutiny for college officials.

Not on that Monday, mind you, but Sweeney and I would later spend a lot of time together, me as a resident in Stockton and Jim in Fresno. Believe it or not, we would eventually come to laugh about the cheerleaders.

I would go down to Fresno prior to the start of a season and meet with his team and coaches to go over the new rules and the ramifications of them. We both eventually would come to like one another.

My first year in the WAC was 1991, and I worked with two different crews, one led by referee Gene Wertz and the other by referee Guy Gibbs. My first game was in Laramie, Wyoming, with the Wertz crew, and we decided to head to a steakhouse for dinner on the Friday night before our Saturday game.

I've mentioned that we had a lot of fun in the Big West Conference, so when the waitress came to the table and asked if she could get me something to drink, I responded first, saying I wanted a vodka tonic. She went around the table to the other officials, and the first three orders went like this: 7UP, Coke, iced tea....

Are you starting to get the picture? I was the only one who was ordering alcohol. You could say things were a little different in the WAC. I remember telling my dad that the WAC was definitely not a party conference, or so I thought.

My second week, I got assigned to the Guy Gibbs crew for

the Penn State–BYU game. We headed up to State College, Pennsylvania, and I ended up taking my dad with me because it was such a big game. Beaver Stadium was the stuff of legends. While we were there, my dad and I took a tour of the Battle of Gettysburg as well as the area around Harrisburg. It was fantastic.

The game wasn't half bad, either. All in all, it proved to be a wonderful experience. After the game, we went to the University Club for a few drinks, and Gibbs and the other guys were already there. Before I knew it, my dad was passed out at the table. When he woke up, he looked up at me and said: "I thought you said that the guys in this conference didn't drink." Oops. I assumed since the Wertz crew didn't drink, that nobody else did, either. Penalize me if you will, but that was a bad call on my part.

Officiating college games was almost like being in college all over again. It was simply crazy. Joe Ornellas was one of the back judges I had when I was a referee. Joe was from Hawaii and would fly over each week for the games. We had a lot of fun together that first year. As you would expect, Joe got paid for being a back judge. But what you might not be able to guess is that Joe actually lost money doing that job.

If you're wondering how that might even be possible, put away your calculator and let me explain. It really came down to two things:

We liked to eat. A lot.

We liked to party. A lot.

When the season was over, Joe's credit card bill was actually higher than the money he took in. That's a recipe for bankruptcy.

"I think I was making pretty good money as an official, something like $10,000 a year, but when we finished that season, I had a bill of $12,400," Ornellas remembered when I asked him about it.

"I still owed $2,400, but that was probably the most fun I've ever had while I was officiating.

When I asked him if the fun we had was worth going into bankruptcy, he laughed. "It was worth every goddamn cent."

While Ornellas swore the next season would be different, I think you already know where this is heading. The night before our first game in 1993, I remember picking him up at the hotel. He told me there would be no more drinking and no more smoking that season, and who was I to argue?

Joe was true to his word—for at least 90 minutes. After that, I found him drunk and smoking cigarettes. Back then, it seemed like it was just as important to have fun as it was to officiate the games.

I remember a game we had at the Air Force Academy one week on a cold fall day. The game was just about to start and I looked up and I saw Ornellas running off the field. I was thinking he must have had to go to the bathroom or something.

"It was very, very cold," Ornellas recalled. "I was thinking I'd go into the locker room, and you know, warm up for a little while. I thought after I warmed up, I'd just catch up wherever you were in the game.

"Well, I came back out there about five minutes later and I saw you hadn't even kicked off yet. I thought to myself, *You son of a bitch*. You were holding the freaking game just for me.

I thought about telling you that I was going back to the locker room to take a shit."

I loved Joe. The crazy Hawaiian's nickname for me was Bub. Why Bub? Well, by this point, you know I had only one testicle. The hydrocele caused the remaining testicle to enlarge. I know—too much information. So BUB stood for Big Ugly Ball. That sums up Joe pretty well.

Working in the WAC, I was fortunate to get to do several bowl games. I remember working two Cotton Bowls, including one as the referee, and it was an incredible experience. But it was the 1994 Gator Bowl in Jacksonville between Tennessee and Virginia Tech that provided me with the craziest postseason memory I have.

That brings me to Dick Pace, the officiating crew host of the 1994 Gator Bowl.

The day before the game, Dick picked me up in his new Cadillac and drove me to the NCAA-mandated meeting that officials were required to attend with both teams. We met with the coaches, the athletic directors, and the TV media to go over preparations for the game. When it was over, Dick drove me back to the Harley Hotel in downtown Jacksonville. As we were approaching the hotel, we were driving down a four-lane, one-way street.

Did I mention the Cadillac was new? Dick chewed tobacco in this new car, so his trusty spittoon was on the floor between the bucket seats. I swear I'm not making this up.

All of a sudden, the esteemed Mr. Pace put on his blinker to turn left. The only problem with that was we were in the far right lane. I was no driving instructor, but I knew the probability of anything good happening was as likely as me hitting the lottery.

We were stopped at a traffic light and I remember telling Dick that he couldn't turn left from the lane we were in. Still looking straight ahead, he muttered something resembling English, but he started backing the car up and we moved two lanes into the No. 2 lane. We still really weren't where we were supposed to be. Then the light turned green.

Do you remember the *Batman* TV show? When Batman or Robin would have a fight with the "bad guys" those big words used to pop up on the screen: *Kapow! Crash! Zowie!*

I'm pretty sure at least one of them flashed before my eyes as Dick attempted to turn left. Somebody was coming fast in the far left lane trying to time the light and plowed right into us, smashing into the door on Dick's side.

Ouch!

The new Cadillac did just about everything but flip over. Dick asked if I was okay and I told him that I was fine. Then I looked down and discovered that the spittoon between those big bucket seats had not been emptied in about a week, because I was covered in tobacco juice. I had clumps of it on the seat between my legs. It looked like the accident had literally scared the crap out of me.

As I got out of the car, bystanders were telling me to wait for the cops to arrive. I realized that we were only a block away from the hotel and decided there was no way I was waiting. I had to get out of those clothes, so I walked up my own Tobacco Road to the hotel.

I'm surprised I didn't vomit from the smell. But I got the clothes off and threw them away. No joke, I threw them away.

That night, I was so sore from the accident that there was a point I wasn't even sure I would be able to work the game the next day.

But I did. Working bowl games is pretty much the same as working playoff games in the NFL. It's a reward. It's an earned honor that you get in college from your supervisor. In my 14-year college officiating career, I was very fortunate to get to work in nine bowl games.

It is part of the reason why I returned to the college game for a short stint in 2010 when I got involved with the Pac-12 to help restructure its program. It's also why I spend time watching and analyzing college football games on Saturdays for FOX. There's just something about the passion that fans have for their college teams. It's a great reminder of days gone by.

College football officials are characters, and that's another reason why it was so fun. I told you about Ornellas, but I need to introduce you to Craig Battaglia. When you look up the word *character* in the dictionary, his picture could easily be right there next to it.

Battaglia was the second-best official I ever worked with at the college level, behind Gatto.

He was a back judge from San Jose and a guy you would definitely want by your side if you had to work the toughest game of your life. He had a take-no-prisoners mentality when he officiated. Some of the things he did with me when he was my back judge were beyond belief.

I remember a time that he got mad at me for something I said or something I did, but I'll be damned if I can remember what it was. He wouldn't speak to me for three weeks. He was on my crew and he wouldn't speak to me. If he had something to say to me, he'd tell another official and then they would relay the message to me.

We were working a game at BYU one Saturday in front of about 60,000 people. BYU scored a touchdown, and we were waiting for the extra point. When an extra point is kicked, the referee doesn't follow the flight of the football, but watches to make sure the kicker wasn't roughed. Then, if he's not roughed, he looks to the back judge, who is underneath the goal post. Usually what happens is that back judge will nod to indicate to the referee that the kick was good, or, if it's not, he signals no good.

Like I said, BYU scored a touchdown and the extra point was kicked, and I looked at Battaglia to find out if the kick was good or not. Did I get a nod? Nope. Did I get a "no good" signal? Nope. I got the bird. Can you believe it? Battaglia flipped me off! With both hands!

"Yes, I did. I know exactly what I did, and I didn't care. I was so tired of your pregame bullshit," Battaglia laughed when I asked him to recall the two flying birds.

I guess I drove my crew pretty hard on game days.

"Hell yeah, you did. From 8:00 AM until the game you wouldn't let up. You were so by-the-book, you didn't let us breathe from bell to bell. We barely had time to go to the bathroom."

That was Battaglia in a nutshell, emphasis on the *nut*, but in a good way.

Funny, just as suddenly as I got the silent treatment, came détente. For whatever reason, right after flipping me off, he just started speaking to me again.

Another time, at the Air Force Academy, a fan was getting on Battaglia pretty good for a call he made on a touchdown play.

"The guy wouldn't let up," Battaglia said. "I turned around and gave him a non-verbal if you know what I mean. The guy kept jawing at me even after the extra point, so I turned around and told him to f— off."

It happened to be Dads' Day and Battaglia had told one of the Cadet's fathers to, uh, f— off.

"Yeah, I got a call on Monday from John Adams (the commissioner of the WAC) asking me if I told a fan to f— off. I told him I had no idea what he was talking about and that he must have gotten bad information."

That was Bagsy.

I'm not sure why, but the Air Force Academy seemed to bring out the worst in Battaglia. One time before a game we were in the locker room and they brought us our paychecks. Battaglia grabbed my check, pulled down his pants, and wiped his butt with it. Then he handed it to me without saying a word.

I told you the man's crazy, but I love him.

Despite all those strange things, like I said before, if I was doing the most difficult game of my life, there's nobody I'd rather have as my back judge.

Battaglia is currently an instructor for the Pac-12 Conference at the back judge position. He was good enough to make it to the NFL but never did. I'm not sure he would have survived, because I bet he might have strangled one of the coaches.

He was a rough, tough guy, but in the NFL, you had to be

able to deal with coaches and administrators who, seemingly, were never happy. It wasn't Bagsy's strong point, but I'd go to war with him anywhere, anytime.

4 THE PROCESS OF REACHING THE PINNACLE

DESPITE HAVING FUN OFFICIATING COLLEGE FOOTBALL, WE STILL had our battles. But that would be nothing compared to taking it to the next level, making it to the N-F-freaking-L. The National Football League—the pinnacle of the officiating world.

The best way for me to describe the process of becoming an NFL official is to just tell you my own story. As I was moving up the ladder as an official, it was definitely something I was thinking about, something I aspired to become, especially after seeing more and more of my friends from the West Coast make it to the NFL.

At the time, you had to apply and send in a letter saying you were interested in becoming an NFL official. Write a letter? What an ancient, foreign concept. By now, you may be able to tweet the league from your phone to let them know you want to be an official.

My letter went to Jerry Seeman, the NFL senior director of officiating, and to Al Hynes, who was in charge of scouting for the league.

Here's the way it worked: the NFL would send you back a form letter response that read: "Thank you for your interest. Send us your college schedule when you get it and we will attempt to send somebody to view and gauge your work."

That was it. It took all of 10 seconds to read.

Then as each new season approached, an official would normally follow up by sending the NFL his impending college schedule. If the league felt the official was worth checking out, they would send someone to scout him.

I first applied in 1990. At that time, I was still in the Big West Conference and I hadn't yet made the move to the WAC, but I started sending in my schedule. However, I never heard anything back. I saw that a lot of my friends were getting to the NFL and I began to wonder why I never got a shot, or at the very least, had somebody from the NFL come watch me.

In 1995 my good friend Tony Corrente got in. I started to believe that at age 45, maybe it wasn't going to happen for me. I started to think that maybe it just wasn't meant to be. I had no idea what the average age of an NFL official was, but I thought I might have been too old. My mind started playing games with me, telling me that maybe I had accomplished all I was going to achieve. I almost had myself convinced that my dream of reaching the NFL was all but over. Or maybe I just wasn't very good.

It's a good thing nobody else could hear my mind yapping away.

By that time, I had completed my fifth season working for the Western Athletic Conference, and one day I got a call from the commissioner, Karl Benson. He caught me totally off guard because he wanted to know if I would be interested in leaving the field to become the supervisor of officials for the WAC.

I asked Benson recently what he saw in me back then that made him believe I could be a supervisor.

"I saw the way you managed the game. I saw the way you managed the crew, and I saw the way you interacted with the media," Benson said.

"But more importantly, I saw how you communicated with the coaches. That's what led me to believe that you could be the perfect supervisor at a time when college football officiating was changing, just like the overall sport was changing.

"I thought you had so much potential, and the way you thought was cutting edge. I think it was a combination of your leadership, your management, your ability to manage the various components of football officiating, and officiating in general."

That would leave me with a tough decision to make. If I accepted, that meant I would be retiring from being an official at 46. I didn't think my career was over on the field, but my mind was telling me that I should take advantage of the opportunity to become the supervisor of officials.

So I accepted the position, deciding that 1995 would be my last season as an official, or so I thought. Before I tell you how I would eventually make it to the NFL, I need to first explain the decision to "un-retire," which eventually led me to where I wanted to go.

I know it sounds confusing. Stay with me...

In September 1995, I had a game at Wyoming, but my crew

and I were staying at the Stouffer Hotel in Denver. So we all made the 130-mile drive to Laramie together and after the game we headed back to Denver. When we got back to the hotel, I discovered an NFL crew also happened to be staying there.

Jerry Seeman was there to see the Broncos play the next day. Coincidentally, Al Hynes, who was in charge of scouting officials for the NFL, had sent a scout to Laramie to evaluate somebody in our Wyoming game. The scout's name was Bama Glass. That's Bama, as in Alabama. I'm not making that up, because, well, you couldn't.

Unfortunately, good ole Bama wasn't there to look at me, but rather another official on my crew. But as I would find out later when Bama got back to Denver, Seeman asked him what he thought of the official that Hynes had sent him to scout.

Glass told Seeman that he didn't like the official and said he didn't think he was NFL material. But, and this would turn out to be a very big *but*, Glass told Seeman that he really liked the referee. The referee, ladies, and gentleman, would be me.

I think it piqued Seeman's curiosity and it bumped me to the top of the list in terms of candidates to be considered by the NFL. All of this went on and I never knew anything about it. I didn't even know Bama Glass was at the Wyoming game.

But three months later, my life changed forever. My remarkable journey to the NFL began when I received a congratulatory phone call from Seeman, who told me I had become a finalist. Now remember, I had already agreed to retire from being an on-the-field official to take the job as supervisor for the WAC officiating program.

That, naturally, would lead to a few complications, but

what's life without a few complications? However, since I was a Bama-Glass-half-full kind of guy, I knew that I would find a way to figure it out. My passion for becoming an NFL official was suddenly becoming a real possibility.

I was anxious and euphoric at the same time. But before I could get truly excited, I needed to make a difficult phone call to Commissioner Benson and explain why I would have to renege on my decision to accept the job as supervisor of officials for the WAC, because I had become an NFL finalist. That meant I would have to continue as an on-the-field official in college.

Luckily for me, Benson graciously allowed me to do that. But there would be a twist, which I'll explain in the next chapter. For that moment, I wanted to celebrate. I had been an official for 25 years, 14 of those in Division I, the highest level of college football. Now, I would be getting a shot at reaching my dream.

When Seeman called, he told me what the process would be like. He said I would get some phone calls and that I'd have to go through an interviewing process. He told me the interviews were nothing to worry about and that I should just enjoy the "process." He kept saying that—enjoy the process. That was easy for him to say.

A couple days later, I got calls from two psychologists back East, who told me they wanted to come to Sacramento for a visit. By then, my days of leasing cars were over. The same goes for my ventures into selling athletic shoes and golf equipment. At that time, I had a little custom embroidery and silk-screening business in Sacramento, and the psychologists told me they'd work around my schedule.

Before they came to Sacramento, I remember getting a phone call to set up the meeting at the Holiday Inn downtown. They told me the meeting would last a few hours.

On the morning of the meeting, I don't know why, but for some reason, the movie *One Flew Over the Cuckoo's Nest* drifted into my head.

But that didn't stop me, and off I went to complete part one of my psychological exam. They sat me in a room and we talked first about life's pressures, and then about football issues and how I would handle certain situations. It was the type of thing that you would expect a psychologist to ask, and I knew exactly what they were doing.

After the meeting, they would prepare a report to let the bosses on Park Avenue know if I was psychologically able to handle the pressures and rigors of becoming an NFL official.

Then it was time for a test, where I had to answer a series of questions. Each question had a sequence of squares that contained objects. One object in one of the squares was missing. By the process of deduction, I had to decide which missing object belonged in the square.

I remember one of the psychologists telling me the test was easy—that there were only 12 questions and that his 10-year-old son completed the test in about five minutes and got all the questions right.

Sure he did.

I got the first one right in no time, and the second didn't take much longer. The third, however, I stumbled on. I sat there and looked at it for quite a while until I figured it out. I was perplexed on the fourth one as well. The questions were multiple choice, so I did have options to pull from.

But before proceeding, I turned to the psychologist and asked again how old his little genius was? Trust me, even if he was Einstein's kid, he wouldn't have finished that test in five minutes. The psychologist laughed at me, all the while watching my every move. They finished the whole process in about three hours, and then I headed back to the shop.

Guess who was there when I got back? My dad. And, of course, he wanted to know everything. I told him I didn't think it went very well. I really didn't feel very good about it. In fact, I told him I wouldn't be surprised if a white-paneled truck pulled up and Nurse Ratched ordered men in white coats to grab me and put me in the back. Then they'd drive off and I'd never be heard from again. We both laughed, but I was only half kidding.

The psychologists apparently didn't agree with my assessment of how it went. Here's a sampling of what they wrote about me in the report they filed to the NFL in December 1995:

> *Mike Pereira is an extremely confident individual, but in no way does he come across as cocky or arrogant....The word "very" could be used in front of almost every descriptive phrase applied to Mike: he is very confident, he is very outgoing, he is very...as he puts it, "I like myself and I'm happy with my life."*
>
> *In terms of internal strengths, Mike was rated a 5 [the highest] on Ego, Strength, Independence, Striving for Excellence, Self-Control, and Resiliency.*

He is quite independent and will take an unpopular stand if he feels it is the right thing to do. He is extremely goal-oriented and feels you get what is due based on your performance.

In terms of observable characteristics, he was rated 5 on Decisiveness, Objectivity, Authoritativeness, Appropriate Cooperativeness, and Ability to Accept Criticism; and 4 on Judgment and Concentration.

His overall ratings were: Performance Characteristics 4.7; Internal Strengths 5.0; Comprehensive Rating: 4.9.

I have to say I liked their report on me a helluva lot more than my own self-evaluation.

While the NFL doesn't use the psychologists anymore, they still use companies like PRADO and XBInsight that provide organizations with assessments to help select, develop, and retain people who fit their culture and contribute to its success.

With the psychologists done with me, I was ready for the FBI. I got a call a few days later from an ex-agent who said he wanted to meet and discuss my background, which included checking into any legal issues I might have had as well as investigating my financial situation. I was kind of surprised at what you had to go through to get to the next level.

Mr. Ex-FBI Man showed up and we met in Stockton. He asked me a ton of questions, and when we were finished, he looked at me and said that everything was good. He said he didn't see any problems. He wished me luck and said that if he needed any more information he would be in touch.

Two days later, my neighbor walked across the street to our

house and asked me if I was okay. She asked if something was going on and began grilling me like I was on a witness stand and she was Gloria Alred. When I asked what was with all the questions, she told me that the FBI had visited her and they had been inquiring about me.

The FBI asked her if she had ever seen any cars pull up to our house in the middle of the night and park for five minutes and then pull away. I guess he wanted to see if there were any indications of wild parties or drug deals going down. That's what my "detective" was doing. He walked through my neighborhood asking my friends and neighbors questions to see if he could uncover anything that would keep me from getting into the NFL.

I obviously passed the sniff test, because a couple weeks later I got another call from Seeman, who requested I come to New York for the second phase of the interviewing process.

So off I went to the Big Apple. When I got there, I sat in the room with Seeman and all his supervisors for about an hour and they asked me a ton of questions, mostly about football. I actually really enjoyed that part of the process. They were getting to know me—and me them.

Seeman concluded the interview by telling me to go back to Sacramento and to continue doing a good job with college football. He told me I'd hear from them, but I shouldn't expect to make it to the NFL that next season. He told me that I was on the NFL's radar now and that they would continue to observe me.

Another thing they told me was that they were going to send me to NFL Europe to see how I did there, before making a commitment to bring me to the NFL.

In the spring of 1996, I did go to NFL Europe for its 16th season and I became a line judge again, the same position I worked in college before becoming a referee. But prior to going to Europe, they sent me to Atlanta for the NFL Europe clinic. We worked scrimmages with the teams that were going to be in the league.

The very first play of the clinic, I remember slipping. It was wet and I fell down. I went home and the next day I got a call from the league asking me if I would switch positions. I was thinking, *That can't be good; one day in and they're already asking me to change positions.*

They wanted to move me off the line of scrimmage to a deep sideline position, and I remember asking them if I was that bad that they had to move me. They said that I wasn't and told me they just wanted to balance out everybody and see if I was willing to try it.

I had never worked at the deep sideline position before, but when you get to this point of the process with the NFL, you never say no to anything. If they had asked me to become an NFL umpire, even though I had never done that before, my response would have been yes. I think anybody would have done just about anything just to get into the club. Thank God they didn't ask me.

My dad seemed much more fascinated by the whole process than I was. At that time, all the mail I was getting from the NFL was coming to the shop where we worked. My dad would meet the mailman every day, and if there was a piece of mail that came to me—addressed to me—from the NFL, he would open it before I had a chance to see it. He was so hopeful that I would make it to the NFL at some point that he would open every letter that came to me from the league.

Who was I to spoil his fun and tell him he was committing a felony?

As the league had told me, getting to the NFL was a process, so I had already resigned myself to the fact that I wasn't going to get in that next season, but then...

It was April 1996 and I received a phone call from Jerry Seeman, who started the conversation by asking me how the weather was in Sacramento. Really? With my nerves starting to get the best of me, he wanted a weather report? What, was I a freaking meteorologist?

By now, you already know how my mind works. I think I might have had ADD before they invented it. Back then we called it being hyper. So my brain was telling me to scream into the phone: *"Who the hell cares about the weather, Jerry? Why are you calling me?"*

Good thing my mouth didn't listen and common sense prevailed over any attention deficit that might have spoiled the conversation. I told him that everything was great and even mustered up some manners and asked how he was. But that would be it for the pleasantries. I just wanted to know why he was calling.

Seeman then said to me what I had been waiting to hear since the first time I put on an official's uniform back in 1971, doing those Pop Warner games in East Palo Alto making $10 a game.

They would be the 16 most important words since my cancer

scare and the 16 most important words since the quarter story:

"Congratulations, Mike, you're in. I'd like to invite you to officiate in the National Football League."

The…National…Football…League.

It doesn't get any better than that, folks. I was nearly speechless. I think I managed to say "wow," but I'm not sure. I do remember I was shaking, because my reason for wanting to be great at something, my passion to reach the pinnacle of my profession, had become a reality.

I stood up, still shaking, and I recall Seeman congratulating me again. I think after the second time he told me, I got two words out: "I accept."

At that moment, Shakespeare I was not.

But then Seeman told me that he didn't want me to tell anybody. I must have sounded like I was a five-year-old, because I think I squealed, "I can't even tell my dad?" He laughed and said I could tell him, but nobody else, because he said he didn't want it out in the media.

I hung up the phone and started jumping and screaming like a schoolboy who had been told he'd made the varsity as a freshman. It was such an incredible accomplishment that words can't do it justice for how good I felt. I wanted to share it with my dad, but he had just left to go play golf at the Van Buskirk Golf Course on the outskirts of Stockton.

You know I couldn't wait, so I called the golf course. I did that because we were still in the prehistoric age, BCP—before cell phones. For all of you youngsters reading this, there really was a time when cell phones didn't exist.

I remember speaking with Felix Claveran, who was the head

golf pro at Van Buskirk. When he answered the phone, I identified myself and asked if my dad had gotten there yet. He told me that he hadn't and I left a message to have my dad call me immediately.

Five minutes later, my dad called.

I told him that I was in.

Leave it to my dad to ask, "In what?" I told him that Jerry Seeman had just called me and that I was in the NFL. There was a long pause, where neither one of us said anything. Probably a good 15, maybe 20 seconds went by and then he finally spoke. "There's just one thing I want you to remember, son..."

Then there was another pause. With each second, tears began to well up in my eyes because I just knew my dad was going to tell me, finally, how proud he was of me for getting to the NFL.

When the silence finally broke, my dad, who was a longtime San Francisco season ticket holder, said: "Son, just don't screw the 49ers."

He then hung up the phone. My dad had a strange way of communicating, as you know. But when he got home, he told me that he walked up to the first tee where all of his buddies were waiting for him. He told me he teed up his ball without saying a word. He then said he hit the longest drive that he had ever hit in his entire life. I loved that. That was my dad's way of saying he was proud of me.

For me, that was my validation that I was finally worth more than the quarter it took to buy a Coke.

Of course, once I was in the NFL, he followed my every move. We took a trip together to New Orleans, where we spent some time with legendary referee Red Cashion. I'll cherish the picture with Red, my dad, and me in the New Orleans Superdome forever, as the 49ers were playing the Saints that day.

The 49ers would play another key role as the relationship between my father and I continued to evolve. The 49ers were hosting the Rams in my second regular-season game as an official. When you're an official, you leave the locker room about 60 minutes before the game, after you know the teams have gone out to the field to warm up. You walk around and observe their actions and get a little exercise, working on a couple drills yourself.

As I said, the game was in San Francisco, at Candlestick Park, and it was an unseasonably warm day. In other words, it was hot as hell. I knew exactly where my dad's seats were as I headed out of the locker room—on the opposite side of the field—so I began walking that way.

And there he was.

My dad was looking at me and I was looking at him. He gave me thumbs-up as I walked by. Much like the phone call I made to my dad when I told him I'd made it to the NFL, tears started welling up in my eyes because my dad was getting to see me work in the NFL.

The tears were just about to make a run for it, heading south down my face, when I realized I needed to pull myself together. I mean, seriously, did I really want people in the NFL to think they had just hired a blubbering fool?

Like most of the stories involving my relationship with my dad, there always seemed to be a twist. At about the 6:00 mark of the second quarter, we were in the middle of a TV timeout and I was just standing at my position when I heard the public address announcer make a statement: "Will Johnny Gainza please report to the first aid station behind section 232."

Gainza, my dad's best friend, was also from Stockton. He and his wife had come to the game with my dad and his wife, though they were sitting in different sections. I quickly looked to Section 232, where my dad and his wife were sitting, and the seats were empty.

My heart started beating like there was a sledgehammer inside my body trying to get out. With six minutes still remaining in the second quarter, what could I do? I couldn't really leave the field. Six minutes in an NFL game can feel like an eternity.

I didn't say anything to anybody, but in my mind I was rationalizing that my dad must have had the "big one," a heart attack, after seeing his son for the first time as an NFL official and passed away.

Twenty minutes passed and I was an emotional mess. When the half ended, I went over to referee Mike Carey and I told him what had happened even before we left the field. Carey told me to follow him and that we would find security because they would know what was going on.

David Hines, the ex-FBI agent who came to interview me in Stockton, was at the game for the NFL Security Department. Carey walked up to him and then told him the story. We had gone to the right place, because Hines knew exactly what was going on.

Remember—it was a very hot day. Hines told me that my dad's wife had eaten some nachos before the game. By the end of the first quarter, those nachos had done a number on her stomach and she was feeling ill. Hines told us that my dad had to take her to the hospital. Then as we were walking away, he yelled back to me that my dad was really pissed off he had to leave the game early.

Hines had given me the phone number for the hospital, so I went into the locker room and gave him a call. Hines was definitely right about my dad being upset. Besides swearing, my dad also swore he would never bring his wife to another game. Ever.

It was my dad's first opportunity to see me officiate in the big time, where his favorite team was playing at his favorite place on earth, Candlestick Park, and his wife passed out and he had to leave early.

That was yet another strange chapter in the ongoing saga between my dad and me. One of the reasons I retired from the NFL after the 2009 season was so I could move back to California and spend more time with him, but unfortunately, he passed away just a few months after I returned.

While I never got to spend the time I wanted with my dad at the end of his life, that first year as an NFL official was an amazing year.

My first game in the NFL, a preseason game between New England and Green Bay at Lambeau Field, might have been the most impactful of any I had in my two years as an official.

I had wondered if I was ready for the big time, ready to work at the NFL level. For good measure, throw in the fact that I was switching positions to side judge. To top it all off, I was about to make an amazing proposal, which you will read about shortly.

Working as a side judge in that game put me on the same side of the field with the head linesman, Earnie Frantz, who would be my partner for the entire season. Frantz was a top-notch head linesman but a guy many would describe as a jerk. Several officials told me that I was in for a long year being with Frantz.

I had never officiated with Frantz, but we had met at the officiating clinic in Dallas in 1996. We spent some time together there and he certainly seemed nice enough, but I was worried because this would be the first of 19 weeks I was going to be with him, and my stomach was in more knots than you'd see at a tug-of-war convention.

"From the moment I met you, I knew you had the right mental makeup to officiate in this game," Frantz told me recently.

The game started, and believe it or not, it seemed easy. It felt like it was almost in slow motion. As the game wore on, my normally negative mind had actually turned positive and was telling me that I could do this. My feet felt like they were 10 feet off the ground.

Midway through the third quarter, I told Franz that I didn't think officiating in the NFL was going to be that tough for me. Then, reality showed up.

Frantz fired back at me that I was a rookie and this was nothing but a scrimmage, a preseason game. Back to earth I fell, both feet firmly back on the turf. But I was still on a high like never before.

The guy who started out at Ravenswood High School doing Pop Warner games in 1971 was an NFL official, doing his first game—the Packers versus the Patriots—at historic Lambeau

Field. The whole scene was surreal.

Despite what everyone had told me, I hit it off immediately with Frantz and we ended up having a great time working together. I would ask him some really stupid questions, but he was always very patient and gave me straightforward answers. We would become the best of friends.

"We clicked as a sideline duo, and it certainly turned out to be a joyous year," Frantz said. "The two of us worked well together and you proved to me that you were a top-notch official."

The day after the Patriots–Packers game, I hopped on an airplane back to Sacramento. I was still on such a high from the night before, I'm pretty sure I could have flown home without any help from the jet.

When I landed, my good friend and inner self, Mr. Impulsive, was waiting for me. And, of course, we didn't head straight home. Instead, we went to a jewelry store. Mr. Impulsive, by the way, had a tendency to get me in trouble.

I had gotten divorced from my first wife, Carin, in 1988, and the new woman in my life was Gail Jones, who had been my girlfriend for eight years. And though we had never really talked about marriage, I felt so fantastic after that first game that Mr. Impulsive and I decided to go for it and I bought an engagement ring.

Then I went home by myself. I told Gail that we were going out to dinner at Harlow's Restaurant in midtown Sacramento to celebrate my debut in the NFL.

That crazy mind of mine was racing, trying to figure out what would be the right moment to propose. I had told her about the wonderful experience the game had been the night before, and then it hit me. I thought I'd be really creative and segue this wonderful football experience into our wonderful relationship.

There I was in mid-sentence when I got brave and got down on my knee. I flipped open the ring box and I proceeded to pop the question.

Gail looked at me, looked at the ring, and then looked back at me again. Time was not flying while I was down there on my knee, and it was definitely not the way I pictured it going. Damn that Mr. Impulsive.

I really didn't think the question, "Will you marry me?" was that hard, but that's what I get for thinking. All that was required was a simple yes or no answer. Whoever said silence is golden certainly wasn't there with me at that moment. I could have read *War and Peace* before she said anything.

Gail looked at the ring one more time and then back to me. I was already anxious waiting for an answer, but then she spoke. Get ready, folks, because her response was a doozy.

"Interesting…"

That's what Gail said. I had just asked the woman who I had been with for eight years to marry me and her response was… "interesting."

I went from popping the question to popping up off the ground. I told her *interesting* wasn't going to get her the ring. I sat back down at the table and we continued to talk some more. I think I stunned her so much she didn't know what to say.

Looking back on it, I asked Gail how big a shock it really was when I proposed.

"I was definitely taken aback because we hadn't really talked about it," my lovely said. "I think 'interesting' bought me some time, so my mind could compute what I was being asked.

"We had been living together for eight years and I was always very comfortable with the way it was because I had already been married.

"In some ways, marriage changed the relationship in my first marriage and I was worried about that affecting us, because we had a really great relationship and I didn't want it to change," Gail said.

Things, however, did change that night, but in a very good way.

We finished dinner and dessert came. And it may have been the best, sweetest dessert I've ever had. No, I don't actually remember what we had for dessert, but Gail finally said the magic word—yes—to my proposal. The next year we got married, and I was the lucky one because I'm married to one of the most beautiful, wonderful women in the world.

It just proved that despite a delay through dinner, with a little patience—something I'm not usually good at—things eventually paid off. And I really can't imagine spending the last 29 years with anybody else.

5   LEAVING THE FIELD FOR GREENER PASTURES

SO GAIL AND I GOT ENGAGED IN 1996, BUT AS I SAID EARLIER, I HAD already officially tied the knot with officiating back in 1971. And since we're looking back, I find it interesting to reflect on my career and the decisions I made to leave on-the-field officiating, not once, but twice.

The first turning point took place during my days at the Western Athletic Conference, which I mentioned in the last chapter. After the 1995 season, I got the call from WAC commissioner Karl Benson, who asked me to leave the field to become an administrator as the supervisor of officials.

You can either thank or curse him—heaven knows some of my Twitter followers will do the latter—because I'm 100 percent convinced that Karl Benson is the man most responsible for me becoming first the head of officiating in the NFL and then a rules expert on television.

The WAC job was clearly an intriguing offer because, as I said, I had applied for the NFL and hadn't really heard anything.

I was vacationing in Hawaii with my buddy, Tony Corrente, and we were discussing the pluses and minuses of leaving the field and becoming the supervisor of the WAC over a few drinks. Corrente was not only my buddy but was also the best man at my wedding to Gail. On top of that, he's currently one of the NFL's best referees.

But let's get back to the mai tais. You might say we had tipped back a few—okay, more than a few—and according to Corrente, I was fascinated by the possibilities of the WAC job.

"It was my job to play devil's advocate," Corrente said when I asked him to recall our conversation in Hawaii. "I remember visiting you in Sacramento and, being an official, you were very well-known there. Besides owning the town, you were having so much fun being on the field, so we talked about why you'd want to give that up.

"On the other hand, the opportunity to take over for John Adams [WAC commissioner] was intriguing. He was a legend and a great leader, and we talked about you stepping in right behind him and picking up that legacy and running with it.

"But there were some things I remember you being distraught about, one of which was having to dismiss some of the more iconic officials as part of the restructuring of the department that would create a new, progressive atmosphere. But some of those guys were good friends that you respected."

That part was difficult, but despite that, I ultimately made the decision to take the job and I called Commissioner Benson before I left Hawaii to tell him I would accept his offer. In my head, and in my heart, I was making the right decision to leave the field after 25 years of officiating. I was ready to embark on a new role as a football officiating supervisor.

But as you now know, that was before I got the call from the NFL. While I was talking to Benson, explaining why I couldn't take his position because I'd become a finalist for an NFL official's job, he asked me a question that would change my life. Now I want you to visualize any left field that you've ever seen, because that's where Benson's question came from.

He asked me if I could do *both* jobs.

Honestly, the idea of doing both never crossed my mind. Could I officiate in the NFL and, at the same time, be the supervisor of officials for the Western Athletic Conference? I explained to Benson that it wasn't likely to happen because most officials don't usually get into the NFL the first year of becoming a finalist.

His brain worked a lot better than mine, though. Benson came back with a plan that was genius. He said that even if I didn't get into the NFL that I could work on the field in the WAC, as well as working as the supervisor. I'd work non-conference games only and I wouldn't be eligible for the conference championship game or any bowl games.

"I thought, *Why not?*" Benson said when I asked him to recall how he came up with the plan.

"I thought there might be some opposition, either within the ranks of the WAC or just in terms of college football in general. You have to remember, I was in my early days in the WAC. Things were changing pretty rapidly at that time, in terms of growth and popularity of college football.

"You weren't coming off the field because you had to come

off the field. You were coming off the field because you thought you had an opportunity to maybe make some changes, specifically, in college football officiating. You had some maverick tendencies, and I liked that."

— —

IT WAS AN INCREDIBLE LEAP OF FAITH BY BENSON TO EVEN THINK about a working relationship like that, where I would do both jobs at once.

You also know that I did get into the NFL my first year, but at the same time, I also took the plunge and became a supervisor, too. I found myself really enjoying the administrative side. But I also really liked being on the field in the NFL.

For the two years I ran the WAC program, I totally changed things around. In March 1996 the WAC expanded to 16 teams. I told Benson that I wanted to visit with all 16 head coaches and athletic directors because I wanted to get some feedback on what changes we needed to make to improve the officiating program. I went to all 16 schools, and when I got back, I restructured how the program was run.

When I was an official in the WAC, I was resentful of the fact that I never scored the highest on the rules test. There were others that scored higher, even though they didn't know half of what I knew about the rules. I finally realized that there were a lot of shenanigans going on when it came to taking the test.

In my first clinic in Las Vegas, I gave a rules test to the staff— but there was one thing I didn't tell them. It might have been a little sneaky, but I didn't inform them that there were four different versions of the test. If they were going to gamble and try to cheat, I was going to catch them. Was it unsportsman-like conduct on my part? I'd say it was more like necessary roughness.

When all of the tests got turned in, I remember Dee Menzies, who worked with me and was responsible for grading the tests, came rushing out of the back room telling me that something must have gone wrong. So wrong that I knew I was right. Dee told me that her answering keys must have been screwed up because the test results were so bad.

I laughed but then explained to Dee that the test results were bad because I had four different versions. She was shocked and so were the officials, who accused me of treating them like kindergarteners. If they were going to act like children, I was going to treat them like children.

What's the one thing that officials need to have? Integrity. I told them they couldn't cheat. They were still not happy, but I think they learned a valuable lesson. I forced them all to study and do makeup exams. It was an interesting time.

As I would watch the video of every game in my little office in Sacramento, I developed a new philosophy of evaluation. I would go through every game and make teaching notes as to what things I wanted called or not called. The reason for that was because I was trying to establish some consistency within the WAC. It was my first dabble on the administrative side, and I found it to be very enjoyable. It would definitely not be my last dabble.

During my first clinic, I also invited all 16 coaches to join the entire WAC officiating group. I was so gullible that I thought I could do anything I wanted. I proceeded to tell the coaches that I wanted to make one thing perfectly clear to them: that swearing on the sideline was no longer going to be permitted. Period. I told them that any foul language used by a coach that was directed at an official would be flagged immediately. I also told the officials that if I found out a coach swore at them and they didn't flag him, I would fire them.

Telling a football coach he can't swear on the sideline is like telling a preacher he can't use the word *amen* in a sermon. That's pretty much impossible on both fronts.

You should have heard the response. Coaches were wailing, saying they weren't going to be able to coach if I didn't let them swear. I cracked up laughing, as did the officials; however, the coaches weren't amused. But, dammit, I was determined to clean things up and establish control.

I'll never forget going to the Fresno State–Utah game in 1996, when Chuck Sisk, a fine side judge, threw a flag on my buddy, Fresno State coach Jim Sweeney, for something he said. I laughed because I knew Sweeney cursed, and I also knew that Sisk was just doing what I had instructed him to do.

After the game, I went into the Fresno State locker room and sat with Sweeney, and we talked about the penalty.

"We can clean this thing up," Sweeney told me, "but I did not call your official a cocksucker."

I didn't believe him for a second, but I played along, asking him if that wasn't the word he used, then he should tell me exactly what he said.

"Knowing that I was going to get a 15-yard penalty anyway, I called him a no-good, *motherfucking* cocksucker," Sweeney said. That was classic Sweeney. We both just sat there laughing our butts off, but the point was made.

The new edict did bring some sense of control to the sidelines in the WAC, but Benson also reminded me why he thought I was somewhat of a "maverick." In 1996 we tried something in the WAC that no other conference in America was doing. And I guess you could say that "something" was not well-liked by everyone.

"You came to me and asked why referees didn't announce the numbers of the offending players on penalties in the college game on television," Benson said. "I thought there was a rule against it but we discovered there wasn't, so I told you to go for it.

"That first weekend, we had four or five home games that we tried it in. The next day, Roy Kramer, the dean of college commissioners, called and asked me what the hell the WAC was doing announcing the numbers of the offending players."

Kramer was the commissioner of the Southeastern Conference, one of, if not the most, powerful football conference in the land. And Benson told me that Kramer didn't take too kindly to us doing it.

"We were kind of known as the wacky WAC," Benson said. "And I told Roy that there wasn't any rule prohibiting us from doing it. He then told me that if we continued, our officials wouldn't be doing any bowl games.

"So we backed off, but I remember you told several officials that they shouldn't be afraid to 'forget' sometimes and announce the numbers. Even in the brief time you were a supervisor, you made a mark on college football officiating."

I continued on as the WAC supervisor of officials and as an

NFL official.

An "interesting" development took place after my first season in the NFL. Gail and I finally got married and were honeymooning in Monterey, California, when I got a call from my NFL boss, Jerry Seeman. He told me that the NFL was doing an in-depth analysis about the officiating program and that he'd like for me to share some of my thoughts with them.

Me? My thoughts? Hell, I'd only been in the league for a year and they wanted to pick my brain? Being so new to the NFL, I asked Seeman, "Why me?"

Seeman told me that they had a panel of 30 guys they were getting opinions from, starting with retired guys, then guys who had been in the league for a while, some for 20 years and some for 10 years. But he said they also wanted to have the perspective of some newer people like myself.

I didn't know where it would lead me at the time, but nevertheless, the NFL sent Joe Bailey to Sacramento in February 1997 to interview me. We sat in the lobby of the downtown Hyatt and we talked for three hours. We discussed a lot of things, from what I was doing with the WAC to what my perception was of how things were being done in the NFL. It was a broad-based conversation with a guy who was essentially a recruiter.

"Right after Super Bowl XXXI that year I got a call from Paul Tagliabue for a meeting to discuss the officiating department and the preparation for Jerry Seeman's retirement," Bailey said when I asked him to recall how the whole process started.

"The first thing I had to do was to figure out the present state of the officiating department. So I had to assess where it stood.

"I interviewed all of the internal people first. Then I interviewed the people who would be influential in making the decision. One was obviously Tagliabue and the other was Roger Goodell, the person that I would have day-to-day contact with.

"We were looking for an individual to transition into the officiating department and then eventually take it over. So, really, it was a succession plan. So we created a master list of potential prospects and I went out and interviewed approximately 30 people."

I had no idea the NFL was looking to hire someone, considering it seemed to be not much more than a review of the league's officiating department because Bailey's firm, Russell Reynolds Associates, did the analysis of workplace environments.

But in reality Bailey had much more knowledge than I imagined.

"I had approximately 23 years of experience in the NFL and that gave me an internal understanding of officiating," Bailey told me. "I had worked with Tex Schramm, the president and general manager of the Cowboys. He was also the head of the Competition Committee for so long that I had a fairly intimate knowledge of the officiating department."

I really liked Bailey and I enjoyed the conversation, but I didn't give it too much thought after he left because I still didn't feel like anything would come of it.

About a month passed and I got another call from the league office, asking me to come to New York and meet with executives. At this point, it still wasn't conveyed to me that this was an interview for a job. But of the original 30-panel members, I was one of only eight that were invited to New York.

Corrente, who had become an NFL official the year before me, had also been invited.

"I remember we were both very curious to see what direction the NFL was going in," Corrente recalled.

"They were talking about a whole new dynamic; I think the key word then was they were looking for a new 'paradigm' and trying to establish what that was. They said they wanted to restructure the office and do all kinds of innovative things."

When we got to New York, they put all of us through a series of one-hour conversations. I spent one hour with Commissioner Tagliabue, one hour with President Neil Austrian, one with Goodell, who was executive vice president and chief operating officer at that time, as well as a few others. I also had one with Seeman.

So what, exactly, was the NFL looking for? Years later I would get the answer from Bailey.

"When you go about searches like this you evaluate people on what their skills and their knowledge are," Bailey said. "So those two buckets are called competencies. You also evaluate people on talent.

"What do they do better than anything else? You interview for motivation, and probably the most important piece of evaluating people is potential. It's not just a plug-and-play person; it's somebody who can grow in the role. The way you do that is that you've got to evaluate them based on whether they've been successful with different kinds of environments and different situations and uncomfortable situations in the past.

"Then, in addition to that, you want people that are properly engaged, determined, curious, et cetera. So that's the real trick to this business. Just like a scout or anything else. It's not hard to figure out how to evaluate where a person is today, but to evaluate where they can go and how well they can do is the challenge."

I can tell you that day in New York was an intense, exhausting day, and on the way to the airport to fly back to Sacramento that night, I thought the whole process had been really intriguing. It was finally clear to me that the league was going to be hiring somebody to work in the officiating department in the New York offices.

"I remember you telling me on the ride back to the airport that you would definitely consider leaving the field, even though you'd only been in the league for one year," Corrente said.

He then played devil's advocate again, something he was good at.

"I also asked why you would leave the field since there was no doubt in my mind you would become an NFL referee. You had also made a splash in your first year as supervisor of officials for the WAC.

"Without hesitation, you told me that you thought you could have a bigger influence and make a bigger contribution to the game of football from Park Avenue than you could in Sacramento."

Yeah, I might have thought and talked big, but I didn't think it would go beyond those meetings. Shows you what I know.

Shortly after I returned from New York, I got a letter from the NFL. It was a job offer from the league asking me to become one of two new supervisors of officials for the NFL. The other was Larry Upson, who had been in the NFL for six years as a line judge. I was stunned—and flattered.

It finally dawned on me what Gail must have felt like when I proposed that day. When I opened the letter from the NFL and saw the job offer, the first thing I thought was...*Interesting*.

Obviously, it would not be an easy decision. I had only been married for a month and I was being asked to move to New York. I really didn't know what to do, but I remember asking everybody I knew for advice.

Jerry Markbreit, one of the greatest referees ever to officiate in the NFL, advised me not to do it. He expressed that I would someday become a referee and that I shouldn't give that opportunity up. He said after 25 years I had finally achieved my dream and asked me if I really wanted to give it up so quickly. He told me he saw something in me.

"We had worked only one game together, but I knew that you had a good reputation. You had worked a lot of bowl games in college and I knew you were well qualified. I felt you had the potential to be one of the best officials in the National Football League," Markbreit told me when I asked him to recall our conversation of 20 years ago.

"In 1990 I had the opportunity to leave the field myself and become the supervisor of officials. I chose not to do it because I loved officiating so much," he continued. "I wasn't sure if I could be a decent supervisor because I knew I would be battling the league every time they wanted to do something I didn't like. So rather than be fired, I stayed on the field."

Knowing now how things turned out, I asked Markbreit if

he would still give me the same advice he did back in 1997.

"I probably would, yes. But I feel that you wouldn't have gotten the notoriety of being an official back then that you do now being on national television. However, being an official is a special talent that a lot of people would like to have and don't. You had it.

"But I can't criticize your decision then or what you're doing now for FOX because you've had tremendous success. It's like you were cut out to do television and the rules thing. There has never been a supervisor that knew the rules any better than you did. You're as good a rules man as anybody I've ever known."

Markbreit wasn't the only one to give me that advice. In fact, almost everybody I talked with told me not to do it. I had a lot of different emotions and thoughts, but I needed to make a decision.

On the plus side, I looked at this as possibly being an end to a lot of negativity that I had been through in my life. If you remember, I talked about dropping out of society after my testicular cancer surgery. Officiating helped me survive that then, and I looked at this offer from the NFL as something that could be the best thing for me at that point in my life.

I also thought that it could be the thing I was looking for, the thing I could be great at. If I could pick the one job in the world I would want, the supervisor of officials position for the NFL would be it.

What would ultimately influence my decision to accept the job was...the Western Athletic Conference.

The year I had spent running the program for the WAC was so enjoyable, even I didn't realize how much until the NFL opportunity came about. I loved the teaching aspect of it as well as dealing with the coaches. I even got involved with the media, trying to help them understand the rules and how the games were officiated.

It was yet another flirtation with the media I would enjoy. You see where this is all heading? Thank you, Mr. Benson.

I played interviewer and asked myself the question, what did I enjoy more—the three hours on the field every NFL Sunday or administering a program throughout the course of the entire week? If this were an exam question, I would have aced it, because it wasn't difficult. I enjoyed the administrative side of my WAC job a lot more than being on the field in either college or the NFL.

I knew I had to do it, but I had some baggage to take care of first. I had recently gotten married and the NFL wanted me to move to New York quickly, in just two months. But I had that embroidery and silk-screening company that I ran with my mom and dad. My dad worked alongside me in all aspects of it and my mom did the books. My mom and dad had divorced many years before, and even though we all worked together, there wasn't a lot of kindness between them.

Believe it or not, their friction actually helped me as an official. No, I'm not drinking Tito's vodka as I write that. The lack of harmony between the two helped keep my skills sharp because I used to have to keep them apart and make sure they didn't get after one another.

It was like conflict resolution, which I think plays a part in officiating, because you're always at odds with someone. You have situations come up between player and player, official and player, as well as official and coach that you have to resolve. It was the exact same thing with my mom and dad.

However, the stumbling block was that the business was all my parents really had at that point. Do I walk out on them and leave the business and leave them high and dry? It was my mom and dad. Despite their differences, they raised me. They gave up a lot for me, and I wasn't going to leave them in the lurch with the business still hanging there. So it came down to this: yes, I desperately wanted the job, but leaving my mom and dad just didn't feel right.

So I decided to turn down the NFL's offer. You read that right; I said no to my dream job.

I remember writing a letter — a rather good one, I thought — to Jerry Seeman thanking him and the NFL for the offer. I told him I was honored and that I really appreciated it. I explained to him the situation about my business and my parents and that I just couldn't walk away from it at that time. I thanked him again but said I couldn't accept. After I made the decision, I felt very good about it and thought I had made the right choice.

I sent the letter FedEx, and the next day I got a call from New York. Not from Seeman but from Joe Bailey, the recruiter, who asked me if I was nuts. I wasn't offended, even though I had only one testicle.

Bailey couldn't believe I was passing up this opportunity. He said I was crazy, that the job was gold for me, that I'd be the next head of officiating. He then told me what I did with the WAC was spectacular. He said I would be wacky to pass this opportunity up. I thanked him for his kind words but told him I had made my decision.

Bailey then gave me one of the nicest compliments I've ever received. He asked me what it would take for me to reconsider. I hadn't really thought about that because it wasn't even a consideration. It wasn't about the money.

Then came the next question that floored me and would change my life yet again.

"What if we hold the job for a year, give you one more year on the field, give you another year to wrap up your business in Stockton and get your parents situated? What would you say then?" Bailey asked.

For Bailey and the NFL to say they would hold the job for me at that time blew me away. Until recently, I didn't know how that decision came about, but when I recently caught up with Bailey, I asked him.

"You can't argue with the reasoning—if somebody has issues from a personal standpoint, the only thing you can do is try and come up with something flexible to help them with that," Bailey remembered.

"I got the buy-in, obviously, from the NFL to do that. I recall talking at great lengths with Goodell about it. They were both, especially Tagliabue, absolutely convinced that you were the right person. Seeman wasn't going anyplace for a few years, so it really didn't hurt the transition. That was the reasoning behind it."

To hear Bailey explain it all makes sense now, but back in 1997, I was still shocked and had the decision to make. I remember when I reached my initial conclusion to take the job or not, I had drawn up a list of pros and cons.

On the left side of the paper, the pros side, there was only one thing listed: *It's the one job in the world I want.*

I didn't need to look at the cons side. I decided at that moment that I was going to do it.

In saying yes, there was an intriguing aspect to my decision. I knew I was going to work on the field for another season, but I also knew the other officials would figure it out quickly, knowing I was one of the finalists and knowing the NFL didn't fill the job.

The way rumors leaked out amongst the officiating staff, I swear some of them could have worked for TMZ if it were around back then. It was pretty much known that I would be moving to the administrative side of the NFL following my second season on the field.

When that season was over, I proceeded to get everything wrapped up with my business, and my parents were totally supportive of me taking the job. They were upset when they found out that I turned down the job in the first place. Like any parents, they wanted to see their kid succeed. So after the Super Bowl was played in January 1998, I got my affairs in order and I moved to New York in March to start my new job as a supervisor for officials for the National Football League.

It felt a little strange because I'm a California guy, but not a big-city California guy. I went from Stockton and Sacramento to New York City. It wasn't like *The Beverly Hillbillies*, but it was close. And even though I was making a brand new start of it—and waking up in a city that never slept—my wife Gail decided to stay in Sacramento. I guess she wasn't convinced I'd make it there, or anywhere for that matter.

She wasn't the only one who had doubts. I found myself

getting homesick after the first few weeks. But a very unlikely place would help me overcome my fears.

Prior to the move, Gail and I visited New York to find me a place to live. We found an apartment on the West Side that was 20 floors up with magnificent views. I looked out over the Hudson River with New Jersey in the background.

We were feeling pretty good about it and decided to go to dinner that night in Little Italy at a place called Angelo's on Mulberry Street. We knew about the place because some people Gail worked with at the Sacramento City Unified School District had eaten there a couple times on a recent visit to New York and had raved about it.

I had made a reservation for 7:15PM, but it was so crowded we ended up not even getting a seat at the bar until 9:15. Gail mentioned to the bartender, Joe, that I was moving to New York to work for the NFL, and he seemed to be the only one who worked at the restaurant that knew anything about football.

We finally got to eat and at the end of the evening Joe introduced me to the owner and the maître d'. It was a fun night and a great place.

I moved to New York a few weeks later, and the first week was absolutely fantastic. I went to some great restaurants and I saw a play on Broadway. I did all the cool things that Midtown Manhattan has to offer.

Then reality set in.

By the second week, I was homesick. I didn't know anybody and I didn't really have any connections to people that worked at the NFL. Most of the people that worked there commuted from outside Manhattan.

I got incredibly lonely one night and decided I would go back to Angelo's. Before I left, I went down to the NFL shop and bought three shirts to take to the guys I had met at the restaurant. When I finally got to the restaurant I saw Joe the bartender and I reintroduced myself and handed him the shirts. He didn't seem very enthusiastic and put the shirts under the counter. I had an uneventful dinner by myself and left.

The following week was worse. I was so lonely I didn't think I was going to make it. I have to admit, I was walking down Park Avenue one night and tears started to well up in my eyes. That's how much I missed home, Gail, and my family.

I thought I would try Angelo's one more time. There was a typical long line to get in, but Antoine, the maître d', recognized me. He pulled me through the line and gave me a big hug. He had gotten one of the shirts I left on my previous visits and yelled for Joe to come over as he was dragging me to the bar. Joe also gave me a big bear hug. It's amazing what three shirts will get you.

It took me a few weeks, but I had finally found my first New York "family." I would end up spending three nights a week there, minimum, and we all became very good friends. I even ended up spending several holidays at Giovanni's house. He was one of the co-owners. The reason he invited me was because he refused to let me be by myself during the holidays.

It was the people from Angelo's, and people like Nancy Behar from the NFL Broadcasting Department, who took me under their wing and helped me get accustomed to New York. They saved me, saved my job, and made it possible for me to survive there.

As far as work goes, it was probably smart that I went to New York by myself, because all I did was work. There really was nothing else for me to do. I was always the first one to get there in the morning and last in the officiating department to leave at night.

There were many skeptics, both inside the officiating world and out, and many people were questioning what qualified me to make administrative decisions after spending only two seasons as an official in the NFL.

I understood the only way to counteract that was to prove that I was worthy to be there and earn their respect through hard work.

But I really did end up loving my job. I rewrote the pass interference rules in my first year so that they would be more understandable to officials. I categorized them to such a degree that officials could explain to players and coaches more specifically what the fouls were. That was accepted very well and is still in the rulebook today.

After my first couple years in the league office, people I knew would ask me, if I had to make the same decision to leave the field again, would my answer be the same?

Thanks to the people at Angelo's and Nancy Behar, who got me comfortable during those very difficult first few weeks, the reply would be the same: absolutely! Despite the stress that came with it, that job was one of the most enjoyable things I've ever done in my life.

6   BREAKING IT DOWN: FINANCES AND THE CBA

AS MUCH AS I LOVED MY JOB OVERSEEING THE NFL OFFICIATING department, I have nearly the same affinity for guys who do it on the field.

But who are these men—and now woman—who make up the group of 122 officials? Well, the first thing you should know is they're part-timers, and that always seems to be a subject of debate. Should they be part-time or full-time? I've previously been an advocate of the officials being part-time, though you will read later on why I might be changing my stripes on that issue.

Why did I think it was good for them to be part-timers? Along with the fact that each officiating crew works only one game a week, they all had found success in their personal lives and professional endeavors prior to being chosen as NFL officials. They learned how to handle success and failure, meaning we had successful people that utilized the experiences they went through off the field, which translated to helping them handle the pressure that was on the field.

Take a guy like Walt Anderson, who is entering his 21st season as an official in 2016. He's now a retired dentist. He's also the officiating coordinator for the Big 12.

But what do some of these guys do in their "other" lives? How about sales managers, the president of a high school, attorneys, retired firefighters, current police officers, a retired federal probation officer, financial advisors, and insurance brokers.

There's even an airline pilot. A guy that's actually on the field Sundays just might be the same guy who is flying you up and down the East Coast during the week. I certainly hope he's not studying the rule book while he's at 36,000 feet, but he might be. That's how seriously these guys take it.

And now, how *she* takes it.

Sarah Thomas became the first full-time female official in the NFL this past season. And I mean the first, because Shannon Eastin, who participated in the 2012 lockout, shouldn't count, because she never went through the process like Sarah did.

Sarah earned her stripes; Shannon didn't. And how did it go in 2015? Pretty much how I expected. After the first few weeks of the season, she disappeared and became just another official, which is a good thing most of the time.

"The thing that I, personally, love about Sarah is that her focus was not on being the first female official in the NFL; her focus was just being an official in the NFL," Dean Blandino, the vice president of officiating, told me.

"Her performance was judged based on what she did on the field, but she's been officiating for 20 years and been on our radar since 2006. She's gotten top-level training and worked her way through the top level of college officiating.

"She was also in our advance program for two years. She did everything that we asked of her. She's shown poise and all the things you look for in an official on the field. The presence and the decisiveness and not being intimidated, she's shown all of that. We've thrown more at her than any other first-year official in the history of the game."

These officials are normal folks, just like you and me. Okay—maybe you.

They're all good people, and I would take the group of 122 NFL officials and put them up against any of the other groups in the NFL including players, coaches, etc. When is the last time you read about an official being charged with assault or child abuse? You don't, because before the NFL makes a decision to hire anybody, it takes a very deep look into his or her background to make sure he or she is beyond reproach. Remember how I detailed what I went through?

The one thing you can't afford in the officiating world is the lone wolf like the NBA found out in 2007 with Tim Donaghy. That situation threw all of us associated with officiating under the bus because Donaghy bet on NBA games, as well as got involved with organized crime. He tarnished the reputation of the entire industry. Not to be deterred, everyone involved in the officiating world continued to perform at an exemplary level, and I feel the industry, as a whole, is impeccable.

So let's dig deeper into the financial side of the NFL officiating world and find out more about how the 122 are compensated.

- What do they get paid?

- What are the retirement benefits?

I'm going to give you an inside look into the finances of being an official and what they are allowed—or not allowed—to do. It's interesting information that very few people get to see.

What drives everything is the current collective bargaining agreement (CBA), negotiated by the NFL Referees Association (NFLRA) and the National Football League during the lockout of 2012. The agreement runs through the 2019 season, but there is a renegotiation period that follows the 2018 season.

In 2015 the NFL paid a total of $19,086,320—$1,800,000 for the preseason, $13,884,320 for the regular season, and $3,402,000 for the postseason—to its officials. That's the pay, the aggregate salaries, paid by the league.

That amount is based on 122 officials, and if the number increases, then the amount of the aggregate salaries will increase.

But you might be surprised to know that it's the NFLRA and not the NFL that determines what each official gets paid in the preseason and regular season. It's the union that decides how that's going to be divided up, based on seniority.

However, in the postseason, the NFL determines what the officials are paid per playoff game and also how the playoff pool is divided up amongst the officials.

So how does the union break down the salary structure for the preseason and regular season? Let's look at this by taking five officials at various stages of their careers.

- **Jeff Triplette**. He's a referee, and 2015 was his 20th season. Triplette is a retired Army Reserve colonel from Oxford, Mississippi. He was awarded the Bronze Star for actions in the Persian Gulf War. Currently, he's president of ArbiterSports.com, a website that assists in assigning officials to various games in multiple sports. Triplette maxed out, meaning once you reach 20 years or higher, the pay is the same. His preseason fee in 2015 was $4,525 per game. His regular-season fee was $10,625. Officials are basically guaranteed 15 regular-season and four preseason games. So Triplette's base pay for 2015 was $177,475.

- **Mark Perlman**. He's a line judge who has been in the league for 15 years and is a teacher. He graduated from Salem College and now resides in Lake Havasu, Arizona. He's a really great line judge who has worked three Super Bowls (2005, 2008, and 2014). A 15-year official earned $3,975 for the preseason and $8,650 for the regular season. His base salary in 2015 was $145,650.

- **Bruce Stritesky**. He's an umpire who's been in the league for 10 years and the pilot I spoke of earlier. He lives in Roanoke, Virginia, and learned to fly when he was just 13 years old. A 10-year official earned $3,675 for preseason games and $7,150 for the regular season. His base salary in 2015 was $121,950.

- **Dave Meslow**. He's a side judge who has been in the league for five years and is a marketing manager. He graduated from Augsburg College in Minneapolis and is from Mahtomedi, Minnesota. His preseason fee is $3,225 and his regular-season rate is $5,550. His base salary in 2015 was $96,150.

- **Sarah Thomas.** She just completed her first year as a line judge. She attended the University of Mobile on a basketball scholarship and resides in Brandon, Mississippi. A first-year official gets $2,775 for preseason and $4,250 for regular-season games. Her base salary for 2015 was $74,850

Now let's look at the postseason. An official who worked the 2015 playoffs in a wild card, divisional round, or conference championship game, as well as the Pro Bowl, received a game check of $7,250. Alternates also got $7,250. An official who worked the Super Bowl got $13,250. The five alternates for the Super Bowl each received $11,250. There's also a bonus pool. The bonus pool is money that is shared by all the officials who qualify for the playoffs, regardless of whether they work or not. That amount works out to approximately $25,000 per official, but it fluctuates depending on how many officials share in the pool, because not all officials are eligible. It's based on years of service or performance.

So an official who worked a divisional game, for example, would get the $7,250 plus a share of the playoff pool. For an official who also worked the Super Bowl, they would get $7,250 for the division game, $13,250 for the Super Bowl, and the pool money as well.

That's definitely an office pool worth getting into. But that's not all. Officials also earn money in other ways:

- Officials have to attend the annual three-day clinic in Dallas, where they get $1,900 per day.

- Each official is required to spend three to four days at a team's training camp and are paid $1,900 per day for that as well.

- Officials now have to travel to New York for two days to take their annual physical, and they are paid $1,900 per day.

- Officials also get a $1,250 travel fee for any games not played during the day on Sunday. By the way, the league provides first-class travel for all officials for every game.

- Officials' hotels are paid for and they receive $310 per diem for the first night and $115 for any subsequent night.

- The white hats, the referees, are paid an extra $14,500 per season for all the additional work they have to do. The referees also get $1,550 for expense money.

- Officials get preparation pay of $2,800 for honing up on the rules and getting in shape. In addition to that, they are reimbursed up to $1,300 for a fitness membership.

- The league also paid the NFLRA for the marketing rights that include names, symbols, emblems, and designs of the union's logos and the name, image, likeness, photograph, voice, signature, as well as biographical information pertaining to all game officials. How much? That would be $650,000. That's not cheap.

That gives you an idea of the salary structure for officials. That alone makes it a pretty good gig. But it doesn't end there. On top of their salaries, the officials have a very generous benefits package.

Let's start with the severance benefit, and that applies to any official that has completed five or more seasons of service. If an official leaves the league for any reason, whether he or she voluntarily resigns, retires, is terminated for job performance, or dies, he or she is entitled to receive a one-time enhanced severance benefit, which is a payment equal to the amount he or she earned the prior season—the preseason, regular-season, postseason game fees and his or her share of the postseason bonus pool.

It's called an enhanced severance because if an official accepts it, he or she has to sign a waiver that says the league is not liable for any issues relating to the official's employment and separation from employment with the NFL.

Then there are the actual retirement benefits. This was the sticking point regarding the 2012 lockout, because prior to that point, officials received a defined benefits pension plan. A defined benefits pension plan is a type of plan in which an employer promises a specified monthly benefit on retirement that is predetermined by a formula based on the employee's earning history, tenure of service, and age, rather than depending directly on individual investment returns.

However, the league wanted to convert to a 401(k) plan instead, which transferred the return on the investment risk from the league to the officials.

The league didn't get everything it asked for in the negotiation. Officials that had a credited year of service in 2011 or before retained their defined benefits pension plan through the 2016 season.

Officials hired in 2012 and after immediately became part of the league's 401(k) contribution. To those, the league contributed $15,000 annually to each official, increasing in increments of $500 per each year of service. After 2016, every official will go to a 401(k) contribution.

Those with the defined benefits pension would get credited $275 per month for years served up to a maximum of 20 years. That means a guy like Jeff Triplette, for example, will get $5,500 a month on the defined benefit when he retires.

That's enough on the financial side; now I want to take you on a covert mission to look behind the veil of secrecy of the collective bargaining agreement. It's all public information, but as your trusty guide, I'm here to turn the legalese—and don't confuse that with Portuguese—into English when detailing the code of conduct guidelines for NFL game officials.

What can they do? And what can't they do? Trust me, there are a lot more don'ts than dos.

- An official can't vote in or publicize any all-league, all-conference, all-opponent team or any similar honorary designation.

- They can't furnish any information regarding a player's ability.

- They can't publicly criticize the league or any member club or ownership, management, or employees of either the club or the NFL, and they certainly cannot chastise any NFL players.

- Officials are not allowed to engage in any type of gambling activity, including betting money or anything of value relating to the outcome of a score of any league game or the outcome of any divisional or conference races. I'll get into more details about gambling later.

- They can't accept a bribe, obviously, or agree to throw or fix any league game. Officials must report to the commissioner if anyone even approaches them about that.

- Officials can't write any articles, give any interviews, or make any public statements, including but not limited to radio, television, the Internet, social media, or any other medium involving their duties as a game official or their relationship with the league without prior consent of the vice president of officiating, who is Dean Blandino.

- They can't engage in communication directly or through a third party with members of the media, fans, or member-club personnel about their duties as a game official or their relationship with the league without also going through the VP of officiating.

- With the new CBA signed in 2012, officials needed to discontinue existing and shall not create any new personal websites, as well as Facebook, Twitter, or any other social media accounts that in any way mention their role as a game official.

- Officials can't request additional tickets (they get two per game they work) or credentials from a team. They can't accept compensation or anything of value for any services or information related to their activities as an official other than the compensation provided under the terms of the CBA.

- They can't engage in any conduct that adversely affects or reflects negatively on the NFL or results in the impairment of public confidence in the honest and orderly conduct of league games or the integrity and good character of a game official.

Obviously, there are a lot of issues when it comes to what officials can't do. Let's discuss alcohol and drug use. I'll make it simple. If an official has a game on Sunday, he or she can't have an alcoholic beverage past midnight Friday. That means no alcohol and no drugs that aren't required for medical reasons. They are not allowed to drink alcohol until they get back to the airport or hotel after the game Sunday.

Are you wondering how the league would know if an official is under the influence of anything?

The officials are subjected to random alcohol and drug testing. Each crew gets tested at least twice a season, and they are not notified about when they will be tested until four hours prior to kickoff.

The NFL takes this very seriously. An official does not want to be caught with alcohol or drugs in his or her system because the discipline is swift and severe. If an official does get caught in one of the random tests, he or she will be suspended immediately without pay for the rest of the season. If they get caught a second time, they will be terminated. During my time as the

VP of officiating, neither of those happened.

Now, let's take a more definitive look at gambling. An official is not allowed to bet on the NFL, but they also can't bet on any game in any team sport, period. When it comes to gambling, the provisions are very explicit. An official also may not enter a horse or dog track or a gambling casino.

Officials cannot engage in any form of gambling during the NFL season. During the offseason, an official can go to a casino, but must alert the league prior to the visit. If they don't, they are fined $1,000 for the first offense, $2,500 for the second, and up to suspension for the third offense.

Lastly, there's fantasy football. An official is also not allowed to participate in fantasy football. They also can't maintain a line of credit with any gambling establishment. I'm sure you understand why the rules are so rigid when it comes to gambling. It's all about the integrity of the game.

What's the discipline if an official gets caught gambling? If an official enters a racetrack or casino during the season, he or she will be subjected to discipline, up to and including a one-game suspension, even if he or she doesn't gamble.

An official who gambles on a team sport at any time during the year will be immediately terminated.

Officials have to get a physical each season, and for the first time in 2015, all officials had to go to New York to have NFL doctors perform the physicals. It's not just physicals, either. They also had to go through agility drills. The NFL wants to make sure that an official is healthy and is agile enough to cover his or her position.

Like I said, there are still a lot more don'ts than dos.

7   AS GOOD AS IT GETS
...OR IS IT?

YES, OFFICIALS MAKE GOOD MONEY, BUT I WILL TELL YOU, WITH THE
pressure and all the tension that comes with the job, these guys
earn every penny.

Believe me; I get it. There's pressure in every job. But when
these officials make it to the NFL, the burden to get it right increases tenfold compared to what they faced at the college level.
Want proof? Look no further than the NFL's television ratings.

The Super Bowl continues to set viewership records, and the
regular-season and playoff numbers continue to grow as well.
More than 100 million people have watched each of the last
six Super Bowls. In 2016, almost 112 million people watched
Denver defeat Carolina in a defensive battle, which was slightly
down from the nearly 115 million people that watched New
England win its fourth Super Bowl in 2015, beating Seattle in a
thrilling finish in the most-watched Super Bowl ever.

While Super Bowl Sunday might need to be added to the
list of national holidays, or at least the day after so people can
recover from their parties, it's not the only game that gets big

numbers.

Check out the ratings for the AFC Championship Game on CBS during the 2016 postseason. More than 53 million people watched the classic matchup of quarterbacks, as Peyton Manning and the Broncos outdueled Tom Brady and the Patriots. It was the second-most-watched AFC Championship Game in the past 39 years.

FOX took in nearly 46 million viewers in Carolina's blowout of Arizona in the 2016 NFC Championship. Can you imagine if it was a close game?

And it wasn't just the playoffs. There were 19 games during the 2015 regular season that delivered an average of 25 million viewers. To give some context of just how popular the NFL is, consider this: Seven of FOX's nine national *regular-season* broadcasts in 2015 delivered a 15.0 rating or better. The sixth game of the NBA Finals, in which Golden State won the championship, got a 13.4.

When you add social media to the mix, officials are scrutinized like never before. It's truly second to none.

Barry Mano, the president of the National Association of Sports Officials, says that the evolution of technology and its intrusion play a big part in today's game.

"Everything is so visible, you just have to simply plan on that," Mano said. "The officials have to go into it knowing that each thing he does or doesn't do is going to be evaluated at the highest levels.

"It's either going to come back to them as kudos or a downgrade, and they have to be willing to accept that kind of criticism and review. If they can't, they shouldn't be doing it."

— —

I think we've established that the "doing it" part is not easy. I can't tell you how much fun I had every time I got to call an official and tell him he had made it to the NFL.

On the flip side, however, not all parts of the job were fun. It was so painful for me when I had to tell an official they would no longer be working in the NFL. It was one of the hardest things I had to do as a boss.

But let's get back to the fun stuff. I got just as big a thrill informing the officials who made it as they did. Often times there were tears because the young official had accomplished his dream.

I remember the feeling I got when Jerry Seeman called me back in 1996 like it was yesterday.

Yesterday, in this case, was 20 years ago, and while I might not remember to take my pills these days, I will never forget the feeling of that phone call. It's as good as it gets.

But, for an official, it's not only the joy of doing the job—it's everything that comes with it, from the pay to the benefits and the excitement you get when you've reached the pinnacle of your profession.

So what was it that we saw in them that got them hired?

Quite frankly, the 122 that are currently in the NFL now were hired because they had it—they had the *it* factor. That is what makes an official stand out.

It's a subject that has been debated for as long as I can remember. And I'll admit—describing exactly what *it* is will give you fits. For me, it goes back to a Conference USA scrimmage

I went to at Southern Methodist University in the early 2000s. I was in the press box with Gerald Austin, who was—and still is—the coordinator of officials for Conference USA. He was watching some young officials work the scrimmage because he was looking for some new guys for his conference.

I asked him what it was that he was looking for and his response summed it up perfectly. Austin said, "I don't know." After many conversations, the scientific formula that Austin and I came up with was this: we don't know what *it* is, but if we saw *it*, we'd know it. Now, I know that sounds like a bunch of bullshit, but it's true. You can't spell *legit* without *it*.

Let's let somebody else try and explain it. Barry Mano describes *it* this way:

"The really good officials get completely immersed in the game itself and what's happening in the game, the flow of the game and the demands of the game at different times.

"It's what they do better than most, and they see better than most," Mano said. "It's pretty interesting. There are officials that see better than the rest of the other officials, and they get more plays right because they see better."

In today's NFL, if I asked football fans which referee was the best, I bet a lot of them would say Gene Steratore. If I asked those same fans to say why they think Steratore is the best official, I don't think any of them would answer that it is because he made good calls on the field.

So let's examine closer what *it* might be.

Steratore's strong, and he's got that look that you would expect from somebody that owns the position. It's a look that, when you see it, gives you confidence in him. It's that look that he gives you, combined with his physical stature and the way he moves. Steratore is also a basketball official and is very athletic.

Part of the *it* factor is definitely how you look, because people will initially judge an official by that. That's why whenever I went to our clinics I would pound the message about pounds into officials' heads — that they had to be in shape to be successful in the NFL. I told them that if they were out of shape the first look that they'd get from a coach would be negative. The first part of it is that you have to be fit.

Here's how Jerry Markbreit, one of the greatest officials in NFL history, described the *it* factor:

"It's someone that is better than the rest, in such an intuitive way, that they perform at a level high above everybody else in a spectacular way.

"The guy is the backbone of an officiating crew. He's the guy that inspires those of lesser abilities to get better."

Another thing that makes Steratore stand out is that he's decisive. When he flips on the microphone and gives his announcement of a foul, he says it with the authority that demonstrates he knows it is the correct call.

When I used to go watch officials work, I didn't care what calls they made. I really didn't. Heck, whether it was a pass interference penalty or holding, I was never sure on first glance if the call was right anyway. I was more concerned if they were decisive in making a call. Did the official grab his flag and throw it with authority?

It's a big part of being a great official, because hesitation leads to suspicion. If an official hesitates, everybody is going to wonder why he made that decision and not really have the confidence in what he called. Decisiveness is clearly a part of being a good official.

Communication is another big key for officials. When I would go to scrimmages, I would especially look to see how the officials connected with players and coaches. Conflict resolution was a big thing for me.

- How do they get involved?
- How do they react when they have a player-to-player confrontation?
- How do they talk to the coaches on the sidelines?

You don't have to be up close and personal to tell if an official has confidence in those situations. I could watch from afar to see if they were relaxed or if they were uptight and uncomfortable. You could tell. A good official always gets along with the people on the sidelines as well as the players.

It's the game within the game that officials have to play. They don't belong to the home team or the visiting team, yet they have to communicate with both. The officials are their own team, the Seven Musketeers if you will—all for one, and one for all.

Like I said, communication was big for me. It's yet another aspect in helping understand what *it* is. Part of the communication process really is professionalism. I don't think you can be a good official on any level without it.

Another thing associated with the *it* factor is rules knowledge.

I don't care what level officials are at when you evaluate them—they need to have the ability to master the rules. By that, I mean they have to have the desire to do so. You can quickly gauge an official's rules knowledge just by spending a little time with him or her. Rules knowledge has to be automatic. If something happens on the field and the officials have to ask if it's legal or not, they're dead. They have to know.

Lastly, an official must have an abundance of courage.

"It's a critical dimension that an official be able to go out there and do what they know is the right thing to do at the right time they need to do it," Mano said.

"The official simply needs to go out there, evaluate the situation without any fear, and make the call based on his knowledge and his positioning on the field," Mano added.

The thing I used to get a kick out of when talking about the *it* factor was this: when we went through the evaluation system in the NFL, 80 percent of an official's grade was based on calls they made on the field and 20 percent was for the subjective areas, which we called the *it* factor.

While nobody discounts the importance of getting the calls right on the field, it seems more significance should be attached to the *it* factor, in my opinion, since that's what gets somebody hired in the first place.

By recognizing the *it* factor, it changed the way we did business in the NFL in terms of hiring new officials. We always sat back and waited for officials to apply, and we would follow their progress, much like what happened to me before I got in. However, when we realized that *it* was what made officials special, we had to commit to doing things a different way.

We explained to our scouts what we felt *it* was:

It was physical stature.

It was professionalism.

It was decisiveness.

It was rules knowledge.

It was courage.

The NFL scouts were told to find guys with those qualities. We didn't necessarily care if the officials they were looking at might have made a bad call, because better play calling is something that can be taught.

But with officials being scrutinized like never before, Dean Blandino, the NFL's vice president of officiating, told me they've taken the search to another level.

"We kind of came up with a little bit of a hybrid; where there is some bird-dogging, where you send somebody out and look at the officials; the other thing is just maybe it's more targeted bird-dogging," Blandino said.

"I'm really looking at that former athlete, that former player, somebody that we could target. We're also trying to have more collaboration with the division II and division III college coordinators because they should be the ones that know."

And what do you do if you find them? Blandino told me about the league's new Advanced Development Program.

"We're taking these officials and trying to re-create something similar to what we used to do with officials and NFL Europe," Blandino said.

"Over 21 weeks, there's a group of 35 officials that are going to mini-camps, that are going to go to training camps, going to spend time with the crew doing the preseason work on the field during the preseason. Then, at the end of their college season, they come back and spend the regular-season weekends with a crew. A lot of what officials do is off the field: the preparation, and the pregame regime. They get that experience. Then when they do come into the league, we feel like they're more ready.

"An official could be in the program from one to six years before they become an NFL official. But the key is, that once they become an NFL official, they would be far more prepared than if they just came straight from college, where they're not getting all of the training they need."

That's really excellent. And while there are some things you can definitely teach, you can't teach *it*. Either you have it, or you don't.

Yes, an official could work on his appearance and get in shape. But in reality, having the character traits that reflect decisiveness, confidence, professionalism, and courage is something that can't be taught.

We told the scouts not to come back until they found officials that have *it*.

So we know what makes a good official and what goes into finding officials with the *it* factor. One thing we also know is that the 122 officials currently working in the NFL are very good at what they do.

It's one thing to be a good official, but how good is the officiating? Those are two different things. And if the officiating isn't as good as it should be, how much room is there for improvement?

A lot of people may not be happy or believe some of the

statements I'm about to make, but they're factual statements.

NFL officials are right 97.5 percent of the time. You read that right, but I'll write it again to make sure your eyes aren't playing tricks on you, and I'll even put it in italics for emphasis.

NFL officials are right 97.5 percent of the time!

How did I reach that conclusion? Prior to the time that I became the vice president of officiating, there was really no accurate way to assess officiating—how good it was or how bad it was. The only way the system was set up was to assess individuals, and it was only based on the times that they threw a flag, or in certain instances, where they decided not to throw a flag when they should have.

I tried to come up with a more accurate way to ascertain the performance of the crew, and I came up with something that I thought was more detailed. I took the total number of plays in a game and then saw how many of those were officiated correctly. From that, I would get a percentage of accuracy. For example, if you had 157 plays, which was the average number of plays per game in 2014, and the officials made four mistakes, that would mean 153 plays were called correctly. Calculated out, that is a 97.45 percent accuracy rate.

But let's take it a step further. That 97.45 figure is based on 157 plays of an entire game. If you actually break down any one of those plays, there are probably 10 or more situations within each play that could present a circumstance where an official would have to make a decision, whether or not to call a foul.

I can hear you all now: "What the heck is Pereira talking about?" It's not calculus, but what's coming might sound like it.

Think about it for a second: Every play has five linemen

blocking. There are five eligible pass receivers that are either blocking or running pass routes. How about the formation? Is it legal? Is either team offside? Is it a catch or is it incomplete? Is it a fumble or is the runner down?

I could go on and on...

So we've talked about the 157 plays per game, and when you figure in the situational possibilities on each play, now you're talking about a potential minimum 1,570 decisions the officials have to make during the course of a game.

And when the officiating department in New York reviews each game, each official, each play, each decision would then get evaluated. That's every single play and every single decision.

If, in fact, it turns out that only four mistakes are made in 1,570 potential decisions, that percentage of accuracy would be beyond phenomenal. But, on the other hand, is it acceptable?

Now that we've covered the statistics and as we head into the 2016 season, I want you fans to open your mind and accept these as basic premises when you start to make judgments from your couch.

Many of you won't know or care who Tim Gleason is, but he understands. Gleason, aka maryrose, is a blogger for *Behind the Steel Curtain,* and he definitely comprehends officiating.

Gleason wrote a blog post in 2008, and I remember reading it and thinking, *Wow, this guy gets it.* His post was titled "The Seven Dynamics of Officiating," which basically described the premises on which officiating is based.

When you try to determine whether you think officiating is good or bad, let me paraphrase some of what Gleason wrote:

1. **WE MUST ASSUME THAT NFL GAMES ARE NOT FIXED.** For starters, let's put that to rest: we must assume that the mistakes made are honest. Every time a bad call affects the outcome of a game, a small gallery of fools screams, "Fix!" Yes, we recently witnessed the Tim Donaghy deal with the NBA, and yes, all professional sports are vulnerable, but nothing peeves me more than people reaching presumptive conclusions that cannot be argued. You can't prove a negative to people who reach conclusions without any evidence to support their presumption, except that an incorrect call was made.

2. **BAD CALLS ARE A ONE-WAY STREET.** When a bad call goes against a team, it is clear that the team got shafted. When a bad call goes in favor of a team, it is one of those iffy, could-go-either-way calls. Even if a bad call is clear, the team will quickly point out other calls in the past that have gone against them. Bad calls against a team change momentum and can alter the outcome of a game. Bad calls in favor wouldn't have changed the outcome anyway and simply even out over the long haul.

3. **OFFICIATING IS THE MOST THANKLESS PROFESSION IN AMERICA.** Officiating might be the only profession that starts at zero and works backward. Officials are never thought of on the positive side of the ledger. Near-perfection is ignored. Anything short of perfection is hung out to dry. For reasons that can only be explained by a social phenomenon, we accept human failures to at least some degree by athletes and coaches. They

drop passes, they miss tackles, they blow coverage, and they make wrong play calls. These are all part of the game. Without human error, there would be no game. But with officiating, we somehow have a built-in zero-tolerance level for any error. They're not accepted to any degree.

4. **THOSE WHO WHINE THE MOST HAVE THE LEAST COM-PREHENSION.** When I see excessive criticism, I want to take those people and put them on the field with a whistle and let them feel the wrath. Officials know exactly how hard it is and how impossible it is to be perfect.

5. **TRANSPARENCY AND ACCOUNTABILITY.** It is quite noticeable that since the Donaghy incident, the NFL has gone to great lengths to be transparent. Fans often scream for "accountability" with officials. What they really mean by that is public lambasting. Fans don't want to concern themselves with an official's batting average. They want them in a public stockade when they make an error. That's what fans really mean by accountability.

6. **FULL-TIME OFFICIALS WOULD NOT IMPROVE THE NFL.** Whenever something bad happens, invariably someone from the gallery will proclaim that the NFL officials should be full-time, as if this billion-dollar league hasn't exhausted that question a thousand times. If the NFL thought somehow taking their day jobs away and looking at more film 40 hours a week would help them get better, the NFL would surely go in that direction.

7. **THE DOWNWARD SPIRAL.** This concerns me the most. It was shameful what happened to Ed Hochuli in the 2008

Chargers–Broncos game. Yes, he blew the call. Yet if you look at his entire body of work, the man is an outstanding referee. Those cowards never put on the stripes and if they did, couldn't carry Hochuli's whistle. Learning that a great official got death threats only makes the officiating profession worse. We need to work on reversing the spiral. We need to see officials in a positive light and not just ignore excellence.

Thanks, Tim. I couldn't have said it any better myself. While I might be changing my mind about No. 6 on Gleason's list, which you will read about later, he really nailed it.

I've already told you that NFL officials are the best this country has to offer. There are none better. The NFL plucks the very best from the college conferences. They already go through a training program that I think could be better, but I'll also get to that later in the chapter on the future of officiating.

I think a lot of people lose focus of how good NFL officials really are. Fans think they're bad sometimes, and yes, the officials do make mistakes. But we have the benefit of watching slow-motion replays of every play and from every angle imaginable.

The official has to make a decision in less than a second from one angle, at the same level as the players. Often officials might get caught in a situation where they are looking through or around players to make a call.

It seems so easy now because technology has made it *appear* easy. I'm telling you that if you put anyone out on the field other than the normal officials, it wouldn't work. That's how difficult the job is.

But don't just take my word for it.

"I'm really concerned that the combination of a generation that's grown up on video games, which is obviously not the real world, and super slow-motion, high-definition television is giving people a completely distorted view of what officiating's about in real time on the field," Bill Polian, the former president and general manager of the Indianapolis Colts, told me recently.

And he was just getting started.

"If we took a person out of the stands, forget about someone who's watching on television, and said, 'Stand down here right next to the line judge. You don't ever have to go on the field, just stand next to him and observe during the course of the game.' First of all, they'd be frightened to death by just the sound of it, much less the intensity, the speed, and the amount of physicality that exists down there. They'd come away convinced that no one but superhumans could ever referee."

What you need to remember is this: perfection is not attainable in officiating. It just isn't.

Everyone needs to get a grip. The game is faster than ever, and even though replay is in the picture, it can't correct everything.

So much of what we're talking about in these situations involves judgment—not facts but judgments that have to be made in a split second as to whether something is legal or illegal.

As I've detailed, the accuracy rate for NFL officials borders on phenomenal. I think that if a person in any other job performed at that level, they'd be in line for a promotion or a raise.

But listen, officials get it. The officiating department in New York gets it. It comes with the territory, and despite the terrain being treacherous to navigate, it doesn't mean that they don't strive for perfection.

I think a lot of that has to do with the fact that the NFL is a once-a-week game. The officiating department has the luxury of looking at every play of every game, including scrutinizing what every official did.

So you want to talk about accountability? We set standards that the officials had to make to work in the playoffs, or in some cases, to keep their jobs. There are still standards, but now they're called "tiered standards." The top tiered standards allow an official to work the Super Bowl and championship games while the officials in the lowest tiered standards don't get to work the playoffs at all. If an official falls into that lower tier for two straight years, they're likely to be replaced.

There were 11 new officials to join the league in 2015. That means that about 10 percent of the staff turned over. That is accountability, and that is being held responsible, along with the fact that each year, officials continue to have background checks and drug tests, just like the players.

The whole notion of the lack of accountability seems strange to me. It seems to be coming from people that know the least about officiating. Gleason wrote in his post that those who whine the loudest know the least, and I think that's true. By the way, that includes many in the media.

It's not a fine whine, either. But I think it has more to do with a fan's rooting interest than anything else.

Maybe you're a fan of the home team and the call goes

against your team.

Maybe it's against the team you bet on.

Maybe it's against your fantasy player and it cost you points.

Whatever the reason is, a fan is going to be upset. It's human nature. But I don't blame them, because to truly take the time to try and understand what goes into officiating on all levels is a foreign concept to most.

Obviously, I'm not talking about just the NFL. I'm talking from Pop Warner on up. But the problem with obsessive whining, as Gleason called it, is that it signals the downward spiral of officiating.

What is that? The downward spiral of officiating is that the negative voices become so loud, fewer people decide to officiate sports because they think, *Why should I?*

I'd say they've got a point. Does somebody really need that abuse?

The pool of people who might be thinking about officiating—even for kids, whether it's on the Pop Warner level or the high school level—won't do it because of the downward spiral of excessive whining.

Some of you might feel I'm at the pulpit now, but I'm not done preaching.

It's got to change. Why? If it doesn't, the consequences will be grim. Pete Morelli, a referee with 19 years' experience, is a fine man who made an error on a decision in replay during a Steelers–Colts playoff game in 2006. Pittsburgh's Troy Polamalu intercepted a Peyton Manning pass that was ruled an interception on the field. But Morelli reversed the decision in replay and ruled it to be an incomplete pass when he should have let the call that was made on the field stand.

It was wrong, and everybody knew it, including Morelli, after the fact. Was he held accountable? Absolutely. He made a big mistake and was downgraded.

But, unfortunately, the whiners got involved way more than they should have. Somebody threw a brick through Morelli's plate-glass window at his home. Somebody else ignited a cherry bomb underneath his car while it was parked in the driveway.

By the way, the Steelers won the game, despite the call. I get the passion that fans have, but this totally crossed the line.

We all need to step back a second, including yours truly, who has become a great slow-motion official, and realize that it's much easier for us to "officiate" like that from afar. These guys have to do it on the field in real time.

Should we be concerned about the excessive whining? Yes, we should, because the perils of officiating out there are worse than they've ever been.

Just ask two families who each lost a loved one—both soccer referees who were killed in 2013 and 2014 by players who were upset with calls the referees had made in the game. We're not talking about Europe here; these fatalities happened in Utah and Michigan. It's unbelievable, and it's unacceptable.

And there's more. In September 2015 a high school official in Marble Falls, Texas, was targeted by two players from John Jay High School, a school in the San Antonio School District, in one of the most despicable acts I have ever seen on a football field.

The first player blindsided the 14-year veteran back judge,

Robert Watts, hitting him in the back. The second player speared him while he was on the ground.

The two players said they were told by assistant coach Mack Breed to do it. Breed told the University Interscholastic League in San Antonio that what he said was that the official "needs to pay" but did not tell players to attack the back judge. Breed said he was surprised when the players hit the official.

Breed got suspended for the rest of the season along with two years' probation. He also resigned from his coaching position. The two players were suspended from playing sports for the rest of the school year. And head coach Gary Guttierez was given two years' probation.

I might be biased, but I think they should have shut down the football program for the rest of the year.

Officials must be protected, regardless of what Watts may have said prior to that, and despite the fact the officials in that game had called multiple unsportsmanlike conduct penalties against John Jay and suspended one of its players. What those players did was inexcusable.

Okay, I'm done preaching, but I felt it was necessary because I'm on the side of every official that steps on every field or steps on every court in every arena. I'm on the side of everybody who dares to put on the striped shirt, be they male, female, or youth.

It's a tough enough job as it is. Let's cut out the whining.

Now, my sermon is over.

8 THE BLAME GAME

FROM EVANGELIZING TO BEING AN INVESTIGATIVE REPORTER, THAT'S how quickly I can change gears. So now I've got breaking news, folks. I've scooped Jay Glazer, Adam Schefter, Chris Mortensen, and all the other insiders. If you want to alert FOX News and CNN, I'm sure those news organizations will want to know.

People, including officials, make mistakes.

I know that will surprise some of you, but as I just detailed in the last chapter, officials make nearly 1,570 decisions per game and they officiate 97.5 percent of the plays correctly.

And then there's that damn 2.5 percent.

I mentioned accountability in the last chapter, but I'm still baffled that people say to me all the time that officials are not held accountable. Excuse me? Are they not held accountable? I don't get it. In your profession, whatever you might be doing, do you have somebody looking over your shoulder every minute of your day? The officials do.

Their mistakes are made on live television in front of millions of people. Are your mistakes magnified like that?

But before I get into specifics of how officials are held accountable, I want to make a revelation that I truly believe—and have believed for a long time:

The NFL, with the exception of the senior vice president of officiating, Dean Blandino, are not big fans of officials or officiating in general.

There it is. I said it. Listen, I don't like saying it, because I love the NFL and loved my time working there. But that's my belief.

Why do I think that? Because officiating is perceived as a negative, and that reflects poorly on the league. And the 2015 season was a perfect example of that. You will seldom hear anybody talk about how great officiating is and how good it is for the NFL. The fact is that any time an official throws a flag, it's a negative. It's somebody doing something wrong, and that translates into the league getting complaints.

It's certainly not a revenue generator. In a league that puffs its chest about how its goal is to have league revenue increased to $25 billion by 2027, officiating is a negative. It doesn't bring in a dime.

I used to joke when I was in the league office that the notion the officiating department didn't bring in any money was flat-out wrong. One year, I sold two rule books for $10 each. That was $20 worth of income to help offset the $30 million or so it takes to run that department.

But let's get back to how officials are held accountable. In my mind, as well as others who have run the NFL's officiating department, accountability always had to do with grades.

That's how you hold officials culpable, and if they don't grade high enough, they don't get to the playoffs, which can be quite lucrative. And if you don't grade high enough and make a certain standard over a period, the next step is getting fired.

That's accountability. But as the great Bob Dylan once sang, "Things Have Changed." And, unfortunately, if you look at a four-week snapshot of the 2015 NFL season, I think that period became a watershed moment for how the league changed its approach to the accountability of its officials. Blameworthiness went from grades to suspensions and then insults.

However, before we get to that, you first have to understand how it got to this point.

I feel it's because the top three people in leadership at the league office responsible for the officiating department have never officiated. Let's start with Commissioner Goodell, followed by Troy Vincent, the executive vice president of football operations, and Blandino.

None of them have ever been officials, so it would be difficult for them to know exactly what it's like to be on the field. And if the 2015 season is any indication, accountability will be handled by the league much differently going forward.

But it all starts and ends with Goodell. As I said, Goodell is not fond of officiating, regardless of what he's said in public, and he certainly didn't like dealing with officiating lockouts, which the league has had to handle twice since 2001. That's why the senior vice president of officiating has to stand up for his officials.

Clearly, I faced negative situations during my time that had people in the league office very upset, but I did not let the league go too far, as evidenced by these next two key moments.

The first took place in week 16 of the 2001 season. Referee Terry McAulay had a game between the Jaguars and Browns in Cleveland, which I will get into in much greater detail in the next chapter, "Plays That Changed NFL History."

But here are the basics. There were less than two minutes left in the game, and the Browns had the ball but were trailing. Cleveland quarterback Tim Couch completed a fourth-down pass that appeared to be a first down, but with no timeouts left, the clock continued to run. Couch ran up to the line of scrimmage to spike the ball for the next play, and after the ball got spiked, the officials signaled the replay official had buzzed down right about the same time as the ball was snapped.

McAulay and his umpire, Carl Paganelli, said that they felt the buzz, and both felt it came right before the snap. McAulay reversed the call because it was clearly incomplete, and because it was a fourth-down play, the ball was awarded to Jacksonville, essentially ending the game.

Cleveland fans went crazy. They felt the play shouldn't have been reviewed because the ball had been snapped. But you could not prove it. It's about the only area in officiating where there's nothing visible to prove when it happened. There's no light that goes on when the buzzer is hit by the replay official— such as, by contrast, the red light that goes off on the shot clock in the NBA.

It was McAulay, Paganelli, and the replay official's word, and I was certainly going to support them. I had to, because I couldn't prove them wrong.

What happened next became known as "Bottlegate." Fans

were so upset that they threw bottles and other objects on the field, and because McAulay feared for the health and safety of his crew, as well as the players, he took the players off the field and said the game was over, even though there were 48 seconds left in the game.

However, McAulay didn't have the authority to do that. McAulay could have temporarily suspended the game, but he had no right to end the game. That purview falls under the power of the commissioner. The league got on the phone with McAulay and told him he had to get the teams back on the field and finish the final 48 meaningless seconds.

We were dealing with an issue that we had never dealt with before—not being able to prove when the officials were buzzed. I didn't give McAulay or his crew a downgrade for reviewing the play because I couldn't prove when they were buzzed. However, in the era of the system of accountability, I gave McAulay a downgrade, an incorrect mechanic for taking teams off the field. Goodell was not satisfied. He wanted McAulay suspended. Suspend him for what? Because he took the teams off the field temporarily while everything but the kitchen sink was being thrown at them? Granted, he shouldn't have announced the game was over, and I gave him the accountability of the downgrade, but I wasn't going to suspend him. I did, however, write him a letter that basically outlined that while the situation was unusual, he was not to do it again. If he did, I told him further discipline would be taken. Believe me, Terry McAulay is a bright man and will never come close to doing that again.

Goodell persisted, but I refused to give in. What happened

next was anything but good. The conversation escalated, and when he was down in front of my office, with others present, he was so frustrated and, I'm sure, getting so much heat from Cleveland that he gave me a hard shove into my door to try and continue the argument about McAulay in my office. Quite frankly, it startled me, and I think it startled him a little because the discussion ended shortly after that.

Despite that, I stood my ground and refused to suspend McAulay. It would have been the wrong thing to do. Even though I worked for the league, I still managed the 119 officials. You have to support your "players," including sticking to your guns when you get shoved by your boss—who, by the way, wasn't yet commissioner then. He was the executive vice president and chief operating officer.

Goodell was, however, the commissioner the next time he wanted to overly discipline an official. At least I got a seven-year reprieve to recover from "the shove" before Goodell-Pereira Round 2 took place. Hey, everything has a nickname in sports, why not me?

It was the second week of the 2008 season, and this one involved perhaps the most recognized referee in the game, Ed Hochuli. Again, I will go into more depth on this in the next chapter, because this also was a play that changed NFL history.

Again, the basics: the game took place in Denver between the Broncos and Chargers. The Chargers were leading, and as the game was nearing an end, Denver quarterback Jay Cutler rolled out, and as he started to pass the ball, it came loose in his hand.

Hochuli ruled that it was an incomplete pass. But when the

first replays were shown, you could clearly see it was a fumble and not an incomplete pass. Although replay allowed Hochuli to reverse the ruling of an incomplete pass to a fumble, the ball was dead as soon as it hit the ground. And the defense was not allowed to recover.

And Hochuli knew it. There was nothing he could do to give the ball to the Chargers. So instead of San Diego getting the ball and letting the clock run out to win the game, Denver got to keep the ball and scored a touchdown and two-point conversion to win the game.

It was a huge missed call by Hochuli, and he was devastated. I gave him the maximum downgrade because he made an error in judgment. Remember, it was just Week 2, and because of the type of downgrade it was—he and his crew cost the Chargers a game—I was curious how it would affect them. Because sometimes the impact of a mistake like that can linger for weeks.

But Hochuli and his crew rebounded and had an unbelievable rest of the season—13 great games that took them from the bottom of the heap after Week 2 and put them near the top at the end of the regular season. So I put them in the playoffs.

When I took the playoff assignments to Goodell to approve, he told me that Hochuli was not to be in the playoffs, based upon the call he made in Week 2. It wasn't quite Goodell–Pereira "The Rematch," but I argued. I couldn't in good conscience keep them out of the playoffs. I'd be sending a message to every crew out there that if they made a critical mistake at the beginning of the year, even if they battled back to have a better overall season than most crews, they'd be held out of the playoffs. That wouldn't have been fair, because they had earned the right to make it under the system.

I told Goodell I wouldn't do it. I knew if I gave in and let something like that happen, it would have been a very poor reflection on me, and I knew I would have lost the confidence of my entire officiating staff.

Which brings me to the 2015 season. The thing that got it all started involved events that transpired from Weeks 3 through 5 that made me feel the line on accountability has moved. Let's go through the details.

Week 3: In a game between the Saints and Panthers, Carolina quarterback Cam Newton publicly called out referee Ed Hochuli after the game. Newton felt like he had been hit late by Saints tackle Tyler Davison, and when he asked Hochuli why he didn't get the call, he claims Hochuli said he was too young to get that call.

Newton had rolled out and thrown a pass near the sideline on the run and got pushed to the ground by Davison. What Hochuli said to him was that he was outside the pocket, and he wasn't going to get that call because he was a runner. Hochuli wasn't allowed to talk publicly about what he said, but he asked the league to hire a professional lip reader because you could see what he said. Looking at the replays, you can see that is, in fact, what he said.

Hochuli is a 27-year referee in the league and very highly respected. He didn't get to plead his case while Newton went public with his claim on two different occasions. In studying tapes of that play, the league said they believed Hochuli and found no evidence of him saying anything to Newton other than what he said he said. Newton, of course, got no discipline.

Week 4: It was a Monday night game between Detroit and Seattle. The Seahawks were clinging to a 13–10 lead with 1:51 left in the game and the Lions driving. On third-and-1 from the Seattle 11-yard line, Detroit quarterback Matthew Stafford hit Calvin Johnson with a short pass, and as he approached the goal line, Seattle safety Kam Chancellor punched the ball out of Johnson's left hand into the end zone. The ball bounced toward the back of the end zone, and rather than recover it, Seahawks linebacker K.J. Wright pushed the ball forward out of bounds.

It was an illegal bat by Wright, and a penalty should have been called. That would have given the ball back to the Lions, with the penalty enforced from the spot of the fumble, which was the half-yard line. That would have put the ball on the quarter-yard line. Instead, the Seahawks got the ball and ran out the clock for a victory. On the replay, you could see back judge Greg Wilson reached for his flag, but decided not to throw it. But Rule 3 states that to have an illegal bat, it must be an intentional striking or punching of the ball with your hand or arm. In this case, it was a little different because it was a push and probably looked a little funny to Wilson. He made a judgment call that it wasn't enough to call illegal batting. He clearly knew the rule but passed on throwing the flag.

Of course, with social media, the news was huge. The league admitted right away that it was a mistake, and Wilson was given a downgrade. I talked with several current officials afterward, and many didn't think it was overt or intentional enough to have a foul called when there were no other players around.

I don't agree. I do think it was a foul and should have been called. If for no other reason than without the push out of bounds, the ball would have bounced in the end zone. The ball doesn't always bounce forward, so you don't really know what might have happened.

Detroit safety James Ihedigbo said after the game that the officials needed to be held more accountable for their mistakes on the field.

There's that word again, *accountable*. Give me a break. I'd be fine with that logic as long as you hold Calvin Johnson accountable for fumbling the ball and Seahawks quarterback Russell Wilson accountable for losing two fumbles earlier in that game.

While I agreed with the downgrade for Greg Wilson, I disagreed with what the league did to him two weeks later in Week 6. They switched him off the high-profile Sunday night game, New England at Indianapolis on NBC, and put him on the Miami at Tennessee game so it wouldn't get talked about on national television in prime time.

Wilson, by the way, is an excellent, veteran back judge, and they switched him off the game. The NFL could have reached out to NBC to ask them to lay off the topic since it had been discussed ad nauseam in the media. Instead, the league switched Wilson off the game, publicly embarrassing him again for a judgment call.

Week 5: I guess you could say time flies when you're entrenched in controversy after controversy, and the NFL had to wait only a week for the next one, this also on Monday night, in a game between the Steelers and Chargers.

In one of the more bizarre things I've seen on a football field, the problem stemmed from a clock issue.

Here was the situation: San Diego had kicked a field goal with 2:56 remaining in the game to take a 20–17 lead. The Chargers kicked off, and the ball went out the back of the end zone for a touchback. As the Steelers offense and Chargers defense were running onto the field, all of a sudden the clock started to run and 18 seconds ticked off, down to 2:38.

The problem? It was during the dead-ball period when no play was going on. But the bigger problem was that nobody saw it. The officials on the field didn't see it. The replay official didn't see it, and neither did either of the teams.

It came to everybody's attention, again, because of social media. Luckily, it didn't affect the outcome of the game, because the Steelers ended up scoring a touchdown on the last play to win the game. The only thing that might have been a little different is that the Steelers could have changed their play selection had they known they had 18 more seconds. Or San Diego would have had 18 seconds to receive a kickoff.

It never should have happened. Whose fault was it? First and foremost, it was the clock operator's fault. The clock operator is hired by the league and paid by the league, and it was his fault.

Now, on the field, that responsibility fell to the side judge, Rob Vernatchi. By the way, the stadium clock, operated by Michael Mothershed in this case, was the official clock. But I get the fact that the side judge is responsible for overseeing the clock.

Vernatchi got notified a day after the game by Blandino that he would get the maximum downgrade, which is a minus-10.

That's certainly understandable. As I said, the side judge is responsible, and somebody on the field had to take the hit. So

Vernatchi was downgraded, as he should have been. However, instead of sticking with the grading system for culpability, here's another example of how times have changed. Two days after being downgraded, Blandino told Vernatchi that he would also be suspended for a game. Suspended for something missed that was very unusual, and in the end, really had no impact on the game. Besides that, no official in his right mind would have suspected that a veteran clock operator would start the clock after the ball became dead on a kickoff.

Vernatchi was suspended and made a public embarrassment of when nothing was being said about the clock operator, Mothershed, who is not only paid by the league but is also a referee in the Pac-12. So it wasn't like he was inexperienced.

This made it official to me—the relationship between the league and its officials had turned. It went from accountability to suspension for something so unusual that a week after it happened, the league adopted a new process that required every crew to record the time of the score after every score inside two minutes of the second quarter and five minutes of the fourth.

It was a new process, because even Blandino admitted it was an unusual circumstance, yet Vernatchi was suspended. But the league seemed to feel it was more important to protect Mothershed, who was responsible for this whole mess to begin with. Eventually Mothershed was let go by the league.

So now, it went from accountability, to suspension, to insult. They made Vernatchi meet with a security person and an NFL lawyer. Why? Because now the league was questioning his integrity, and I guess wanted to make sure he didn't have a bet on the game. Why else would you ask Vernatchi to do that?

That wasn't just an attack on Vernatchi; the league was questioning the integrity of all 122 officials as well. But here's maybe the worst part—whatever credibility the league leadership of Goodell, Vincent, and Blandino had in the eyes of the officials vanished much quicker than those 18 seconds.

I'm a big fan of Blandino's, but it's a fine line when your leader in something like officiating has not done what the people he is leading do. They made the right choice to bring him in. They made the right choice to make him the VP of officiating, but I think he made a bad decision on this one, if it was indeed his decision.

What he did was throw Vernatchi under the bus because of the heat that I know came from his bosses.

Between the two years I spent on the field in the NFL, along with the 12 more I spent in the office, I had not seen a darker period than the league was going through then—when accountability went from grading to an attack on integrity.

If you want to suspend somebody, I'm fine with that if it's for cause. A suspension for calling a player names on the field, I get it. Firing an official for putting his Super Bowl tickets on eBay and trying to sell them at a profit, certainly. And firing an official for cashing in his first-class plane ticket and pocketing the difference between a coach and first class ticket is totally understandable. The latter two actually happened under my watch.

But this wasn't right—and I wasn't the only one who thought so.

"Suspending sports officials is a distinctly bad idea. Mistakes are made in every game by players, coaches, and officials," said

Barry Mano, president of the National Association of Sports Officials. "Some have little to no impact and some loom large. We seem to have gotten to the point, as it relates to officials, that any mistake is to be redressed. No 'bad deed' can remain unpunished.

"The knee-jerk reaction to a real or believed mistake is to publicly suspend," Mano continued. "Suspending an official will not lead to a better performance by that official or the others on the staff. It will bring fear into the room. That drives morale down. Suspensions make no sense, other than in a PR director's playbook. Suspensions are a public dressing down."

And for those who think, *Oh, that's just Pereira ranting again*, I'm not the only smart person who thought that.

Scott Green, a former NFL referee who spent 23 years in the league, including working three Super Bowls, wrote a critical story in *USA Today* saying Vernatchi's suspension was indicative of the Goodell regime. He called it an arbitrary punishment of an individual for a fast public-relations fix.

Green also characterized it as a reactive approach for short-term satisfaction for one team's fans but said that it didn't address improvement. Instead of rhetoric about strong-arming officials as a group to accept more discipline, Green said that the NFL needs to evaluate how its officiating department is administered.

But if you thought Weeks 3 through 5 got everybody upset, that would just be a tremor compared to the earthquake of criticism that would shake the league after several more faux pas in Weeks 6, 7, 10, 11, 12, 13, and 15.

Let's take a closer look:

Week 6: At the beginning of the 2014 season, the league office began to get much more involved from its command center in New York with the replay decisions that were being made on the field. Here's an example from Week 6 in 2015 of a highly questionable call that took place in the Bears–Lions game.

Here was the situation: Detroit had a 14–13 lead and the ball at the Chicago 3-yard line with 58 seconds to play in the first half. Lions quarterback Matt Stafford threw a pass to Golden Tate, who caught it at the goal line and was hit by the Bears' Kyle Fuller as he broke the plane. The ball popped loose and appeared to be intercepted by Jonathan Anderson for a touchback. In fact, it was ruled an interception on the field.

Instead, it was overturned to a touchdown. The question was, did Tate maintain control long enough to become a runner, to be able to ward off contact? I don't think he did. The ball had already started to come loose before the "third foot" was on the ground.

The league pointed out at the start of the 2014 season that it was adamant about sticking with the calls made on the field unless there was clear visual evidence to the contrary. On this play, I don't think it was clear and obvious that Tate had become a runner. Even Blandino publicly stated that it was close and later admitted to his officials that if he had to do it over again, he wouldn't have reversed the call. The touchdown gave Detroit a 21–13 halftime lead. In the end Detroit won by three, 37–34, so one could argue that the Tate play turned out to be the difference in the game.

Here's the issue I have. Did the league's involvement on that play, combined with the influence it has on all reviews, open

Pandora's box? Who challenges Blandino and the league? Are they above reproach? Who holds them accountable?

I know I wouldn't have wanted to be responsible for making those decisions. I felt that my role as the VP of officiating was to be the buffer between the officials and the teams. The officials are a neutral party that doesn't have any contact with the teams during the week. They are perceived to be neutral and are not allowed to work a team more than twice in a season to make sure there is a lack of familiarity.

But that's not the case in the league office. Do you want the league office making decisions on who wins and who loses? There's already a perception that the league office "protects" certain teams.

Now the conspiracy theorists can come out of the woodwork with accusations that the league, not just the officials, has a say in who wins and loses games.

That was an ugly four-week period for the league and for Blandino, a period in which I thought he had lost the officiating group.

While I was badgered and abused at times during my time with the league, I always did my best to stick up for the officials. I'm not sure Blandino could say the same during that period. As you'll read later, however, by season's end, he may have learned a valuable lesson.

Week 7: In the Baltimore–Arizona game, the Ravens were called for an illegal formation penalty on a reserve offensive lineman while they were in the red zone. The problem with the penalty was that John Urschel ran straight toward the huddle and looked to referee Ron Torbert while motioning to his jersey, signaling he was eligible. Ravens quarterback Joe Flacco also pointed out Urschel to the crew to try and emphasize the point, and Torbert seemed to acknowledge what they were doing.

So you can just guess what happened next. Urschel caught a six-yard pass and the Ravens were called for an illegal formation. The drive stalled and they had to settle for a field goal in a 26–18 loss.

It did seem rather unusual, considering Torbert seemed to acknowledge Urschel reporting. Torbert looked directly at Urschel and then he reached down to turn on his microphone, which is what normally happens, so he could announce the position change.

However, the league said Torbert was clarifying a number of a player from a previous play and he did not recognize the action as Urschel reporting. The league then notified the officials that they must do a better job of recognizing when all substitutions come in if there is any type of acknowledgement or request to change positions that are contrary to their number.

Week 10: The Ravens were on the short end of another missed call that cost them a game won by Jacksonville 22–20.

The Jaguars were trailing 20–19 in the closing seconds of the game. Jacksonville quarterback Blake Bortles was sacked by Elvis Dumervil and pulled down by the face mask with no time left on the clock. However, when the ball was snapped with less than 10 seconds remaining in the game, one of the offensive linemen wasn't set and should have been called for a false start by Pete Morelli's crew.

If the penalty had been called like it should have been, there would have been a 10-second runoff and the game would have ended with the Ravens winning because the Jaguars were out of timeouts.

However, since there was a defensive foul called on the last play of the game, the period was extended, and after the enforcement of a 15-yard penalty, the Jags kicked a 53-yard field goal on the game's final play to win the game.

This may have been the costliest mistake of the season because it cost the Ravens the game. I'm not one to normally say that one play or one call makes a difference in the outcome of the game, but in this case, I think it did.

Since the officials didn't shut down the play, the Jaguars ended up getting another play and kicking a field goal, which, to me, was the difference between winning and losing, as my friend Mike Shanahan used to say.

Week 11: There were three calls by referee Gene Steratore's crew that caused much scrutiny in the glare of the Monday spotlight in a game between the Bills and Patriots.

The first came early in the third quarter when Patriots quarterback Tom Brady hit Danny Amendola on a 14-yard reception at the New England 45. Amendola had a clear field in front of him, seemingly headed for a touchdown, but an inadvertent whistle ended the play at the spot of the catch. The Patriots would wind up missing a 54-yard field goal on the possession.

Nobody ever wants to hear an inadvertent whistle, especially an official. It's the worst thing you can do. I'd be lying if I said I had never done it myself, because I did do it in a major college football game and was devastated by it. You have to show restraint, and a whistle like this was certainly a costly mistake. Steratore got together with his crew and made an intelligent decision in allowing the completion to stand even though the whistle came while the ball was still in the air. It was a decision that was consistent with fumbles versus down-by-contact rulings. You allow the catch or recovery, but you don't allow any advance. Inadvertent whistles are really tough to deal with when you're an official because you anticipated, and therefore, did something as opposed to waiting to let it happen.

The second also came in the third quarter on a six-yard touchdown run by the Patriots' James White. The Patriots quick-snapped the ball while the Bills were trying to make substitutions.

Patriots tight end Scott Chandler was running onto the field for the play but changed course and retreated to the sideline. The Bills tried countering with substitutions, and Jerry Hughes was 15 yards behind the Patriots line of scrimmage. The ball should never have been snapped, as the Bills should have been given time to get their substitutions into the game, even though technically the Patriots didn't substitute.

The whole substitution process has become something that's very difficult for officials with the quick snapping that teams are using nowadays, because it's not just the clear substitution, but it's a simulated substitution that gives the opportunity for the defense to match up if they need to. Including the end zones, the field is 120 yards long, and when a player enters or leaves the field, it might be difficult to spot, especially when the ball is down deep in a team's territory, which was the case on this play.

I can see how this was missed. But the officials have to be cognizant of players running on or off the field and any type of substitution process. If the offense substitutes or they even simulate the substitution, the defense gets a right to match up and the umpire has to stand over the ball and wait for play to begin until that happens.

And finally, the third one came on the game's final play of a 20–13 win by the Patriots. Buffalo quarterback Tyrod Taylor hit Sammy Watkins at the Bills' own 48-yard line. Watkins went out of bounds with two seconds remaining and the Bills should have had a shot at throwing a Hail Mary pass. However, the head linesman signaled for the clock to continue to run and time ran out. The official, in only his second season in the NFL, in my opinion mistakenly applied the college rule, saying Watkins was down in bounds when he first hit the ground.

The officials should have stopped the clock. Instead, the official kept the clock running, and time expired. Would it have made a difference for the Bills? You never know with a Hail Mary.

In fact, when a receiver goes to the ground without being touched and rolls out of bounds, the clock should stop in that situation. If he intentionally gives himself up and goes to the ground, which is what they said in the pool report, then the clock would remain running, but that clearly wasn't the case here.

Watkins caught the ball near the sideline, went to the ground, rolled over, and his momentum took him out of bounds untouched. The Bills should have had one more play.

Week 12: Unfortunately, the Arizona–San Francisco game

was not pretty. Referee Pete Morelli's crew's had several problems during the game, most notably, losing track of downs and taking a down away on one of the Cardinals' possessions that caused nearly a five-minute delay. Arizona coach Bruce Arians said afterward about the officials: "They can't count to three." The league was so upset by that crew's performance, it reassigned them from Week 13's primetime, Sunday night game between the Colts and Steelers to an afternoon game.

It seems to me that every year, there is a crew that has a dark cloud that follows them wherever they go. That was certainly the case with Morelli's crew. This game represented the type of season this crew was having. It was a simple play and the defense had 13 men on the field and the crew didn't get it shut down before the ball was snapped.

Since they didn't, the play transpired, which involved a penalty on the defense. That would have made it first-and-5, which should have been a simple penalty enforcement for too many men on the field. The flags were late, a discussion ensued, the penalty was then enforced, and they rolled the down to the second down, saying basically that the penalty occurred between downs and not during the first-down play.

It was wrong, and it obviously cost Arizona a down. One of the worst mistakes, from an officiating standpoint, is giving a team an extra down or shorting them a down. You can understand why Arians was upset.

It's the type of administrative mistake that the league looked into and eventually decided to use replay to correct administrative mistakes in the playoffs. This was a critical mistake by Morelli's crew.

Week 13: Detroit was the scene of the next controversy. And it came in another primetime game, this one between the Packers and the Lions.

The Packers were trailing 23–21 very late in the game. As Packers quarterback Aaron Rodgers was scrambling desperately on what appeared to be the game's final play, Lions defensive end Devin Taylor's right hand hit Rodgers' face mask, causing Rodgers' helmet to rotate. It wasn't a violent facemask pull, but it was enough for Carl Cheffers' crew to call a penalty, giving the Packers an untimed down, since time had expired. And on the next play Rodgers threw a 61-yard touchdown pass to tight end Richard Rodgers, giving the Packers the miracle victory.

I'm just going to say it like it is: this face mask call was extremely technical, too technical to call. You could try to defend it and say that Taylor got a thumb in the mask and it turned the head slightly, but in fact, the thumb slid out early and quickly, and in order to have a 15-yard facemask penalty, you needed to see a twist, a turn, a pull, a push—and really none of those occurred.

In real time, it did look like it could have been, but it wasn't. Not only did Cheffers throw a flag, so did the head linesman. But slow motion showed that it was not enough to be a face mask. I said afterward it would have been much easier to defend why it wasn't called than why it was called.

This was basically the last play of the game, and it gave the Packers an extra down and the ability to beat Detroit on the Hail Mary, which they did.

Week 15: The hits seemed to just keep on coming for the

NFL's officiating department during the 2015 season and you could say the same thing for Giants receiver Odell Beckham Jr. and Panthers cornerback Josh Norman when New York squared off with Carolina.

What started out as a marquee matchup between two very talented players ended up as a disaster and a national discussion point as both players went at each other like it was a UFC fight. I thought both players crossed the line on several occasions. Beckham was called for three unnecessary roughness penalties, two on one series in the third quarter. Norman also drew an unnecessary roughness penalty on that same drive.

It was as if those two were playing in a game by themselves, because neither seemed to care about how their actions affected their teams.

Many in the national media, including Joe Buck on FOX's broadcast, criticized referee Terry McAulay and his crew for not ejecting both players.

The NFL released a statement afterward that said: "The disqualification of a player is a judgment made by the on-field officials. The actions of the players involved in unsportsman-like conduct will be reviewed as per the standard protocol that is followed in all situations of this type throughout the season."

Beckham was later suspended for a game and Norman was fined $26,000.

Something that people need to understand is that it's in the DNA of the officials not to eject someone unless it's clearly a non-football act. The two things in terms of player-to-player ejection that they are looking at are punches with closed fists and kicks. Those are two things that would merit an ejection. The other thing that merits an ejection is contact with a game official. It's not mandatory. It doesn't have to be an ejection, but if it's severe enough then it is an ejection.

I get it that people thought that the officials should have ejected Beckham and probably Norman, too. I think the officials, much like in the wild-card playoff game that got out of hand between the Bengals and the Steelers, did everything they could to try to keep control.

I think the people who didn't do everything they could to try to keep control were the players and the coaches. I get McAulay and his crew not throwing out Beckham, even though everyone talked about the big helmet-to-helmet shot by Beckham when Norman was leaning over the pile.

While I can't get into officials' heads, I think the thing that probably swayed them toward not ejecting Beckham for that hit was that it seemed to have no effect. Norman popped right up and went right after Beckham. If he had been down and out and unconscious on the ground, then they probably would have tossed Beckham.

The unique thing to me was how the league handled this whole situation. It came out and said that it called the replay booth to remind McAulay and his crew that they have the ability to eject players.

Does the league really think Terry McAulay didn't know that? He's refereed three Super Bowls. He knows that he has the ability to eject players. Again, the idea is not to eject players unless they have to. The other unusual thing was the officials' union coming out and making a statement that it felt that Beckham should have been ejected, even though executive director Jim Quirk felt that the interpretation of what he was saying wasn't correct. It was criticism from the officials' own group, which McAulay didn't take lightly and said he was not going to be a part of the union.

People asked me if, indeed, McAulay could drop out of the union. The answer is simple: no. In order for an official to work in the NFL under the collective bargaining agreement, he or she has to be a member of the union. Officials don't have to participate, but the dues are taken out of their paychecks by the league. Like it or not, McAulay has to be a part of the union, but he certainly doesn't have to participate. But McAulay is pretty headstrong, and I can imagine that he will have no participation going forward.

Here's my summation of the season of discontent.

The interesting thing as I look back on this seismic shift in the officiating world is that an official was suspended in Week 5 for a call that didn't affect the outcome of a game, yet an official missed a call in Week 10 that did have a direct bearing on the outcome and he wasn't suspended.

I think it's pretty easy to realize that suspensions don't do any good. The suspension didn't take away the mistake, yet mistakes continued to happen.

All of a sudden in Week 10, there was no suspension. I do believe that the league and Blandino realized that suspensions achieve nothing. They're just a PR move, and the public relations that you get is not worth the negative relationship that comes between the league and its officials.

I can't even begin to calculate how many times I was asked

during the bad stretch what was going on with officiating in the NFL why all of this was happening.

It was something that I had to reflect on because I really was having a hard time figuring it out myself. When I thought about it through the eyes of an official, I looked at the officiating roster and saw how young it had become. The league has hired 22 new officials in the last two years. That represents approximately a fifth of the staff, a fifth that had either no experience or just one year of experience heading into the 2015 season.

You look at that turnover and you start thinking about things like why is it that an official is not allowed to work a Super Bowl until he's got five complete seasons under his belt? Most officials will tell you that it takes almost five full years to get to the point where they can be completely comfortable officiating given the speed of the game. It's difficult and people sometimes forget that.

So with 22 new officials in just two years, is it any wonder this happened during the 2015 season? That's a lot of turnover.

Let's look at Pete Morelli's crew, which we know struggled. He had a second-year back judge and a first-year line judge in Sarah Thomas. Does that affect the veterans that you have on your crew? I think it does.

Veterans work with the newer officials and those that are trying to get used to the speed of the game, and maybe, while trying to watch over others, it affects their own performance. I'm not saying I'm not a proponent of turnover, because I do think there should be turnover. I just think you've got to be careful of turning over so many at one time.

Former Broncos and Redskins coach Mike Shanahan likened it to when he first got into coaching.

"You get up in the game and you lose focus of what your job is. It takes just a split second and it's over. You don't get a chance to catch up," Shanahan told me. "I can't tell you how many times it's happened to me with coaching. You can tell the officials that have been in the league for a while versus the officials that haven't been, just like coaches."

By the way, the turnover that transpired the last two seasons is not over. There's going to be more and more in the next couple years, with the staff becoming much younger. It may be that there will be more periods like this where they struggle.

The good news is that the more experience this young group gets, the better off they're going to be. So I think that bodes well for the future, which is a good thing. Early on, though, they may struggle with a few growing pains.

Another thing that factors into the equation is the turnover in the administrative ranks as well. Hell, look at the turnover in the NFL's officiating department. There have been three different vice presidents—myself, Carl Johnson, and now Dean Blandino—in a six-year period. It's not that the messages are necessarily different, but the way those messages are communicated to officials is, and the way that training videos are done is different. You're getting a different presentation from different people. I think all those factors contributed to what took place with officiating during the 2015 season.

While there are always going to be mistakes, I think as the season came to a close, the officials avoided any more catastrophes. They avoided the trainwrecks all the way through the

Super Bowl, so that aspect of it is good and it gives the league, Dean Blandino, and officiating as a whole something to build on heading into the 2016 season.

9 PLAYS THAT CHANGED NFL HISTORY

I'VE TALKED ENOUGH ABOUT THE UGLINESS. AT THE END OF THE DAY, I always hoped that the officials were never mentioned during the course of a game. If that happened, that meant they had done their jobs.

That's because the game is the thing. The players, the teams, and the coaches are whom people pay to see—and, in some cases, even the owners.

Throughout the storied history of the NFL, there have been many memorable games, plays, and moments that led directly to rule changes that have literally changed the game, and in turn, the course of professional football.

It's time for a stroll down memory lane—and it's a good thing it's a stroll, because I'm not sure I can go much faster at this point.

THE IMMACULATE RECEPTION
DECEMBER 23, 1972

FIRST UP ON OUR TREK IS THREE RIVERS STADIUM FOR A GAME BE-tween the Oakland Raiders and Pittsburgh Steelers. It was the site of one of the most famous plays in NFL history: the Immaculate Reception.

With 30 seconds left in the game and the Steelers trailing 7–6, Pittsburgh quarterback Terry Bradshaw threw a pass to Frenchy Fuqua, who was hit by Jack Tatum simultaneously as the ball got to him. The ball shot up into the air and then was scooped up by Franco Harris at the Steelers' 40-yard line, and he ran it 60 yards for the game-winning touchdown.

It was a very controversial play that more than 40 years later is still being debated. Why? Because when the ball was caught by Harris it was just inches, if that much, from hitting the ground. And the other big question was, did Tatum touch the ball? If Tatum didn't touch it, the play would have been ruled illegal, because the ball would have been touched consecutively by Fuqua and Harris, who were both offensive players.

But that led to a rule change. The rule, at that point, stated that two eligible receivers could not consecutively touch the ball.

A year later the rule was changed to say it was legal for two eligible receivers to touch the ball consecutively.

So many questions remain to this day. I'm afraid we'll never really know if the ball hit the ground before Harris caught it. And I'm not even sure instant replay would have solved the controversy if it was around in 1972.

I've looked at the play 100 times and I can't tell if the ball hit the ground, or who touched the ball first, Fuqua or Tatum. After my further review, the play stands.

THE HOLY ROLLER
SEPTEMBER 10, 1978

CONTROVERSY AND THE RAIDERS SEEM TO GO TOGETHER LIKE PEA-
nut butter and jelly. I'm not saying you couldn't have one
without the other, but it certainly appears they're made for one
another.

So it's only fitting that the Raiders would again be embroiled
in a controversial play that resulted in yet another rule being
changed.

The site was San Diego, the year was 1978, and the Raiders
were visiting the Chargers. The Raiders trailed 20–14, with
10 seconds remaining in the game. They had the ball at the
Chargers' 10-yard line and quarterback Ken Stabler dropped
back to pass. It appeared as though Stabler was about to get
sacked, and as he attempted to pass, he fumbled the ball forward. Raiders running back Pete Banaszak tried to pick up the
ball, but couldn't, and with the ball still loose, tight end Dave
Casper would try his hand—or should I say foot—at recovering the ball.

When Casper tried to pick up the ball, he accidentally kicked
it forward into the end zone. He then fell on the ball in the end
zone, giving the Raiders a touchdown and a 21–20 victory.

I interviewed Jerry Markbreit, who was the referee in that
game, about that play. It was only Markbreit's second year in
the NFL and, believe it or not, it was the first game he had ever
worked that was on national television.

"I was feeling pretty good about myself," Markbreit recalled. "Everything was going along great. I had made three or
four calls that I felt were really solid. I looked up at the clock

and there were 10 seconds left in the game. Then…

"Stabler dropped back, he got boxed in, and the ball pops out. I couldn't see exactly how the ball came out. Since then, I've seen it a thousand times from the front and he flipped the ball forward. I couldn't see it then, of course, but as a referee, if you don't know pass/fumble, you go fumble, which is what I ruled.

"Well, it was bad. It was muffed, it was kicked, and it wound up in the end zone and it ended up being ruled a touchdown. Of course, everybody went crazy, especially the Chargers. I thought I had made one of the great calls."

Markbreit told me that even after looking at the play a thousand times, he felt that it was impossible to see what really happened because there was somebody in the way of the camera. But he thinks Stabler flipped it forward.

Rule makers didn't find that play to be fair to the Chargers, so they instituted "the forward fumble rule" for the 1979 season. That stated a fumble on fourth down or inside two minutes to play, in either the second or fourth quarter, could only be recovered, and advanced, by the fumbling player.

After my further review, I agree with Jerry—Stabler did flip the ball forward and it should have been ruled an incomplete pass, not a fumble. Stabler's arm was clearly moving forward in an attempt to throw a pass when the ball came loose.

The Raiders should have lost.

While the play in the Raiders–Steelers game became known as the Immaculate Reception, San Diego fans dubbed this one the Immaculate Deception.

THE SNOWPLOW GAME
DECEMBER 12, 1982

"LET IT SNOW, LET IT SNOW, LET IT SNOW..."

I'm dating myself, but those words were part of a song that was sung by the legendary Dean Martin back in the '50s. They could have easily applied to a game between the Miami Dolphins and the New England Patriots that was played in Foxborough, Massachusetts.

The weather outside was frightful and there was nothing delightful about the heavy snowstorm that began falling before the game started.

Because of that, an emergency ground rule was established on the spot, which allowed the officials to call a timeout and have the ground crew clear the area where the yard markers were with a snowplow.

However, it was snowing so hard, the crew had difficulty keeping the field clean for any length of time. Fast-forward to the fourth quarter. The game was scoreless with a little more than four minutes to play. The Patriots were lining up to kick a potential game-winning 33-yard field goal when Patriots coach Ron Meyer ordered the snowplow to clear the area behind the line of scrimmage so his kicker, John Smith, could have a much easier time kicking the ball. Smith made the field goal and the Patriots won 3–0.

Upon my further review, the officials did nothing wrong. The NFL changed the rule after that season, and to this day, you can't clear the kicking area for an attempted field goal during the game with anything other than your hands or feet.

THE COIN TOSS
NOVEMBER 26, 1998

I'VE ALWAYS BEEN FASCINATED BY HOW A PLAY CAN HAVE A NAME attached to it, and I definitely had a few during my time overseeing the officiating department, starting with the Coin Toss Game.

Isn't Thanksgiving supposed to be a day of giving thanks?

I took a holiday trip home to the West Coast in November 1998 to be with Gail, and we had plans to go to a friend's house for Thanksgiving dinner. When I walked in, people started yelling at me—and not in that good way when they are happy to see you.

The Detroit Lions play on Thanksgiving Day about as often as somebody mentions Motown during the Grammy Awards—in other words, a lot. It was no different that year.

Pittsburgh was visiting Detroit, and it had been a good game that was tied 16–16 at the end of regulation.

Phil Luckett was the referee, and during the coin toss for the overtime, controversy struck. How can you have controversy on a coin toss? Oh, let me tell you.

Jerome Bettis was a captain of the Steelers, and the visiting team gets to choose between heads or tails. Luckett's microphone appeared to only pick up Bettis saying "tails" when he tossed the coin.

The coin toss came out tails and Luckett awarded the ball to the Lions. Luckett said that Bettis first said heads and then tails, which resulted in mass confusion on the field.

At the time, that's how the coin toss was done. The player would call his choice as the coin was in the air. It sounded pretty clear that Bettis said "tails," but if you listen really closely it sounds like he starts saying heads and then switches to tails.

The Lions got the ball and, on their first possession, kicked a field goal to win the game 19–16.

Upon my further review, I can't prove what was said and what wasn't said. But as confusing as it was, I would have seriously considered a do-over, retossing the coin.

As you might imagine, that led to a rule change. Captains are now required to make their choice before the coin is tossed.

Looking back now, it might seem insignificant, but it wasn't in 1998. It was one of those simple plays that changed the game.

THE MUSIC CITY MIRACLE
JANUARY 8, 2000

GOOD OL' NASHVILLE IS THE SITE OF OUR NEXT PLAY. IT WAS THE 1999 season and the game took place between the Buffalo Bills and Tennessee Titans.

It was a wild-card playoff game, and the result was anything but music to my ears.

The Bills had just kicked a field goal to take a 16–15 lead with 16 seconds left to play in the game. On the ensuing kickoff, Titans tight end Frank Wycheck caught the ball and was advancing it up the sideline when he stopped, then threw the ball completely across the field to Kevin Dyson, who ran 75 yards to score a touchdown.

The most improbable touchdown gave the Titans a 22–16 victory. However, at first glance, it looked like Wycheck had thrown the ball forward to Dyson, but the ruling on the field was that it had not been a forward pass.

"We practiced that play every Saturday," former Titans coach Jeff Fisher told me when I recently asked him to recall the play. "But here's the interesting thing about that play: Dyson was third on the depth chart at that point. But Derrick Mason was out with a concussion and Anthony Dorsett was cramping, so I told Kevin to get ready. I told him to stay five yards behind the ball and to stay outside the numbers because we were coming to him."

The line judge who made the call was Byron Boston. From the goal line, Boston hustled to try and get in the best position possible so he could make the call. He ruled that the pass was backward and legal. Replay looked at the play to see if it could be determined if the pass was forward or backward. After the review, replay indicated that the ball might have been parallel, but they couldn't tell if was forward or not, so the play stood as it was called on the field.

"I remember seeing Boston point backward, that was the key," said Fisher. "Had he not done that, who knows what would have happened? But he had gotten himself into position. Waiting for the decision on the challenge was tough, but I thought it would be difficult to overturn."

You know the word *fan* comes from *fanatic*!

Bills fans were so irate they hired engineers in Buffalo to send diagrams to the league office, showing that it was a forward pass. I remember looking at the videos and it was obvious to me that the pass wasn't forward, but the whole motion forward versus backward and what is parallel helped redefine the rule.

As a result of that play, two things were clarified. One: in order for a pass to be forward, it must be forward from the point where the passer releases the ball to where it first touches another player or the ground. If the pass is deemed to be parallel, the pass is considered to be backward.

Second: it reaffirmed the rule that stated in order to change something on instant replay, the referee needed to have clear, indisputable visual evidence to reverse a call. That wasn't the case in the Music City Miracle.

Upon my further review, get over it, Buffalo fans. The ruling on the field was correct. It was not an illegal forward pass.

Therefore, it remained a really great play in NFL history, a huge play in a playoff game that's still talked about to this day. That rule adaptation had a big effect on the game.

I asked Fisher if he still gets asked about that play.

"It still comes up all the time. As a matter of fact, there were 66,000 people in the stadium that day, but there are probably 100,000 who say they were actually there and saw it," Fisher laughed.

THE BERT EMANUEL RULE
JANUARY 23, 2000

HOW ABOUT HAVING A RULE REFERRED TO BY YOUR NAME?

Ladies and gentlemen, let me introduce you to Bert Emanuel, born in Kansas City, Missouri.

Emanuel played for eight years in the NFL with five teams, including Tampa Bay. But none of those years and none of the plays were as important as one he participated in during the 1999 NFC Championship Game between the Bucs and the St. Louis Rams.

The Bucs were trailing the Rams 11–6 when Emanuel made

a diving, 13-yard reception to the St. Louis 22-yard line with 47 seconds to play in the game.

Tampa Bay called a timeout and the Emanuel catch gave the Bucs a realistic chance to continue the potential game-winning drive.

During the timeout, the replay booth stopped the game to review the play. It was then determined the ball touched the ground when Emanuel was attempting to make the catch. The call was reversed to an incomplete pass and the Rams held on to win 11–6.

Did Emanuel maintain control of the ball? Yes.

Did he lose possession of the ball? No.

But it was reversed to an incomplete pass because the ball touched the ground. With the rule the way it was then, it stated that in the attempt to make a catch, if the ball touched the ground, the pass was incomplete.

At the Competition Committee meeting the following season, which just happened to be cochaired by Tampa Bay general manager Rich McKay, the committee felt that it wasn't fair that a guy stretched out to make a great catch and it was overturned to incomplete just because the ball touched the ground, even though he controlled it and didn't lose possession.

The committee took a look at several plays from the 1999 season, since that was the first year instant replay was used, and they decided to change the rule. The new rule stated that even if the ball touched the ground, it would remain a catch if the receiver maintained control of the ball. It seemed logical at the time because we didn't want to take great plays out of the game.

That rule change has led to one of the most confusing aspects of the game. Very few people today can agree on what is and what isn't a catch. Just ask Calvin Johnson and Dez Bryant, two players who were recently involved in enormously controversial plays.

Upon my further review, this rule fell into the "damned if you do, damned if you don't" category. If a rule change created as much confusion as this rule did, then we would have been better off not making a change at all.

Instant replay has negatively affected this rule because it dissects every element of the catch. Did a receiver maintain control of the ball? Did he maintain control long enough to perform an act common to the game? When does the process of the catch end?

So many areas of judgment are involved within replay that it was probably better to leave it out of the replay rule and not make it reviewable. Let the officials make the decision in real-time based on common sense. The way it is now, the rule trumps common sense.

But it's too late to go back. So now, going by the current rule that states in the process of going to the ground, the receiver must maintain possession of the ball when he hits the ground. Forget about whether the receiver lunges or performs any act common to the game on his way to the ground. If the ball comes loose when the receiver hits the ground, it's an incomplete pass. Period.

If the receiver wants to lunge, let him lunge. But if he loses control of the ball when he hits the ground, the pass is incomplete. By the way, the rule was not changed heading into the 2016 season.

BOTTLEGATE
DECEMBER 16, 2001

I WILL NEVER FORGET THIS DAY. I WAS IN THE LOCKER ROOM TALK-ing to an official after a game at the old Giants Stadium in New Jersey when someone came up to me and said, "Fans are throwing bottles at your officials in Cleveland."

Sure they are, and pigs are flying out at LaGuardia Airport, I thought to myself.

Then I looked up at a television monitor and I was shocked. It was a game between the Jaguars and the Browns, and yes, indeed, fans were throwing bottles at my officials. To this day, the mere thought of bottles and the Dawg Pound makes me twitch.

As I mentioned in the last chapter, Jacksonville was leading late in the game 15–10, but Cleveland was driving for a poten-tial game-winning touchdown.

On fourth-and-1 from inside the Jacksonville 20-yard line, Browns quarterback Tim Couch appeared to complete a pass to Quincy Morgan for a first down with 48 seconds to play. With no timeouts, Couch spiked the ball to stop the clock and started walking over to the sideline when officials began to dis-cuss Morgan's catch.

Referee Terry McAulay went to the replay monitor on the sideline to review the pass prior to the spike. Everyone was upset because the rule states you can't review a play once the ball is legally snapped.

However, according to McAulay, he and his umpire Carl Paganelli received the buzz from the replay booth right about the time the ball was snapped. Their reaction time was such that it looked like they were shutting down the play after the spike.

McAulay reversed the first down to an incomplete pass, giving the ball to Jacksonville. At that point, for all intents and purposes, the game was over.

However, for the fans, it was just the beginning. They started throwing bottles and other debris. The officials, as well as the players and personnel on the field, were dodging things that were being thrown at them, so McAulay said the game was over because it wasn't safe.

But a referee is not allowed to make that kind of decision. He does not have the authority to terminate a game; only the commissioner, Paul Tagliabue at the time, can make that determination.

We had to get in touch with McAulay, the Browns, and the Jaguars to tell them to go back out on the field and finish the game.

The game concluded with the Jags running two more plays, and they walked away with a 15–10 win. McAulay and his crew, and I'd say many others around the league, learned a very valuable lesson that day. Only the commissioner, or his designated representative, has the power to call off a game.

Upon my further review, McAulay was wrong for declaring the game over. That much is a given. What was interesting to me was that everything an official does can basically be proven by video—except when the replay official initiates a review. Did he do it before the ball was snapped or after? I can only take their word for it, which was that the replay official's buzz was just prior to the ball being snapped.

I will say, philosophically, we've always said in replay that any buzz that comes close to the ball being snapped, the officials are to lean in the direction of the buzz occuring before the ball is snapped.

One interesting thing that came out of this play was we found out something we didn't know: there was more than a one-second delay from the time the replay official initiated the buzz until the referee received it. I believe that would have made a difference in how this play was handled. The League then had the system updated the following season to eliminate as much of the delay as possible.

Three stadiums—in Pittsburgh, Minnesota, and Green Bay— banned the selling of bottled beer the following week.

THE TUCK RULE
JANUARY 19, 2001

WHAT'S BETTER THAN WATCHING FOOTBALL IN THE SNOW? HITTING the lotto jackpot.

Okay, you got me, but there are few things as exceptional as seeing football played in the snow. It's almost as if God intended football to be played that way.

I was in a hotel room in St. Louis, just hanging out waiting for the NFC divisional game that would be played the next day between the Rams and the Packers.

Snow was forecasted in New England for the game between the Raiders and the Patriots, so I thought I'd kick back, open a bottle of wine, and enjoy a great matchup in the AFC divisional playoffs.

In the fourth quarter of a really entertaining game, I was two-thirds of the way through completing the process of finishing a bottle of wine.

With a little less than two minutes to play in the game, the Raiders led 13–10, but the Patriots had the ball on the Raiders' 42-yard line.

Patriots quarterback Tom Brady dropped back to pass and was hit by Raiders cornerback Charles Woodson.

The ball came loose and it was ruled to be a fumble recovered by the Raiders. When I saw the play on TV, it looked like a fumble to me; however, after I watched the first replay, I thought, *Damn, that's going to be reversed to an incomplete pass.*

As I continued to watch the screen, I saw that referee Walt Coleman stopped the game and announced that the play was under review. And I knew exactly what was coming next.

I was actually staring at my cell phone and I knew when Coleman returned from looking underneath the hood to make his announcement, my cell phone was going to blow up with calls.

Within 30 seconds of the call being reversed to an incomplete pass, my phone started ringing like never before, and thus, the infamous Yuck Play, I mean Tuck Play, was born.

The call was reversed to an incomplete pass after the officials determined that the ball came loose before Brady had tucked the ball back all the way into his body, therefore making it an incomplete pass.

With 32 seconds left in the game, Patriots kicker Adam Vinatieri kicked a game-tying 45-yard field goal to send the game into overtime. The Patriots eventually won 16–13.

Upon my further review, here's the thing: it's a rule that never made sense to me. Even Coleman said it felt like a fumble, but by rule, it was a classic tuck play and the ruling in replay was correct.

It took a long time to get that rule changed, but it finally happened in 2013. If that same exact play happened today, it would be ruled a fumble. I certainly took a lot of grief over that play because I defended Coleman's decision. But that was the rule.

Nobody, however, who was either a member or a fan of the Raiders will ever let that play go.

"I'm still annoyed by the call; I'm still angry," former Raiders chief executive Amy Trask said to me when I caught up with her recently.

"Let it go? I've always thought that's the fun of sports. There are so many parts of our life where we need to let things go—really serious, tragic things. But the fun thing about sports is that we don't have to.

"And that was the wrong call. People think when I say that I'm angry about the Tuck Rule, I don't agree that there was a Tuck Rule. No, I understand what the Tuck Rule was. I believe it was inappropriately applied."

Obviously talk of the Tuck struck a nerve with Amy, but I get it.

"You got me worked up all over again," Trask laughed. "But if you look at the pictures of Brady, he's got both hands on the ball and he has the ball pulled all the way back into his chest. I'm not denying there was a Tuck Rule at the time. I'm saying I don't believe it was appropriately applied.

"The other thing is this, and this has nothing to do with the

Mike's family portrait (from left: Al (Dad), Lydia (Mom), Linda (sister), and Mike).

Mike and his sister, Linda, as children.

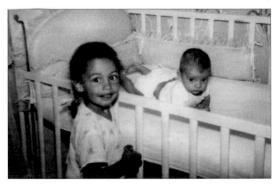

Mike as an infant, with his sister, Linda.

Mike (top row, third from right) and his Little League team in Hoover Tyler Little League.

Mike as a child with his mom, Lydia, and his sister, Linda.

Mike with Lefty Gomez in Anchorage, Alaska, in 1973.

Mike's first officiating uniform in Pop Warner football.

Mike in his early years as a high school official.

Mike signaling incomplete at a small college football game.

Mike's dad (standing) and his college crew.

Mike as a hitter at Santa Clara.

Mike and his dad when Mike was playing for Santa Clara.

Mike at Santa Clara doing what he did best—bunting.

Mike and his dad with Red Cashion at a
Seattle Seahawks vs. New Orleans Saints
game.

Mike sharply attired in Alaska as a
member of the Anchorage Glacier
Pilots.

Mike as a freshman basketball
player at Santa Clara with
teammate Wilbert Miles.

Mike and former Buffalo Bills coach Marv
Levy after Steve Tasker's ejection.

Mike and his wife, Gail, with former New York City mayor Rudy Giuliani at V Foundation Dinner.

Mike in his NFL league office. (Referee magazine)

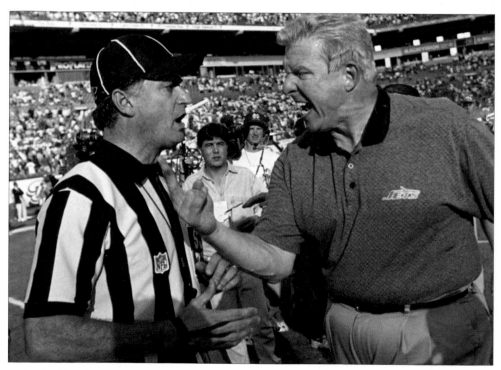

It looks like former New York Jets coach Bill Parcells is screaming at Mike in this famous photo, but he was actually upset with referee Tom Sifferman, who was cropped out of the picture. (AP Images)

Mike working in the NFL War Room. (Referee magazine)

Mike and Dean Blandino, the current NFL VP of Officiating.

Mike and CBS Sports' Jen Sabatelle.

Mike and Cris Collinsworth at Super Bowl XLIII (Arizona vs. Pittsburgh).

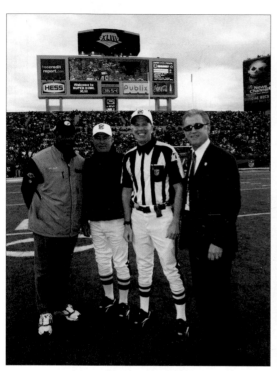

Mike at Super Bowl XLIII with referees Tery McAulay and Ron Winter and Pittsburgh Steelers coach Mike Tomlin.

Mike and former Arizona Cardinals head coach Ken Whisenhunt at Super Bowl XLIII (Arizona vs. Pittsburgh).

Jumbotron acknowledgment at Super Bowl XLVIII congratulating Mike on his years of service. However, it was one year longer than he really served—it should have been 14 years.

heart of the Tuck Rule, but another reason that makes it so hard to swallow is that call, that play, was just inside of the two-minute warning. Had that play occurred even a few seconds earlier, it was game over because New England had no timeouts left. They couldn't have challenged.

"I will go to my death not thinking it was the right call. You got me totally fucking worked up about it all over again."

I guess that means she will never let it go.

But before I left the league, I asked the Competition Committee to change that rule and got nowhere because they said it would add so much gray area to a rule that was basically black and white. God forbid you would change a rule to add common sense.

Thank heavens the rule finally got changed.

THE ED HOCHULI PASS-FUMBLE GAME
SEPTEMBER 14, 2008

YOU KNOW THAT FEELING YOU GET IN THE PIT OF YOUR STOMACH when you make a mistake and there's nothing you can do to correct it?

There's no amount of antacid you can take to make yourself feel better.

Welcome to referee Ed Hochuli's nightmare. As I also mentioned in the last chapter, the game took place in Denver between the Chargers and the Broncos, and it was one of the most interesting plays I've ever been involved with.

The Broncos trailed 38–31 with 1:17 left in the game, but had the ball, second-and-1 from the Chargers' 1-yard line.

Denver quarterback Jay Cutler was attempting to pass the

ball and it slipped out of his hand just prior to his hand moving forward, and it appeared to be a fumble that was recovered by San Diego linebacker Tim Dobbins. Game over.

However, Hochuli blew his whistle and ruled the pass was incomplete and the play was over. The replay official initiated a review and Hochuli went under the hood. He knew at that point that he made a mistake, and while he could reverse his ruling from an incomplete pass to a fumble, he could not give the ball to the Chargers. The only thing he could do was to put the ball back at the spot of the fumble with Denver retaining possession.

He was devastated, because he knew immediately that he had made the wrong call and there was no way for him to give the ball to San Diego, which would have essentially ended the game.

Two plays later Cutler completed a four-yard pass to Eddie Royal for a touchdown and then converted on a two-point conversion to give the Broncos a 39–38 victory.

I knew Ed about as well as anybody, and I knew how devastated he would be. One of the things I instituted when I began running the officiating department was to install phones into the officials' locker rooms at each stadium so I could contact them either before or after a game in case there was a concern or a problem.

I'd say there was both a concern and a problem in this case.

Hochuli's call cost San Diego the game, and I knew how badly he would feel, so by the time Ed got to the officials' locker room, I was already waiting on the phone to talk to him. He got on the phone with me and I immediately pointed out all the good he had done for the NFL and all the great things he had done as an official.

I explained to him that there was a reason that I put officials who were struggling on his crew, that there was a reason I always gave him first-year officials—because I knew with his preparation and his work ethic, he would make them better. I didn't want him to feel like his career was ruined with one missed call.

He was destroyed, so I had hope that by the time the phone call was over, Ed would understand just how important and valuable he was not only to me, but also to the officiating department.

It's just one more example of how serious the officials take their jobs, and I knew I had to talk him off the ledge.

The following season, we changed the rule to prevent that from happening again. From that point on, when a quarterback pass-fumble play was ruled an incomplete pass but, in fact, was a fumble, the ball could be awarded to the recovering team, even though the team wouldn't be allowed to advance the ball. It's the same for a quarterback pass-fumble play now, as it is with a runner that is ruled down by contact when, in fact, it was a fumble.

While that didn't make Ed feel any better, and he doesn't take too kindly to it, it became known as the Ed Hochuli Rule.

Upon my further review, even the best make mistakes. It wasn't the first and it won't be the last. But you have to look at a person's total body of work to determine his value.

Hochuli missed the call and he and his crew suffered a substantial downgrade. It was enough to knock most crews out of the playoffs, but not Hochuli's.

But as I said before, this crew battled back and ended up working a wild-card game that postseason, much to Commissioner Roger Goodell's chagrin. Due to the magnitude of the mistake, Goodell didn't want Hochuli or his crew in the postseason.

But based upon their overall season performance, how could I not put them in the playoffs? They battled their asses off and earned it over the final 14 weeks of the season. What would that have said to an officiating crew if I told them that since they had made a mistake in Week 2, they wouldn't make the postseason?

It would say that I suck as a boss. It wouldn't be right and it wouldn't be fair.

Needless to say, Goodell and I didn't always see eye-to-eye on things.

DEFLATEGATE
JANUARY 18, 2015

WHO WOULD HAVE THOUGHT THAT A SIMPLE, MEANINGLESS INTERception could alter the course of NFL history?

Yes, it led to a rule change, but the significance of history being reshaped involved the air being let out of the reputations of several very prominent people.

Let's start with the play. It took place in the AFC Championship Game between Indianapolis and New England.

The Patriots led 14–0 and there was a little more than nine minutes left in the second quarter when quarterback Tom Brady attempted a pass to Rob Gronkowski that was intercepted by the Colts' D'Qwell Jackson. When Jackson got to the sideline, he handed the ball to the Colts' equipment manager.

The equipment manager didn't think the ball had the proper amount of air in it and notified NFL Gameday Operations.

NFL rules state that the air pressure of game balls is required to be between 12.5 and 13.5 pounds per square inch. At halftime, NFL officials inspected the footballs, and initial reports said that 11 of the 12 balls used by the Patriots were below the minimum amount. But other reports refuted that, citing only one ball was underinflated by two pounds while "several" other balls were found to be roughly one pound underinflated, and "several more" were either right at, or barely beneath, the correct inflation mark.

What does air pressure in footballs have to do with history?

You may not believe it, but you're about to find out. A ball with less air pressure in it is supposedly easier to grip. So the presumption was that Brady had the ball boys take some of the air out of the balls. In other words, cheating. At least that's what I call it.

The balls were reinflated at halftime, but the Colts might have been better off not saying anything, as Brady actually played better, leading the Patriots to a 45–7 rout of Indianapolis.

The NFL hired independent investigator Ted Wells to lead the probe, and when he was finished, he concluded there was "substantial and credible evidence" that Brady knew Patriots employees were deflating footballs and that he failed to cooperate in the investigation.

NFL commissioner Roger Goodell suspended Brady for four games, fined the Patriots and owner Robert Kraft $1 million, and docked the team two draft choices.

Now, let's get to those reputations. Kraft and Brady have

been a part of one of the most successful franchises in NFL history, as they've appeared in six Super Bowls since 2001 and won four of them.

Did the punishment fit the crime? I think most people said no. But, in this case, I didn't agree with "most people." Surprised? Don't be, because from my standpoint, you have to put it into historical context.

Plain and simple, the Patriots have done some shady things.

Deflategate wouldn't be the first -*gate* to make the league irate with the Patriots. That happened in 2007 with Spygate. That's when the Patriots illegally taped their opponents from the field, taped their plays and their signals.

New England ended up getting harshly punished by Goodell, coughing up $500,000 and a first-round draft choice while coach Bill Belichick got fined $250,000. A lot of people thought that punishment fit the crime, and so did I. By the way, the Patriots were told that if they did anything else in the future that affected the integrity of the game, they'd be dealt with even more harshly.

There were other issues that came up with the Patriots that we had to deal with when I was in the league office. None of them were proven, but the complaints had to do with the coach-to-quarterback system—that in key times of the game, the system would have technical problems when Patriots' opponents had the ball and would come back on when the Patriots had the ball. Again, those accusations were never proven.

I'm not done. This wasn't proven either, but there were accusations of the Patriots filming the Rams' walkthrough prior to Super Bowl XXXVI in 2002.

In 2015 Kurt Warner, who was the Rams' quarterback during that Super Bowl, still had his suspicions about the Patriots.

"I don't want to believe that there was anything outside of their team beat our team," Warner told the *New York Daily News*. "That's what I want to believe, but there's a sliver of doubt. Was there any advantage they gained in any game? Not just our Super Bowl game, but maybe it was a game before that helped them get to the Super Bowl. All of those things enter your mind."

Deceitful is something that comes to my mind.

Certainly you would have to look at this and say it's a trend—a trend that no matter how you slice it was either cheating or breaking the rules.

When you look at all the incidents with the Patriots, there's obviously a history of negativity. And it's the same owner, the same coach, and the same quarterback involved with each one.

So Kraft, Brady, and their coach, Bill Belichick, have had their reputations tarnished by all these allegations.

But Goodell is no saint in this, either. The decisions he made during the 2014 season, and now beyond, have not been kind to the commissioner.

There was the mishandling of two controversies, one with Ray Rice and the other with Adrian Peterson. And then came Deflategate.

Brady gave 10 hours of testimony during his appeal before Goodell on June 23, 2015. On July 28, the NFL announced it would uphold the four-game suspension.

When the testimony of the hearing was released, several in the media reported that Goodell's claims of why he upheld the suspension misrepresented what the evidence showed.

Despite Judge Richard Berman urging the two sides to settle their differences, they could not, and on September 3, Judge Berman threw out Brady's suspension on the grounds of a lack of fair due process.

The NFL appealed the ruling, but Brady was allowed to play to start the season. The NFL's appeal was heard in March 2016 and then it was up to three judges to determine the outcome. A month later, a federal appeals court, by a 2–1 vote, overturned Berman's decision and ruled that Brady must serve a four-game suspension imposed by the NFL. Brady filed an appeal near the end of May with the United States Court of Appeals for the Second Circuit, asking for a hearing based on the fact that Goodell "ignored highly pertinent rules in the collective bargaining agreement on tampering with equipment," according to his lawyer, Theodore B. Olsen. His lawyer also stated that Goodell changed his reason for penalizing Brady without giving him a chance to defend himself. The Court of Appeals rejected the motion in July, leading Brady's legal team to consider appealing to the U.S. Supreme Court.

So what kind of changes did Deflategate bring to the game? The biggest was how the footballs were prepared before the game—how they were measured and checked, along with logging those measurements.

The jurisdiction of who was in charge of the footballs was also changed to fall under a league-employed person called the kicking ball coordinator. NFL security would then escort the kicking ball coordinator, an official, and the footballs to the field before the balls would be released to the ball boys of each team.

I will say that the league reacts to situations like this in certain ways. Was it an overreaction in terms of the ball thing? Of course it was. This issue of air pressure in footballs actually got to federal court, for God's sake.

But here's the thing: You're talking about the integrity of the game, and Goodell looked at things differently that happened off the field versus things that happened on it.

He believed that the game played inside the boundary lines must be played on a level field. Anything done to affect the integrity of the game on the field is a very serious offense. Under his administration, the idea was to make discipline so strong that it would deter teams from doing it again. He did it with Bountygate in 2012 and he did it with Deflategate in 2015.

I always felt that players' safety was a big issue with Goodell as well. There were a lot of people that didn't like the rules that were put through, but he really did want players to play more years in the NFL. He wanted their careers extended.

But in the end, I think it's reasonable to think that no owner, team, or player will ever trust the league investigating anything again. And I wouldn't have said this a few years ago, but I think Goodell's days as commissioner may end sooner rather than later.

THE TESTAVERDE PHANTOM TOUCHDOWN
DECEMBER 6, 1998

I KNOW THIS IS OUT OF SEQUENCE, BUT THERE'S A REASON. THIS play led to the most significant rule change during my time in the league office.

People talk about the pressure of playing in the National Football League; I've talked about the pressure of officiating in the NFL; But in my 12 years in the league office, the biggest play that changed the course of history in the NFL took place in my very first season as the supervisor of the officials.

The game took place in New York between the Seahawks and the Jets. Entering the game, the Seattle coaching staff was under pressure to win the game.

How much pressure? I'll let you decide. The Seahawks were heading into the last game of the season and still had a shot at making the playoffs.

With a win, they were in. With a loss...

Prior to the season, the Seattle coaching staff was told by management if they didn't make the playoffs, they'd be looking for a new line of work in the unemployment line.

The Seahawks led late in the game 31–26, but the Jets had the ball, fourth-and-goal from the 5-yard line with 27 seconds left.

Jets quarterback Vinny Testaverde called a quarterback draw up the middle and was tackled at the goal line. Head linesman Earnie Frantz called it a touchdown.

The only problem was...it wasn't a touchdown.

The ball never crossed the goal line; only Testaverde's hand did. Frantz himself stated that he confused the hand with the ball when he ruled it a touchdown.

"I think what I did was actually react to the hand that broke the plane and I got confused and thought the ball was in his hand," Frantz told me recently. "I was wrong, and when I saw it afterwards on replay I was devastated."

With no instant replay that season, the game was over. The Jets won 32–31.

Seattle went home, out of the playoffs. Seahawks coach Dennis Erickson, along with his entire coaching staff, got fired.

Frantz, in my mind, was one of the greatest head linesmen in the history of the game. He worked three Super Bowls, three joyous moments in his career. However, the phantom touchdown call would haunt him.

To say Frantz was distressed would not even come close to describing the agony he felt. It nearly destroyed him. The impact of the incorrect call was almost too much for him to handle. Frantz threatened never to officiate again.

"Nobody wants to make a mistake of that magnitude. I went back to my place in Dallas and shut the door, pulled the blinds, and really didn't come out of my apartment for a couple of days," Frantz said.

"I thought that was really going to be my last game. I told [director of officiating] Jerry Seeman that I was going to resign. He told me I was too good an official to resign. He said I had made a mistake and he told me that I was going to Jacksonville the following week to work the first round of the playoffs. Without Jerry treating me like that, I think I may have walked away. He saved my career."

In fact, this was another example of overcoming a huge mistake, as Frantz came back the following season and worked Super Bowl XXXIV between St. Louis and Tennessee.

But the missed call solidified the need for instant replay and it returned, as we know it today, the next season.

10 FINALLY, "INSTANT" GRATIFICATION

WITHOUT QUESTION, INSTANT REPLAY WAS THE BIGGEST CHANGE during my time with the NFL, and I had a front-row seat for something that would truly alter the course of professional football history.

The year was 1999, and as I said, instant replay would return, but it wasn't the first time it had been utilized in the NFL. It was first put in for the 1986 season, and it was used for a five-year period until 1991.

To understand how the NFL got to this point, we need to go back and trace the origins of instant replay. The concept really began in 1983 when Art McNally, the supervisor of officials, was working on it with Tex Schramm of the Dallas Cowboys, who was on the Competition Committee.

Discussions had been taking place about having officials get more plays called correctly on the field. McNally and Schramm experimented for a period of three years (1983–85) by putting together a system of instant replay during games using those old VCR machines. You remember those, right? They were the machines that you always saw the flashing 12:00 because no-body knew how to program those damn clocks.

That system was not used, but the two of them would sit in a booth and see how efficiently they could correct calls.

In 1986, they put a system in place where the replay official would be in the press box using the VCRs. The official could call down to the field in an attempt to correct a mistake or con-firm a call that was made.

But instant replay was full of flaws and not a well-thought-out system. While the intent to correct obvious mistakes was a good thing, there were no time limits for reviewing a play and no limits to the number of times that you could stop the game.

Once, in Dallas in 1989, the game was stopped 14 times be-cause of instant replay. That imploded the system, because it took away the flow of the game. That was the beginning of the end.

You might say that the replay official, L.T. Bonner, had a quick trigger—uh, buzzer—finger. Like I said, he stopped the game 14 times to review decisions that were made on the field. Those stoppages caused delays of approximately 30 minutes.

In Bonner's only reversal, he moved the spot of the ball by two yards. When Referee Jerry Markbreit was asked after-ward about being second-guessed so much, he replied: "No comment."

"No comment" spoke volumes for everybody because no-body liked instant replay—the coaches, the players, the offi-cials, and even fans were not fans of it.

It destroyed the tempo of the game, and it wrecked the of-ficiating because officials played no part in the system. The officials became tentative because they knew "big brother" in the press box had the ability to change a call.

I don't need to explain how the officials felt about it. You had a system that was bound to implode, which it did in 1991. The pace of the game was the primary reason, but you had a lack of buy-in from the officials being a key component as well.

So out it went until 1999. But the same murmurs that were being talked about in 1983—about getting more calls right on the field—picked up steam again during the time that instant replay wasn't being used.

But it was the Testaverde play in 1998 that we talked about in the last chapter, along with the entire Seahawks coaching staff getting fired, that got the ball rolling again. After the '98 season, the league office was determined to bring it back.

The key thing was, how could we bring it back and avoid the issues that had happened with the old system that was used from 1986 to '91?

The Competition Committee was certainly and clearly involved in the decision. Dennis Lewin, who was the head of NFL broadcasting at the time, also knew the networks would be involved, because that's where the video would come from for the officials to review.

To address the issue of the flow of the game, the challenge system came about. Each team got two challenges, which meant you were looking at a possibility of only four challenges per game. We also looked at the possibility that teams couldn't challenge in the last two minutes of either half, because in those critical times of the game, we felt the decisions should be left in the hands of the replay officials to stop the game if they felt there was a mistake that was made in a reviewable category.

The reason that was done was twofold. We didn't want coaches to throw a challenge flag just to stop the clock. That was a fear we had. The other concern was that if a team was out of challenges or timeouts, they couldn't get an obvious error corrected in the last two minutes, the most critical time of the game.

The Competition Committee agreed that was the best way to go. It was a good system that proved to work because, even today, you're still looking at less than two stops per game. The average for the 2014 season was 1.7 stops per game, which is not that intrusive to the flow of the game. And it was even better during the 2015 season, with the average number of stops down to 1.6 per game.

The other issue was going to be how to get the officials to buy in.

How? By empowering them to officiate the game. We put sideline monitors on the field so that the officials could review the video before making a decision. We said we'd put the decision in their hands and let them decide whether to confirm a call or reverse it. They were in. They liked the fact a decision wasn't being made by a guy upstairs in an air-conditioned booth who was wearing a three-piece suit. It was still on the officials to make the final call.

Another part of instant replay that seldom gets talked about is how the officiating department would look at the decisions that were made in replay after the fact. We decided that if an official had his call reversed, it would have been deemed that he made the correct call originally.

In other words, the official would not be downgraded for making an incorrect call. Replay clearly became their friend.

Then, it was time to look at the equipment. How could you upgrade from two VCRs, which is what was used in the past?

The way it worked was as follows: if there was a review, the replay official would stop one VCR and keep the second one running. He would look back on the first VCR and then stop the second one if a replay came. Obviously, it was the best they had at the time, but it wouldn't be sufficient moving forward.

Dean Blandino, the current SVP of officiating, was already in the league office at that point and was our technology guru. He became the foremost expert on replay.

"They got a bunch of vendors together, these big technology companies, to basically show off their wares and show us what they could do with replay. What we wanted was the ability to record the television feed electronically and then have the ability to access the different angles quickly," Blandino said when I asked him to recall the process we went through.

"There was this smaller company, Leitch, which is a Canadian company that was based in Toronto. They had this touchscreen technology program that allowed you to capture the TV feed and record it. Then each time there was a new replay or new play, you basically hit a button. It would mark a point in that video and a still frame would pop up on a touchscreen, and then you could access any angle by hitting the touchscreen. That was their take on how to do a replay review, and it was ultimately the best system for us to move forward with at that time."

The equipment was expensive. We started in standard

definition and would eventually move to high-definition. That was really the first step to try and get everything right since the system was blown up in 1991.

We met with the Competition Committee to talk about how to impose limits, which is how we came up with the coaches' challenge system, in which a coach could get only two challenges per game.

"Yeah, I think that was another selling point to the system because, again, when you look at what we learned from the past, when you look at the old system, the number of stoppages, there was no limit," Blandino said.

"I think it was important that we limited the number of times that the game could be stopped for instant replays. It wasn't designed for the officials to reofficiate every play. You're not going to get every play right via replay. That was a key component to the new rule."

The legendary George Young, who was the former general manager of the New York Giants, happened to be head of the football operations department at the time. And he was not a big advocate of instant replay.

How old-school was George? Let me put it this way: think the leather helmet era and you will definitely get the picture. It was kind of ironic that his last name was Young.

Nevertheless, one time I had what I thought was a great idea, which come to think of it, wasn't all that unusual because I thought all my ideas were great. Though I'm only partially kidding, it was so great I can't even remember exactly what it was at this point. But what I do recall is that I was pumped to tell George.

I just knew he was going to like it and it would be one of the first major changes during my time there that would have made the league better. Or so I thought. I described in full detail what my plan was and he told me it was a great idea. I began to get really excited...until he added that I should forget about it.

What? I didn't understand; he said it was a great idea. He told me as good an idea as it was, it was something that was never going to happen. When I asked him why, he responded with this gem: "Don't you now what N-F-L stands for?"

My naïve mind started racing and I thought No Family Life, because the job does demand a lot of your time. My thoughts then drifted to the No Fun League, thinking that rules were starting to be put in place to prevent players from celebrating something fun.

I then got an answer that would totally floor me. George Young said that the NFL stood for *No Fucking Logic.* At that point, I grew to love the man.

As I said, "Old-School" George wasn't a big fan of replay and he used to carry a manila folder where he kept all of his replay information. The folder wasn't labeled on the tab like most manila folders, but on the outside, in big letters, Young's folder read: THE MONSTER GROWS.

Young had been through the first replay system once before as GM of the Giants and was very concerned where replay would be headed in the future, and how it might end up interfering with the game.

Even though I wasn't against replay, I was concerned about it affecting the flow of the game. I thought it also sent a bad message that you might be able to correct every mistake in the game, when that was—and still is—virtually impossible.

If you'd like, you can call me "Old School" Mike because I was concerned that more and more plays were going to be reviewed. It's a complex system that has led to decisions that clearly have affected the outcome of games.

The Bert Emanuel play in 1999 and the Dez Bryant play in 2015—plays that were ruled one way on the field and reversed in replay—are good examples. A controversial play, however, that wasn't reversed was a Calvin Johnson ruling of an incomplete pass in the end zone in a Detroit–Chicago game in 2010.

During the 2014 season, a new wrinkle would come into play. Blandino, along with his staff in New York with a state-of-the-art command center, would now be involved in the decision-making process. The referees still had the right to make the final decision, but Blandino and his staff would look at plays that were being reviewed with the referees in hopes of making predictable and faster decisions.

"That was done to create more consistency in the decision-making process and to be more efficient," Blandino said. "The technology got to a point where you could bring the television feeds back to New York, but the key was the ability to bring them back in real time because we couldn't afford a delay. When we first opened the command center in 2002, we were getting DirecTV feeds that were 5 to 10 seconds behind what was actually happening. That wasn't going to work if we were going to be involved in making the decisions along with the referee. We had to be able to get those TV feeds back to us within milliseconds in terms of delay. That's what we had to have."

Did the input from New York have an impact in the

decision-making process? Does it snow during the winter in Green Bay? The answers to both are, of course, yes.

With Blandino and his group involved, 34 percent of all replay reviews in 2014 led to reversals, down from 43 percent in 2013. That reinforced the standard that calls shouldn't be reversed unless there is indisputable visual evidence, or as Blandino likes to call it, clear and obvious visual evidence.

It was interesting; however, the reversals shot back up in 2015 to 42.4 percent. The question is why? It's hard to pin down an answer because I do believe the referee and the crew in New York feel the video has to be clear and obvious to overturn a call.

But when you're looking at 415 total reviews in 2015, it's understandable that a few wrong decisions were made because, in reality, so much of instant replay now involves judgment.

I also think it's an indication that staying with clear and obvious visual evidence as the criterion, more mistakes were being made, and that led to more reversals.

But you're looking at only two years worth of data—34 percent of replay reviews in 2014, and it was up 8 percent to 42.4 in 2015. Will the upward trend continue? I don't think so—not only will the young officiating staff improve and make fewer mistakes, but I also think Blandino's crew in New York will also get better because they will get a set standard in their mind of what clear and obvious is.

So like it or not, instant replay is here to stay. Is it good? Is it bad? Does it make a difference? The answers would be: yes, no, and yes.

I asked Blandino where things might be headed in the future.

"When you talk about technology and where it's going, you think, *What are the next steps?* We've explored multiple-channel replay systems, where you're not waiting for TV to show you the shot you need to make a decision. As it stands now, the TV truck will decide what angles go to air, and those are the only angles we can use," Blandino said.

"You do have the ability to, on a multichannel system, take in multiple camera angles and not have to wait for TV to show them. As soon as the play ends, there would be four or five different angles to look at, then run them in sync so we could look at a play from five different angles at the same time and then focus on whatever angle we think is best. We're experimenting with that."

Technology is clearly having an impact, and with all the experimenting that's going on, it's only going to get better and better.

But beware of the monster. It's already a beast and growing fast.

There's also a sentiment floating around from some coaches, including Bill Belichick, who started the idea, that coaches should get to challenge anything they want—whether it's a play clock that has expired, an offside penalty, or an interference call.

That idea could be good for the game and good for getting more mistakes corrected—but at what cost?

While Belichick says that you're not going to add any more challenges than are currently allowed (two per game, plus a third if the coach wins the first two challenges), I completely disagree. He's not really looking at the big picture. If you look at stats from the 2015 season, there was less than one coaches' challenge per game (0.78). If you open it up and allow them to challenge anything, I guarantee you that number will go from 0.78 to 4 because they are going to challenge the obvious, even though there might not be any significance to the play.

And they really don't have to. Coaches hardly have to challenge anymore, as the replay official is now responsible for initiating the review if a scoring play occurs or if there's a turnover.

I have a real problem allowing coaches to challenge everything. The length of the games will increase *dramatically*. Games might last so long they will make the Oscars seem like a short show.

The pacing of the game as it is now, with penalties, replays, and endless commercial breaks, already seems choppy to me. And a change like that would only make it worse.

Although it's being discussed, I don't think it will happen. People just have to accept the fact that mistakes are going to be made.

The bottom line is this: if you can correct an obvious error that has a major impact on the game, then it's good for the game.

Even "Old School" Mike wouldn't argue with that.

11 THE GOLDEN RULES...AND HOW TO CHANGE THEM

Yes, technology had finally invaded the NFL in a big way, causing us all to live by new rules.

Speaking of rules, during my nine years overseeing the officiating department, I was involved in getting 76 rules changed.

That was almost as many as the uniform number I wore as an NFL official, which was 77. And though subconsciously I might not have been shooting for my number, I did fall only one short.

But if you think back to the chapter on plays that changed the NFL, the one rule I was always pushing to get changed before I left the league was the Tuck Rule. Eventually, that rule did get changed the way I wanted, so if you want to count that as No. 77 on my ledger, you go right ahead.

So what's the process of changing rules?

When I took over in 2001, after working under Jerry Seeman for three years, I wanted to change rules to make the game better and to bring the rule book more in line with the game. The previous philosophy was not to change the rules.

I remember then-Seattle coach Mike Holmgren telling me that just because a controversial play happens one time didn't mean we needed to change a particular rule. He said that if a play had only happened one time in 20 or 30 years, we shouldn't overreact and change it.

I disagreed with that philosophy. I believed that if something happened in a game that showed there was a loophole in one of the rules, then we should change it, regardless of how many times it happened.

The NFL's Competition Committee had the power to propose rule changes to the owners and set points of emphasis. I ran afoul of the Committee when they decided to make defensive holding and illegal contact points of emphasis in 2004, much like they did again in 2014. It didn't make sense to me, and I said so.

In officiating, in every area other than player safety, if an action by a player did not create an advantage, then the official didn't call a foul even if it was technically against the rules.

When it came to defensive holding, the committee said any jersey grab on a receiver was to be called a foul, even if it didn't restrict the receiver's ability to run his route. It was the same way with illegal contact. Any contact beyond five yards was to be flagged even if didn't affect the receiver.

I raised my concern about these points-of-emphasis fouls, as I knew it was going to create so many more penalties for quick jersey grabs or slight contact that had nothing to do with the play.

I was chastised for disagreeing with the committee. They probably weren't used to having the vice president of officiating stand up and voice his opinion. I remember being called on the carpet by NFL management for disagreeing with the committee members. It wouldn't be the last time they disagreed with me.

However, I felt it was part of my job to challenge the committee on things. We didn't always see eye-to-eye, but I think that was all part of coming to a good conclusion about a rule or a point of emphasis.

To give you an idea of how "radical" my thinking was, as I mentioned, there were 76 new rules passed during my tenure. In the three years prior, when I worked as the supervisor under Seeman, only six rules were changed.

So how do you actually get a rule changed? Believe it or not, you don't need a court order to do it. Historically, I'd say that probably 75 percent of them come through the officiating department.

I was known as a rule changer, so I'd take suggestions from anybody if I thought it was a good idea. Besides my own thoughts, I'd get input from other officials, and sometimes even from fans. Then I would present the proposed change to the Competition Committee and they'd look at it for consideration.

Most of the time, I would have a video of plays on which I wanted to change the rule so I could explain the rationale to the committee. They would consider it and then decide whether or not to write a rule-change proposal. If they did, it would then get submitted to membership.

The eight-member Competition Committee—made up of coaches, club executives, and owners—doesn't make or change rules. All it can do is present the proposal to ownership. Then it's up to the owners to vote a rule in or out, and it takes three-quarters approval to get a rule passed. In other words, 24 of the NFL's 32 teams (75 percent) would have to vote in favor of the change for it to pass.

Another way to get a rule passed is for a team to propose it directly to membership. If that happens, it has to get voted on regardless of how the Competition Committee feels. The only way it won't get presented is if the team that proposed it decides to withdraw it.

The other thing to consider is that the Competition Committee sends out a survey to all 32 teams. The survey goes to head coaches, general managers, and ownership. The survey not only addresses rules but other issues as well, such as roster sizes, scheduling, and more.

For example, teams might have been asked if they felt pass interference was being officiated consistently. If not, did they have any suggestions on how to improve it? The committee would then track the answers that could deal with anything from false starts to illegal motion or defensive holding.

From these surveys, if the committee saw a preponderance of concerns about a particular rule or issue, they could propose a change based on that information.

The other thing the committee does is look at a lot of video from the previous season. It reviews anything from player safety issues to injuries. If the committee sees a trend, it might propose a rule change based on that tendency. The play of Dallas safety Roy Williams in 2004 was a perfect example of that. The Competition Committee watched a significant number of major lower leg injuries, four of which were caused by the way Williams tackled players.

Instead of wrapping up and tackling, Williams would grab inside the collar of the shoulder pads and pull the runner down backward. Without any input from clubs or the officiating department, the committee looked at that technique as something that should be banned.

"There were a lot of injuries as a result of the horse-collar tackle," Rams coach Jeff Fisher, who was on the committee, recalled when I asked him about it. "Those are the types of plays that the committee looks at...the peel-back blocks, the low blocks, things like that. We try and write or adjust rules to protect the players."

Write and adjust they did as the committee proposed the Horse Collar Rule, and as with most player safety rules, it passed for the next season (2005) because no owner wants to vote against a player safety rule. That was the feeling then, and it's no different today.

As I said earlier, anybody could propose a rule change, even fans, and I bet a few of you had that *You're crazy, Pereira* look on your face when you read it. But it's true. I have seen letters written from fans for proposed rules changes that were put into a Competition Committee report.

The NFL really does have an open-ended policy where clubs, the officiating department, the committee, and yes, even fans, can propose a rule change. The changing of rules was, and still is, a good thing. It makes the game better...and safer.

But the NFL was about to experience a changing of the guard at the VP of officiating position in 2001—a new sheriff in town, if you will, a sheriff that liked to change rules, despite a sometimes reluctant Competition Committee.

12   A NEW SHERIFF—AND NEW RULES—IN TOWN

YOU KNOW, SOME PEOPLE SAY I LOOK LIKE BARRY WEISS FROM THE popular show *Storage Wars* on the A&E Network. I actually get that a lot.

But I want you to think outside the box a little, folks, now that I had become the VP of officiating.

The Competition Committee must have known they were going to have their hands full with me taking over. The guys on the committee already knew that I had rewritten the rule on pass interference and they had to know that was only the beginning.

I wonder if they thought I was this hired gun or something, a rebel with a cause. I was definitely not there to make their day. I was there to try to make the NFL—and the rules—better.

Six rules were changed during my first year in 2001. Remember there were just six rules total changed over the previous three years.

However, changing any rule is a collaborative effort, and I needed buy-in from the league, the Competition Committee, and the clubs.

Here's a year-by-year look at the number of rules that were changed during my time in charge of the officiating department, highlighted by some of the most important rules that were changed and why they were changed. But let me warn you: it might be time for a bathroom break because this chapter is *long*.

2001: SIX RULES CHANGED

INSTANT REPLAY

I KNOW WE'VE GONE OVER THE HISTORY OF INSTANT REPLAY, BUT IN the review of the rules by year, I also want to give you the specifics on how it evolved during my nine years.

The first thing we tried to get pushed through was to get instant replay passed on a permanent basis. As I've said, we had tried it, went away from it, and brought it back again in 1999 on a year-by-year basis.

I felt that instant replay wasn't going away and instead of doing it year-by-year, we should at the very least make it multi-year, or better still, permanent.

But nobody wanted to make it permanent. The committee was still concerned there were other ramifications we hadn't realized yet that could make it better. They also felt that if we tried to make it permanent, we might not get the required 24 votes to pass it. Replay then may have been eliminated. However, they did agree to a multiyear proposal and we got instant replay approved for three years. That was the first official rule change under my reign of terror.

I was off and gunning, I mean running.

MOMENTUM PLAY

THIS CHANGE CAME ABOUT BECAUSE OF ONE PLAY. IT HAPPENED only once, and we felt the end result of the play just wasn't fair.

It was Saturday, December 16, 2000, and the Raiders were playing the Seahawks on a cold, 50-degree, rainy Seattle day. Is there any other kind of day in Seattle?

Oakland was leading Seattle 24–19 with 2:40 left in the game. The Seahawks had the ball and had a second-and-20 from their own 19-yard line.

Ricky Watters carried the ball 53 yards to the Oakland 28-yard line and was tackled by Charles Woodson, who knocked the ball out of Watters' hand. The ball scooted forward all the way to Oakland's 2-yard line and it was recovered by the Raiders' Marquez Pope. Because the ground was wet and slippery, his momentum caused him to slide into the end zone. He was then touched by Seattle's James Williams and the play was ruled a safety, which cut the Raiders' lead to 24–21.

Oakland then had to kick the ball off to Seattle, which eventually led to a winning touchdown—a Jon Kitna nine-yard pass to Darrell Jackson.

So Pope made a good play by recovering a fumble, but because of the wet and sloppy conditions, he slid into the end zone and the Raiders had a safety called against them, which contributed to the loss.

"The rule says that on a fumble, momentum can't carry you into the end zone," Seattle coach Mike Holmgren said at the time. "Don't ask me why it's different for an interception versus a fumble, but that's just the rule."

Holmgren was right. There was no momentum rule for

fumble recoveries, only a momentum rule for intercepted passes.

If a defensive player intercepted a pass, for example, at his 5-yard line and his momentum carried him into the end zone where the ball became dead, he would get the momentum spot. That means the ball would be spotted where the ball was intercepted at the 5. But it did not include fumble recoveries or the fielding of kicks, so it was clearly an unfair rule.

The proposal to the committee was that we take this play and include fumble recoveries and possession of kicks into the same category as pass interceptions, and it passed. It was a rule change that made sense.

CATCHING AN ILLEGAL FORWARD PASS

HERE ARE SOME EXAMPLES OF PLAYS THAT NEVER MADE SENSE to me.

A quarterback from one yard beyond the line of scrimmage throws an illegal forward pass that is caught by an eligible receiver, who advances the ball down the field. By rule, the play is ruled dead as soon as the receiver catches the pass.

Or how about a quarterback who throws a legal forward pass that is caught by a big, burly ineligible lineman, who then heads up the field? By rule, that play is also dead at the spot, right where the lineman catches the ball.

I felt that it didn't make sense because the rule seemed like it was protecting the fouling team. I felt that way because if you played it through like a regular reception, there was always an opportunity for the defense to make a play and force a fumble and get the ball.

By ruling the play over when the pass was caught, it protected the offense and it forced the officials to make a decision that was contrary to the basic rules of the game.

That's because there was a pass receiver that was not down and a ball that had never touched the ground. In any other situation, other than it being an illegal forward pass or an ineligible player, the play would have continued.

But by this strange rule, the play was over.

The committee agreed it was strange and the rule ended up getting passed, which basically said that the ball would remain alive and not dead until the end of the play. Another good rule change.

I was just getting started. I had to pace myself, so out of the six rule changes that came in this year, some were just simple penalty enforcements and that's why I'm not going to take the time to go over them.

2002: SEVEN RULES CHANGED

PYLON RULE

WE WERE ON A ROLL WITH SIX IN 2001, BUT 2002 WOULD PROVE TO be an even better offseason with seven rules passed.

The first one was interesting because it was a Thanksgiving Day game in Detroit with the Lions hosting the Packers. Where else would a Thanksgiving Day game be but in Detroit? That's about as automatic as an assembly line at the Ford plant, considering the Lions haven't missed playing in a Thanksgiving Day game since 1945.

Here was the situation: there were 33 seconds left in the game and the Packers were leading 29–21. The Lions had the ball, second-and-8 from the Green Bay 29-yard line. Detroit quarterback Mike McMahon dropped back to pass and completed what appeared to be a 29-yard touchdown pass to Lamont Warren.

Warren was near the sideline at the goal line and one foot came down in bounds while the second foot touched the pylon before coming down in bounds in the end zone. But the ruling on the field was an incomplete pass.

John Madden, who was part of the FOX broadcast team with Pat Summerall, argued that the play should have been ruled a touchdown. He said Warren got both feet down and the ball was inside the pylon. He virtually ignored the fact that Warren touched the pylon with his right foot before it came down in bounds in the end zone.

Madden also thought the play should have been reviewed from the booth, but it wasn't. The Lions didn't call a timeout and snapped the ball so quickly that it nullified any chance for the play to be reviewed.

There was actually no need for a review, as the replay official clearly confirmed that Warren's foot had touched the pylon, making the pass incomplete.

Madden was incorrect in his assessment of the play; however, the millions of people who were watching believed him.

Could this have been a little foreshadowing? Maybe this was a sign that my future was in television, where I could help both fans and announcers understand the rules.

The Lions did end up scoring a touchdown with 10 seconds left in the game but ended up missing the two-point conversion and lost 29–27.

But that left us with an interesting question during the off-season. Should a player touching the pylon be considered out of bounds, especially in terms of completing a catch?

We felt the answer was no. We changed the rule to say that a player touching the pylon did not put him out of bounds. The only thing that puts him out of bounds is when he actually touches the ground out of bounds, or touches something else out of bounds, but not the pylon.

So Madden would eventually be right, just at the wrong time. He was just a year too soon.

DEAD-BALL FOUL

THERE WAS TERMINOLOGY IN THE RULE BOOK THAT ONLY A REFEREE could love. We had something called "continuing action." What the heck is that?

If a foul occurred in the continuing action after a play was over, it was considered to be part of the play and a live-ball foul, not a dead-ball foul, even though the foul occurred after the ball had clearly become dead.

I bet what I just described is continuing to confuse you. Don't worry; you're not alone. It didn't make sense to a lot of people. As a result, officials would have to ask how long continuing action lasts.

Even the Competition Committee was confused. And if it didn't make sense to them, then I knew I had a real chance of getting something changed that would simplify a rule.

From that point on, you either had live-ball or dead-ball fouls, period. If it was a dead ball, then the down counted and the referee would enforce the penalties. We also threw in a caveat that if you had a dead-ball foul after a first down was gained, you would not penalize the offense twice by starting first-and-25. The offense would be penalized 15 yards, but they would start first-and-10 instead of first-and-25.

CHOP BLOCK

BY 2002 PLAYER SAFETY WAS AT THE FOREFRONT OF EVERYBODY'S mind and there were a lot of issues involving special teams that were difficult for people to understand. It's a very complex part of the game.

So I got together with special teams coordinators Chuck Priefer of the Lions and Mike Westhoff, who had coached with the Dolphins and Jets. By working closely with them, we were able to make some sense of particular blocks and get some rules passed. In this instance, what I'm referring to is the chop block.

Those are combination high-low blocks that are illegal on certain running plays and all passing plays, but kicking plays were not covered by the rule.

So the Competition Committee looked at chop blocks on kicking plays, especially on the outside edge by offensive teams against defenders who were rushing the kick. They decided to make the rule the same as it was on a pass so teams couldn't chop block, period. By the way, the NFL eliminated all chop blocks in 2016.

CLOCK STOPPING AFTER QB SACKS

TICK, TOCK…TICK, TOCK…WHEN DO YOU STOP THE CLOCK?

The last rule change in 2002 came because we had a rule in the book that said when the quarterback was sacked behind the line of scrimmage, the game clock would stop.

The theory of stopping the clock on quarterback sacks was that if you had receivers that had gone far downfield on a pass route, you'd stop the clock in order to give them time to get back on their side of the line of scrimmage and not have unused clock time. I didn't really agree with that rationale.

Nevertheless, that was the rule. I really wanted to get that out, but I always ran into a roadblock because the league was happy with the number of plays per game, which averaged about 150 during the prior season.

There weren't that many sacks in a game—4.67 per game in 2001. But if you didn't stop the clock after a sack, you would consume about 10 seconds of game time per sack. That would equate to approximately 47 seconds that the clock would continue running.

I can tell you the Competition Committee didn't like the idea of less playing time and fewer plays. But I pressed the issue, saying that inside of two minutes left in either the game or the second quarter, that you actually penalize the defense for making a good play. By that I meant, if the defense sacks the quarterback and you stop the clock, the offense gains the advantage of more playing time.

The committee discussed it and decided they would make the exception that on a quarterback sack inside of two minutes, the clock wouldn't stop, but outside of two minutes it still would.

By 2013 the rule was standardized to make it applicable throughout the entire game. Now the clock never stops after a quarterback sack.

2003: FIVE RULES CHANGED

10-SECOND RUNOFF

OF ALL MY YEARS IN THE LEAGUE OFFICE, 2003 PROVED TO BE MY slowest as far as getting rules changed. Only five were altered that season, none of which really had that much significance. You've heard of players having an off year; this was mine.

I think most football fans understand the 10-second runoff rule. That's where if you have certain fouls called before the snap and the clock is running, then 10 seconds are automatically run off the clock. This predominantly occurred on false starts.

The rule also applies to certain live-ball fouls, specifically, on intentionally grounding and an illegal forward pass.

But coaches argued that if they had a timeout, why shouldn't they be able to use it in order to save the 10 seconds? It seemed to make sense to everybody, and that never happens, so it passed.

George Young was not always right.

THE ELIMINATION OF BACK-TO-BACK ONSIDE KICKS

THE NEXT RULE THAT CHANGED WAS THE ELIMINATION OF A SEC-ond consecutive onside kick attempt.

The rule stated that inside five minutes of the fourth quarter, if a team failed to execute a successful onside kick, then the kicking team would automatically get a second chance to kick it after a five-yard penalty.

In other words, if a team kicked the ball toward the sidelines and it went out of bounds untouched or last touched by the kicking team, they'd get a do-over.

What? How many things do we get a second chance at when we fail the first time? When did taking a mulligan in football become accepted? It didn't make sense to me.

Pittsburgh coach Bill Cowher was a strong proponent of this rule, and I remember asking him to explain the rationale behind his thinking. He said he thought that the onside kick was one of the most exciting plays in football and gave a team that was behind another opportunity to catch up.

I countered that by telling him an incomplete pass to the end zone was also an exciting play, but a team didn't get an extra down inside five minutes just because they were behind.

This was a tough rule to get through, but certainly in my mind, it was a very solid rule change.

2004: NINE RULES CHANGED

INSTANT REPLAY

I TRIED TO GET INSTANT REPLAY THROUGH AGAIN, THIS TIME PERMAnently, but couldn't pull it off. However, we did manage to get it extended for five more years through the 2008 season.

The committee was hesitant about making too many structural changes before it became permanent, so we basically left it as it was, but you would see some minor tweaks sneak their way in during the next couple years.

ALLOWING COACHES TO CALL TIMEOUTS
FROM THE SIDELINES

THIS ONE WAS INTERESTING. I BEGAN LOOKING AT THE COLLEGE game and its rules, and I really liked the one where they allowed coaches to call timeouts.

Hey, if something proved to be successful even though it was at a level below the NFL, why not?

I thought the college rule on this made a lot of sense. Instead of a coach in the NFL having to scream to a player to call a timeout—or to send in a substitute to an official to call a timeout—just let the coach do it. Coaches in the NBA and college basketball called timeouts all the time.

So why would we go through the nonsense of having to

communicate that request through somebody else, especially when the official might be standing right in front of a coach?

While this all seemed pretty sensible, the unintended consequences would eventually rear their ugly heads. Because when it passed, coaches starting calling timeouts for things we didn't anticipate—or like—such as freezing the kicker.

So instead of a player calling a timeout in the middle of the field where everybody could see it, coaches now could do it standing next to an official from an area that wasn't on camera.

Coaches would wait until the last second right before the ball was snapped and call a timeout. Yet the play would go off and the kick would be made or missed, but nevertheless, the play didn't count because the coach had called a timeout. Sometimes their decisions to freeze the kicker backfired, as the kicker missed the first attempt but got a second chance and made it. It just didn't feel right to us and it wasn't the intent of the rule.

There were coaches like Tony Dungy who said he would never freeze the kicker in that manner. He argued that why would he want to give the kicker a practice kick? The committee felt like there was enough of a risk involved with the decision backfiring, they decided to leave the rule the way it was.

Part of the reason we didn't alter the rule was because we really didn't know at what point to address when a coach shouldn't be allowed to call a timeout in an attempt to freeze a kicker.

The other element of this rule was to let the coach leave the coaching box to call a timeout. At that point, coaches totally stopped relying on players to call a timeout. We allowed them leave the box for that and to throw a challenge flag before a snap.

If it had been my choice, looking back at it now, I might

not have proposed this rule. If I could have looked through a crystal ball and seen how things turned out, I probably would have changed my mind.

But then again, if I could see through a crystal ball, I would have gotten winning lottery numbers instead and not had to worry about any silly rules.

UNSPORTSMANLIKE CONDUCT: CARRYING FOREIGN OBJECTS FOR THE PURPOSE OF CELEBRATING

THE LAST RULE CHANGE WITH ANY SIGNIFICANCE IN 2004 CAME because the committee was reacting to a touchdown that was scored by then–San Francisco wide receiver Terrell Owens.

The touchdown actually happened on October 14, 2002, when the 49ers were playing in a Monday night game against the Seahawks. No stranger to celebrations, or controversy for that matter, Owens pulled a Sharpie marker out of his sock after scoring and signed a football, then handed it to a fan.

I'll admit I'm a purist, and sometimes that didn't make me very popular in the eyes of many people. I don't like individual choreographed demonstrations. I believe that football, just like most of the major sports in this country, is a team game.

College football players are pure. They're not allowed to demonstrate after a play. If they score a touchdown, they are not allowed to spike the ball. They are supposed to hand the ball to an official or drop it. There are no prolonged demonstrations allowed.

The NFL, on the other hand, had crossed over to entertainment.

We had players doing things just to get on SportsCenter. They were planning demonstrations during the week so they could get face time on TV, and I was completely against that principle.

Okay, make me president of the No Fun League fan club if you must, but I feel if a receiver catches a touchdown pass, instead of doing some kind of dance routine, he should run to his quarterback and celebrate with him since he was the one who threw him the ball. Then after that, he should celebrate with his offensive line for giving the quarterback the protection to have time to throw him the ball. It's a team game.

While the committee and I didn't always see eye-to-eye on demonstrations, in this particular case, they felt that carrying a hard object on a player's body that was not part of his uniform should be illegal, and that included Sharpies.

The committee also said that if an object a player was carrying was deemed to be dangerous or hazardous, the player would be ejected.

What is hazardous? We discussed it, and felt that if the object was hard and not pliable, something you couldn't bend, that it should be considered harmful to both the player that possessed it and the player who tried to tackle him. That would be considered hazardous and also lead to an ejection.

It was really the first change to address this issue of what I called unsportsmanlike conduct.

2005: 13 RULES CHANGED

ELIMINATING EXCESS TIMEOUTS
OUTSIDE TWO MINUTES

WHO SAID 13 IS AN UNLUCKY NUMBER? IT WASN'T FOR ME, AS I SET my record with 13 rules changes. And while it would be my all-time high for a season, not a lot of them were significant.

But the first rule changed that season was an interesting one.

Pardon me, but I'd like to change *interesting* to *bizarre*. That's because it was a rule that was based on teams getting a timeout when they didn't have any left.

Excuse me?

The rule stated that if a team had used all of its timeouts and it was outside two minutes left in either half, they could actually buy a fourth timeout.

I said it was bizarre, didn't I?

It was kind of like a barter system taking place on the football field. If a coach had used his three allotted timeouts in a half, he could ask the referee for a fourth one. The official would allow it and then tell the coach it would cost his team a five-yard penalty. In many cases, getting the clock stopped was way more important than a five-yard penalty.

So coaches could literally usurp the rules and take a penalty, stopping the clock until the next play started. Mission accomplished if you're a coach.

I thought it was a stupid rule. A new rule was passed so that it would no longer be allowed, eliminating the excess timeout. The new rule stated that each team would get three timeouts per half. Period.

HORSE COLLAR

PART OF THE COMPETITION COMMITTEE'S ROLE IS TO LOOK AT MAjor injuries that occur throughout a season and to examine how they happened.

As a result of that, the horse-collar rule was probably the most significant change made for the 2005 season.

The committee reviews upper body, shoulder, knees, and ankle injuries while scrutinizing the penalties as well. I remember hearing the committee's "oohs and ahs" when they were look-ing at the technique that Dallas safety Roy Williams was using in tackling players sometimes during the 2004 season.

"I remember we were in Hawaii," Rams coach Jeff Fisher recalled. "We watched a couple of his plays and then we called our video guy and had him go back and look at some other plays. He put a tape together and we noticed a trend."

Williams would grab a player inside the back of the shoulder pads and drag him down, which resulted in four major injuries caused by him alone—and six overall—during the previous sea-son. Believe it or not, that included two tackles, which resulted in two injuries caused by Williams in one game.

No individual or team expressed a concern to the committee, but the committee knew it had to address it. The committee was just doing its job, and the horse-collar rule was implemented.

The rule stated that a player could not grab inside the shoulder pads and immediately pull a runner to the ground. The following season, an amendment was added to include tackles by the back collar or the side of the jersey. In 2016, the rule was expanded to make it illegal to tackle a player by grabbing the nameplate.

It was further expanded to say that a tackler didn't have to pull an opposing player all the way to the ground, just toward the ground, to make it illegal. The committee felt that this tack-ling technique was so serious it wanted it eliminated.

I've always respected the Competition Committee for tak-ing the time to look at all the injuries to see how they occur and to see if it can see any trends. And that's exactly how it came up with this rule.

PROTECTION FOR THE KICKER/PUNTER

THE COMMITTEE ALSO REVIEWED A PLAY THAT OFFSEASON THAT RE-sulted in a concussion and broken jaw for Giants punter Jeff Feagles.

Feagles punted the ball and was running down the field to cover the play when he was blindsided by Philadelphia's Jeremiah Trotter on a helmet-to-helmet hit. It was a legal hit then because Feagles was not considered to be a defenseless player.

When the committee saw that injury, they felt they needed to give some special protection to kickers, and so they made them defenseless, which said that you could not hit them in the head or neck area with your helmet, shoulder, or forearm.

This was another good example of a player safety rule that came from looking at injuries.

2006: 12 RULES CHANGED

I might have taken this new-sheriff-in-town thing a little too seriously in 2005, going overboard with 13 rules changes. So we cut it back…to 12 in 2006, with some pretty significant ones, including tweaking instant replay because it was taking too long for referees to make decisions.

INSTANT REPLAY

THE WAY REPLAY WAS ORIGINALLY SET UP, ONCE THE REFEREE DISAP-peared under the hood to review whether he was going to stay with the call on the field or reverse it, he had 90 seconds to make up his mind.

Some people felt the referee abused the 90-second rule, and that was probably true sometimes. But remember, the 90 seconds was just to make a decision. If the referee was going to reverse the call, he could stay as long as he needed to get the correct yard line set, get the down and yardage right, and get the clock time precise.

But in trying to cut the overall time of replay stoppages, we felt we could shave off 30 of the 90 seconds allotted and that would still leave the referees enough time to make a decision.

While some officials didn't think 60 seconds was enough time, here is why we made the decision to cut it. We felt if a referee couldn't make up his mind in 60 seconds, then he should leave the play as it was originally called on the field because obviously it wasn't indisputable.

The other critical change was that if a ruling on the field was made that a runner was down by contact before he fumbled, we would allow a review or a challenge of the play.

To give you a bit of history, it was a one-way rule when instant replay began in 1999. In other words, if a play was ruled to be a fumble on the field, a referee could go into replay and reverse it if the runner was down before the ball came out.

However, you couldn't do the reverse of that. If the referee ruled that the runner was down, you could not reverse it to a fumble because the play had been killed, or as some liked to say, the whistle had been blown. Therefore, that aspect wasn't reviewable. You couldn't correct the mistake when it was obvious that the player had fumbled.

We looked at this with the Competition Committee for a long time, and the biggest concern with making this change was that the rule was telling players to play through the ruling of a dead ball, which is in direct conflict of what coaches normally tell players—which is to stop playing when the whistle blows.

We also thought if we allowed this play to be reviewed, and we allowed the referee to give the ball to the recovering team, we might be exposing players to more injuries because they would be playing through the whistle.

Some players might stop when the whistle blows and some might not, leaving some to be in very vulnerable situations that could potentially create more injuries. But in looking at all of the applicable plays from the 2005 season where a runner was ruled down and a fumble occurred, the recovery was almost immediate—even before a whistle was blown.

For a one-year experiment, the committee and ownership agreed to let this play be reviewable—to essentially review it through the ruling and give the ball to the recovering team even though the play had been blown dead. One key point: the recovery of the ball had to be in the immediate action after the fumble.

Now that meant you could give the ball to the recovering team, but only at the spot where they recovered it, with no advancement because the ruling killed the play. It was still the fairest thing we could do and it worked, and is clearly a central part of replay today.

HITS TO KNEES OF THE QUARTERBACK

ANY MEASURE OF A TEAM'S SUCCESS IN THE NFL USUALLY STARTS AT the quarterback position. As the quarterback goes...

So another critical change for the 2006 season was made based on concerns regarding low hits on the quarterback.

It was an injury suffered by former Bengals quarterback Carson Palmer that prompted this rule change. Palmer, in the first round of the AFC playoffs against Pittsburgh the previous season, completed a 66-yard pass to rookie receiver Chris

Henry. It was the longest completion in Bengals playoff history.

However, as Palmer released the pass, Steelers defensive tackle Kimo von Oelhoffen was pushed from behind while diving in an attempt to tackle Palmer, hitting and severely injuring his knee.

Was the hit avoidable? Was it not? Was it coming off a block?

There was some vague wording in the rule book regarding low hits, but the Competition Committee modified the existing rule to prohibit defenders from hitting a quarterback at or below the knee when he was in a passing posture with one or both feet on the ground, unless they were blocked into him.

That made it a pretty stringent target for hits on the quarterback. A defender couldn't go high or go low. The target had to be somewhere below the nape of the neck or the top of the *V* of the jersey and had to be above the knee.

Throughout the course of recent history, for obvious reasons, more and more protection has been brought in to insulate the quarterback. The committee was very aware that in many cases the quarterback was and is the face of the franchise.

Remember, the committee is made up of owners, coaches, and club executives who know how important quarterbacks are. Many times their own livelihoods were based on how well the quarterback played.

This rule would get adjusted and strengthened again in 2009 when the "Tom Brady Rule" was implemented. Brady suffered a season-ending knee injury in the first game of 2008, when Kansas City's Bernard Pollard was blocked to the ground and then made a desperation lunge from the ground, hitting Brady in his left knee, tearing his ACL and MCL.

The modified rule stated that a player who went to the ground, whether blocked or not, could not then lunge into the knee area of the quarterback.

PROTECTION OF THE LONG SNAPPER

CLEARLY, THE QUARTERBACK IS THE MOST PROTECTED PLAYER ON THE field, but this rule also raised another interesting point. Special teams coordinators brought up concerns about the protection of long snappers on extra-point tries and field-goal attempts.

Centers were getting defensive players lining up directly over them and then getting nailed before they had a chance to protect themselves.

A rule was already in place on extra-point tries and field-goal attempts that stated a defensive player could not drive a helmet into the knee area of a center.

The committee decided to give them further protection by saying that a defender couldn't line up over a center. That meant a defensive player on the line of scrimmage would have to line up with his helmet outside the shoulders of the center.

It was far more difficult for the defender to hit the center head-on in the back of the head or neck from the new position. It would later be revised again to include requiring the defender's entire body to be lined up outside the shoulder pads of the center.

UNSPORTSMANLIKE CONDUCT: DEMONSTRATIONS AND PROPS

AS PART OF THE COMMITTEE'S THOUGHTS—OKAY, MOSTLY MINE—WE decided to put much more strength behind the unsportsmanlike conduct rule.

You can call me no fun if you'd like, but for me, it still goes back to the purity of the game. So we specifically categorized some of the things players do that would no longer be allowed.

For example, players would no longer be able to go to the ground for any kind of celebration or demonstration. They had to stay on their feet. The only thing that was permitted was a player going to the ground to pray or to thank God. And even that would lead to some confusion down the road.

Next, players couldn't use a prop. They couldn't use the ball for anything other than what it was, a football. Imagine that. They couldn't use it as a bottle of beer and try to pop open the top and drink it. You couldn't put the ball down and putt it, for example, with a pylon from the end zone.

I was very vocal about making these unsportsmanlike conduct penalties, as well as one that totally frustrated me—the throat slash.

The first time that I can recall seeing the gesture was by Green Bay quarterback Brett Favre in 1999.

I hadn't seen it before, but along with Favre, other players such as Tampa Bay's Warren Sapp, the New York Jets' Keyshawn Johnson, and Seattle's Ricky Watters were also doing it.

Later on that year, I got a tape from an official who wanted me to watch his work from a high school game to see if I could give him any pointers.

So I'm watching the tape, and after a defender sacked the quarterback, he got up and gave the throat-slash sign.

That just validated to me that young people emulate what their heroes in sports do. And the more we allowed it in the NFL, the more it was going to trickle down, and I didn't think it was good sportsmanship and it didn't say good things about the game.

I've always felt that the league had an obligation to the lower levels of football, and to kids, in general, to represent itself in the best way possible and not to allow these silly gestures. You would never have seen players like Walter Payton or Barry Sanders make those types of gestures or classless acts on the field.

The league lived up to its obligation and sent a memo out to all 32 teams, banning the throat slash.

2007: EIGHT RULES CHANGED

By the 2007 season, I knew my days were numbered at the NFL, so it was time to ease up a bit.

ELIMINATION OF CROWD NOISE RULE

ONE RULE THAT I WAS DYING TO GET RID OF WAS THE CROWD NOISE rule. There was a rule on the books that said if the home crowd was too loud and the opposing quarterback was not able to communicate his signals, he could request the referee to stop the game and warn the crowd to be quiet. If the crowd didn't cooperate, it could cost the home team a timeout, and if it continued, a penalty.

It hadn't really been called since 1989 when the Bengals were playing the Saints in a preseason game in New Orleans. In that game, with the crowd roaring like only they can in the Bayou, Bengals quarterback Boomer Esiason turned to referee Dick Hantak and asked for a crowd-noise timeout, and it was granted.

Hantak made an announcement to the crowd to quiet down or else the Saints would be charged with a timeout.

You don't have to be a rocket scientist to figure out what happened next. Bingo, they got louder. All it did was fire the crowd up even more.

When Esiason went under center again, you might as well have sent a 747 over his head, because the noise became as loud as a jet engine. He looked back at Hantak and the game was stopped again.

It became a mockery of the system, and it was not going to work. As it turned out, it wasn't Esiason who was really behind this, but rather his coach, Sam Wyche. Wyche instructed Esiason to ask Hantak for the crowd-noise timeout.

Despite it not working then, the rule stayed on the books for nearly 18 more years before it was changed. By this time, teams had already gone to the silent-count strategy, so crowd noise didn't really make any difference. Therefore, we eliminated the rule.

ILLEGAL TOUCHING OF A PASS

WE WENT BACK TO THE COLLEGE GAME FOR HELP ON THIS ONE. I may not have been a good student in college, but who said that you can't teach an old dog new tricks?

Basically, the rule for both college and the NFL had stated that if a pass was first touched by an ineligible offensive player, whether it was on purpose or by accident, then it was illegal touching.

The NCAA changed its rule to say this in 2006: if the ball was unintentionally touched by an ineligible player then it was no longer a foul.

That was a good change in my opinion, because it seemed rather senseless to call it a foul when the ball tipped off the shoulder pad of a lineman. There was, obviously, no intent because the player wouldn't have seen the ball.

So the NFL followed suit and the committee went ahead with the change for the 2007 season.

INSTANT REPLAY PERMANENT

IN ALL MY YEARS AS THE HEAD OF THE NFL'S OFFICIATING DEPART ment, I'm not sure I had a more difficult time—or a more significant rule—to get passed.

Although instant replay had been adopted for a period of five years, which would have taken it through the 2008 season, the committee felt like they finally had enough votes to make it permanent after the 2006 season, so they put it up for a vote.

One of the concerns had always been if we could get the 24 votes necessary (out of 32 teams) to make it permanent. We weren't sure if a lot of owners were still sitting on the fence at this point, but we took a chance.

And March 27, 2007, would become a day I would never forget. Because a rule we had been pushing for since 1999 finally became permanent. The owners voted 30–2 to make instant replay an enduring fixture of the NFL.

For me, it would be the signature moment of my time at the NFL.

2008: NINE RULES CHANGED

ELIMINATING THE FORCE-OUT

A LONG TIME HAD BEEN SPENT DISCUSSING THIS INTERESTING RULE change. I hated the rule, and I'll explain why later.

The force-out rule dealt with airborne receivers who would

control a pass near the sideline and then be driven out of bounds by a defender. If officials deemed that the receiver would have come down in bounds without contact by a defender, they could award the receiver a catch under what was termed a "force-out."

The theory behind eliminating the force-out rule was that we felt the defender had made a good, clean play and was being punished for it. He had blocked the receiver, who was in control of the ball, out of bounds, without committing pass interference or unnecessary roughness.

Not only did it seem like the defense was being penalized for making a good play, but it was an extremely difficult play for officials to call. The official had to make a judgment of whether or not the player actually would have gotten both feet down in bounds or if he would have come down out of bounds without the contact. And for good measure, throw in the official would also have to determine if a defender was intentionally knocking the receiver out of bounds or if he was making a legitimate play on the ball, in which case, it wouldn't be deemed a force-out.

Because it was so subjective, it was a rule that was not reviewable in replay.

Despite a lot of objections, the committee proposed the elimination of the rule. A receiver would have to come down with both feet in bounds for it to be a catch. Those opposed felt like we were taking a portion of the offense out of the game, and we all know how important offense is to the NFL.

However, the catch-and-carry rule would still apply. I know you're all probably thinking: *Now what the heck is that?*

That's a rule that says if a receiver is in bounds as he's being wrapped up by a defender before he comes down, and then is carried to the sideline and dumped out of bounds, that's still a catch.

Although my tenure on the field was short, I always felt the force-out rule was one of the most difficult to call and factored into probably the hardest call I ever had to make.

The 1997 season was only my second in the NFL, but I was assigned to the AFC Divisional Playoff Game in Kansas City between the Broncos and Chiefs.

Denver won the game 14–10, but there was a key play in the third quarter that would end up being the difference in the game...and I made the call, along with head linesman Terry Gierke.

About five minutes into the third quarter, KC was trailing 7–0 but driving the ball down the field. The Chiefs took the ball from their own 30 down to the Broncos' 3-yard line. But on third-and-goal, KC quarterback Elvis Grbac attempted a pass to Tony Gonzalez near the sideline in the end zone. Gonzalez went airborne to control the ball and then was knocked out of bounds by a defender, who was trying to intercept the pass.

I felt like Gonzalez came down with this hand out of bounds and that it wasn't a force-out, so I ruled it to be an incomplete pass. The fact that the defender was playing the ball and did not push Gonzalez out of bounds eliminated the possibility of the force-out in my mind.

Jerry Markbreit was the referee in that game and came up to me afterward in the locker room and gave me a hug and a kiss... on the lips.

"I'm a kisser. My family and all of my relatives were kissers on the lips," Markbreit would tell me years later when recalling the game.

"I was so excited for you because you had made the call of the day. It was a historic call, a second-year guy making a ball-buster of a call that you were right on. It was something special. It was me telling you how proud I was of you."

OPTION TO DEFER THE COIN TOSS
BACK TO THE COLLEGE GAME ONCE MORE...

It didn't matter which team won the coin toss; I felt it should have the opportunity to defer its choice until the second-half kickoff.

The college rule had it that way, and it was really the exception to the rule when a team that won the opening toss didn't defer. It was obvious to me to give the winner of the coin toss the choice because they might prefer to have the ball to start the second half as opposed to the first half.

I liked the fact there were elements of strategy involved with the decision, and while this rule was presented to the committee several times before, it didn't make it to a vote until 2008.

The rule passed and is now a staple of the coin toss rule.

And though most coaches were against it because I think they felt like it was one more element they had to make a decision on, more and more teams now defer to the second half.

In the first season after the new rule went into effect, teams deferred 7.8 percent of the time, and it has steadily continued to rise every season since. In 2011 the number of deferrals rose to 41.2 percent and to 55.4 percent the following season. After the 2014 season, those numbers had reached an incredible 65.6

percent. But are you sitting down? Just like health care costs, those numbers continued to rise in 2015, with teams deferring a staggering 82.5 percent of the time after winning the coin toss.

ELIMINATION OF THE FIVE-YARD FACE MASK

HAVE I MENTIONED THAT YOU CAN LEARN A LOT IN COLLEGE? WE also learned a lot from the college game.

The NCAA eliminated the five-yard face mask rule in 2007. The NFL decided to follow suit and eliminate it. Why? Because the five-yard face mask penalty was called incidental, which meant there was a grab but no twist, turn, or pull. Therefore, it was not a player safety issue.

It was another confusing thing for the officials to try and determine. Instead of officials having to make a decision of whether the grab of the mask was a 5- or 15-yard penalty, the 5-yard penalty was eliminated.

The rule was passed, leaving only a 15-yard face mask penalty, which stated that grabbing the face mask must include a twist, turn, push, or pull and that the second action is what would cause the penalty.

You know, it wasn't always a one-way street, the NFL taking from the college game. The college game, for example, adopted the NFL's horse-collar rule for its 2008 season.

COACH- TO-DEFENSIVE PLAYER COMMUNICATION

WHAT'S GOOD FOR THE GOOSE....

The NFL had implemented a coach-to-quarterback communication system, where the two could communicate in between plays and talk up until there were 15 seconds left on the play clock.

In 2008 the league looked at equity between the offense and the defense. With defensive coaches, including Jeff Fisher, on the Competition Committee, they argued that the defense should be allowed to do the same thing—a defensive coach should be able to communicate with one player, just as the offense did.

"Here's the history behind it," Fisher told me. "Once the coach-to-quarterback rule got passed, advance scouts would watch the opposing team's defense to scout their signals. So teams took advantage of that, and one player in particular—Peyton Manning—was so good and quick at picking up the defensive signals, we had to do something about it.

"The offense wasn't signaling in a play, but the defense was signaling and offenses were picking up on it. So we talked about it on the committee and determined from an equity standpoint, the right thing to do was let the coach talk to the middle linebacker and tie the two rules together."

The rule passed, as it should have been.

2009: SEVEN RULES CHANGED

PLAYER SAFETY: FORMATION ON ONSIDE KICKS

KICKOFFS BECAME A BIG PLAYER SAFETY ISSUE DURING MY FINAL season as the vice president of officiating. It became clear when looking at injuries there was a higher number of concussions on kickoffs, both onside and regular.

So restrictions were put on the formation of the kicking team on onside kicks that stated a team attempting an onside kick must have at least three players on each side of the field that lined up outside the hash marks. And one of those three had to be lined up on or outside the yard-line number.

What it did was prevent a team bunching up together on both sides of the kicker, creating a potential massive collision where the ball was kicked.

Prior to this, a change had been made to further prevent an overload on one side of the field, which required the kicking team to have at least four players on each side of the kicker when the ball was kicked.

ELIMINATION OF THE THREE-PLAYER WEDGE

THE BASIC WEDGE WAS ELIMINATED FOR THE 2009 SEASON, BUT not in its entirety.

The wedge formation was used on kickoffs, where the receiving team would get monster-sized players, lined up shoulder-to-shoulder on the same yard line with the intent of moving upfield to block for the returner.

You had these massive three- to four-player wedges blocking smaller players, who many times were injured in trying to break up the wedge. But the committee also noticed players on the wedge getting hurt as well, because helmet-to-helmet contact was not a foul. That's because it was deemed there was no defenseless player situation involved.

If you go back to the 2007 season, even though it wasn't an illegal wedge, Buffalo's Kevin Everett suffered a paralyzing injury on a type of collision that was very similar to what would frequently happen as a result of a wedge.

Trying to make kickoffs as safe as possible, the committee implemented a new rule to eliminate a wedge that involved more than two people.

MOVING THE KICKOFF BACK TO THE 35-YARD LINE

THE KICKOFF RETURN CAN BE A VERY EXCITING PLAY, AND THE philosophy of the league prior to 2009 was that it wanted kickoff returns.

However, as kickers got better and better and kicked it farther and farther, we began to see more and more touchbacks.

The committee first moved the kickoff line from the 40-yard line to the 35 in 1974 and eventually to the 30 in 1994. When it was moved to the 30-yard line, the number of kicks returned improved to 80 percent.

But as players got bigger and faster, the injuries continued to mount as a result of kickoffs and the committee returned the kickoff line back to the 35-yard line in 2011.

And the increase in touchbacks was dramatic.

In 2010 only 16.4 percent of kickoffs resulted in a touchback. But in 2011 the number of touchbacks rose to 43.5 percent and jumped to 50.2 percent in 2014. But in 2015, the number of touchbacks reached an all-time high of 55.9 percent. In 2016, touchbacks on kickoffs will result in the ball being placed at the 25-yard line. That will encourage more touchbacks.

While fans might not like it, safety has clearly become a priority and the league is content with the increased number of touchbacks.

THE BLINDSIDE BLOCK

PLAYER SAFETY HAS BECOME PARAMOUNT IN THE NFL. HERE WE have another player safety rule eliminating blindside blocks to the head or neck area.

What's a blindside block? It's really simple. It's a player nailing another player that doesn't see him coming, either from the side or from behind. It was later amended in 2014 to include the front as well.

The new rule was implemented to give the defenseless player protection. That meant a player would no longer be allowed to blindside another player in the head or neck area with the helmet, shoulder, or forearm.

This was a good thing, folks. Because I can tell you from watching a lot of film, there were many eye-squinting, vicious hits put on a lot of players.

HITS ON DEFENSELESS PLAYERS

Continuing on with the defenseless player theme, we established clear, definitive language as to illegal hits on defenseless receivers.

Just as in blindside blocks, a defensive player couldn't hit a receiver in the head or neck area with his helmet, shoulder, or forearm and he couldn't lower his head and make initial contact with the crown of his helmet, hitting the receiver anywhere on his body.

The emphasis was an attempt to protect the receivers that are obviously in an unprotected position, placing the responsibility and total liability on the defender.

We totally understood that it would make it harder to play defense, but leaving the offensive player in a very vulnerable position to be hit in that manner was not good for either player because of the risk of injury to both. And it certainly wasn't good for the game.

MAKING QUARTERBACK PASS-FUMBLE
PLAYS REVIEWABLE

LASTLY—AND I KNOW, AS I MENTIONED EARLIER, THAT HE HATES TO hear it referred to this way—we have a rule that would become known as the Ed Hochuli Rule.

It was another tweak in replay where we expanded what could be reviewed on a quarterback pass-fumble play to correct a mistake like the one that Hochuli made in the Chargers–Broncos game in 2008.

With San Diego leading 38–31 with a minute left in the game, and the Broncos at the Chargers' 1-yard line, Hochuli ruled that Denver quarterback Jay Cutler had thrown an incomplete pass. But replays clearly showed it was a fumble that was recovered by the Chargers. Denver was allowed to keep the ball and moments later scored a touchdown and game-winning two-point conversion to come away with a 39–38 victory.

The play was reviewed and reversed to a fumble, but unlike a review of a fumble vs. a runner being down by contact, the rule did not allow Hochuli to give the ball to the Chargers. The ball was dead at the spot of the fumble.

With the implementation of this tweak in the rules, plays like this became reviewable all the way to the point where you could give the recovering team the ball.

So those were the important rule changes on my watch, and as you can see, I was not afraid to change rules because I wanted them to make sense.

I liked the fact that we adopted some of the college rules to make them similar in both games. I would like to see even more rules shared between the NFL and NCAA.

I've often been asked over the years if I could change one rule that I couldn't get passed, what would it be?

I'd probably say it was the Tuck Rule, because it didn't make any sense to me. Though it was correctly reversed in 2001 when the play occurred, it didn't seem logical.

It was obvious that Patriots quarterback Tom Brady was not attempting to throw the ball when it got knocked loose against the Raiders in an AFC divisional playoff game.

But the rule made it an incomplete pass. I wasn't able to get it changed while I was in office at the NFL, but it did get changed for the 2014 season. Now that the Tuck Rule has been taken care of, I don't have to worry about it.

So let me focus on another rule that still drives me crazy to this day—the pass interference rule. I really tried to convince the Competition Committee that the rule was too punitive. That's because the rule matches what I think is the hardest call an official has to make with the most punitive penalty yardage. In my opinion, that's a recipe for disaster.

I looked at too many calls during my time with the NFL that were made and the end result turned into a 40-yard penalty—and there were many times the call was incorrect.

I'm an advocate of the college rule, where pass interference is a maximum 15-yard penalty.

In the NFL, a personal foul that threatened a player's safety results in a maximum 15-yard penalty, but a defender could pull a receiver's jersey on a long pass route and be penalized for 40 yards.

Everybody is on the move on that type of play—the offensive player, the defensive player, and the official—with the official having too many variables to deal with.

If the pass is in the air, has it arrived yet? Was the contact before the ball arrived or was it just as the ball arrived? Was it catchable? By rule, did the contact by the defender significantly hinder the receiver?

Those are a lot of decisions that have to be made that I don't feel warrant potential penalty yardage of that magnitude.

But I never made any progress with the committee.

Why? It was because the committee was fearful if we went with the college rule, it would take away the deep vertical passing game in the NFL.

Are you kidding me? Do they not watch college games on Saturday? College teams are passing the ball more than ever.

Here's the tendency: if a defender is close enough to the receiver to commit pass interference, he makes a play on the ball. I can count on one hand the number of times in my career that I have seen a defender in the open field intentionally tackle a receiver who might be a yard or so in front of him. It just doesn't happen.

I would even have gone so far as to adopt the Arena Football League pass interference rule, which made it a spot foul only if the defender intentionally tackled the receiver. But the committee wanted no part of it.

So if you made me commissioner for a day, the pass interference rule is the one I'd change. But being commissioner, even for one day, has no appeal to me. I'd rather be on a golf course.

13   THE NFL'S CAST OF CHARACTERS

I DIDN'T WANT TO BE COMMISSIONER, LIKE I SAID, BUT I WONDER how some of my conversations with various owners, general managers, and coaches might have been different if I had been.

Commissioner or not, my dealings with most in the NFL were always entertaining and memorable.

I moved to New York in 1998 and, if you remember, initially my wife Gail decided to stay in Sacramento because she really liked her job as executive assistant to the superintendent of the Sacramento School District. She wasn't sure I'd last in New York.

But I did take every opportunity I could to fly to the West Coast to see her. I decided to combine one of the trips home with a visit to the Raiders training camp, which wasn't that far away in Napa Valley.

It was the second time the NFL had sent me to the Raiders training camp, the first being during my rookie season as an official in 1996. But this was the first time I was going as a supervisor. I remember being full of enthusiasm and confidence.

I walked up to infamous owner Al Davis and said, rather innocently: "Hello Mr. Davis, I'm Mike Pereira, supervisor of officials…"

"I know who you are," Davis said with a disgusted look on his face. "You fucked us in the game last year in Kansas City. You know you did. You know you fucked us in that game, and I will not forget that you fucked us in that game."

You know how I like to talk, but I was speechless. I was stunned that Davis would talk to somebody from the league office that way. I guess I was also a little naïve because I would learn quickly that Davis' relationship with the NFL was colder than a walk down Park Avenue in February.

Here's the thing; I had nothing to do with the Raiders–Chiefs game that Davis was talking about in 1997, a game lost by the Raiders 28–27. I wasn't even there, but I guess I was guilty by association.

When I got back to New York, I remember telling Jerry Seeman about my visit, and he seemed pretty upset by it. Seeman wrote a letter to Commissioner Paul Tagliabue, making me document every detail of what Davis said. It's no secret Commissioners Pete Rozelle and Tagliabue were not big fans. Davis wasn't just a thorn in the league's side…he was a cactus.

I never heard where it went beyond that because I never expected, nor received, any apology from Davis. But my relationship with the Raiders took an unlikely turn from an improbable person: Amy Trask. She was the chief executive of the Raiders, and when I went to meet with their coaching staff in the spring, I was informed that she wanted to meet with me.

There was, obviously, no love lost between the Raiders

and the officiating department, and after my meeting with the coaches you'll never guess what Trask wanted to talk to me about. While I was expecting to get more bashing of the league, what I got from her was that she wanted to talk about illegal contact.

The chief executive of the Raiders was questioning me about an illegal contact play from the year before. I explained to her how illegal contact was a foul that occurred before a pass was thrown. It's not like a pass interference penalty, where the foul occurs while the ball is in the air. We chatted a little bit longer about the play in question and she accepted my explanation. I was really impressed with her knowledge of the game.

"I remember when that conversation concluded that I thought we could have a very honest, healthy, robust dialogue," Trask said when I asked her to recall my visit.

"We could agree, we could disagree, or we could simply agree to disagree. It was clear to me that you and I were not always going to agree on things, but I felt very good that you were willing to have a conversation with me and when it was over, felt that we understood one another."

Although some within and outside the Raiders organization won't want to hear it, I came to respect Trask more than any person involved with that team. We actually ended up developing a pretty good friendship. After becoming the VP of officiating, I used to spend every Sunday in the command center in New York, and if a call went against the Raiders, we would joke around the office about how long it would take before I got an email from Amy.

We'd watch my phone, and sure enough, within 25 seconds,

I'd get the "what-kind-of-call-was-that?" email from Amy. If I didn't respond right away, she would start re-emailing me about every 15 seconds.

"You and I had some very, very fierce disagreements and very significant differences of opinion, but I always—as much as I wanted to strangle you—enjoyed our dialogues and our disagreements," Trask laughed.

"During a game, if I saw something, either a call or non-call, I would just sit there in the suite and just hit resend, resend, resend, until I got a response."

It became a tradition between Amy and me, a love-hate-love relationship. To this day, she is still somebody I consider a very good friend and an astute football person, as demonstrated by her role at CBS.

While things weren't always so humorous with Amy, some of my interactions with others around the NFL were quite hysterical.

Enter former Detroit coach Wayne Fontes.

It was one of my first preseason games during my rookie year as an official, and part of the head linesman and side judge's pregame responsibilities were to see the visiting coach 90 minutes prior to kickoff. The officials have a set list of questions they normally go over with the coaches, including inquiring if there are any special plays they might be considering so they don't catch officials by surprise.

We went looking for Coach Fontes in his office and he was already out on the field. When we found him, head linesman Earnie Frantz told me to ask Coach Fontes the questions. It was the first time I had to ask the pregame questions of a head coach, and I was very nervous. With Frantz standing behind me, I asked Fontes if the Lions had any plans of running any special plays that the officials needed to know about.

"Yes, we do," Fontes said. And there I am, at the ready, with a note card and pencil in hand to write down his every word.

"We are going to run a screen pass from our own end zone," he continued. "Our quarterback is going to drop deep into the end zone; he's then going to throw a pass off the face of the first deck in the stadium. It will bounce off the façade back onto the field, hit the right upright, and then our running back is going to catch it and run for a touchdown."

I fell for it, hook, line and sinker. I wrote down everything until he said the ball would hit the right upright. I looked up to see Fontes and Frantz laughing their butts off. If it had been an audition to play the village idiot, I would have definitely gotten the part.

"That was to make a fool out of you, and Fontes did exactly what he intended to do," laughed Frantz.

I have to admit, it was pretty funny.

Not all my encounters would be so amusing, especially when it came to dealing with a coach such as Bill Parcells. It was my second year in the league and I had a game in Miami with the Dolphins and New York Jets, whom Parcells coached at the time.

The game was winding down in the fourth quarter, with Miami leading 24–17, but the Jets were driving. On a fourth-down play, Jets quarterback Glenn Foley attempted a pass to Wayne Chrebet, who was going to the ground as he caught the ball. His knees were on the ground and then he launched forward, sticking both arms out in an attempt to get the first down, but the ball popped out when he hit the ground. I was on the opposite side of the field, but the official closest to the play ruled the pass incomplete. There wasn't any instant replay that year, and Parcells lost it. He went nuts.

Even though it wasn't my call, I was in front of the Jets bench and I got an earful on the sideline. Make that three or four earfuls. I think my ears were so embarrassed by what Parcells said to me they turned red.

It didn't end after that, even though the game did.

Parcells made a mad dash toward field judge Tom Sifferman, who made the call. I was only in my second year and I was worried that he might say or do something to Sifferman that he'd regret, so I ran with him. I got between the two of them so Parcells wouldn't get himself in any trouble. He railed on Sifferman pretty good, too. Then he left.

The funny thing about it is the next day a photo appeared in newspapers across the country that showed Parcells yelling at me. But there was no Sifferman in the picture. An Associated Press photographer had taken the shot, but Sifferman had been cut out of it so it looked like Parcells was yelling at me. He had already done plenty of that earlier.

However, since it was just Parcells and I in the photo, it looked like it was me that was getting flak for making the call.

There's one more amazing part to this story. When I got home from work that Monday I had a voice mail from Parcells. He had called to apologize, saying what he said Sunday was totally unacceptable. He also said he was embarrassed by his actions and that he was sincerely sorry. That shows you what kind of guy Bill Parcells is. For all the emotion and pressure that these guys are under, a man's true colors come out when he takes the time to make a phone call like that to apologize.

A footnote about Parcells: when he came back to coach with the Dallas Cowboys in 2003, I had already moved on to the league office. I saw him at the league meetings and he stopped to tell me that I'd be happy he was back in the league because he would never call and complain about the officiating. He didn't want a player or an assistant coach to think that way. He told me officials don't cause teams to lose, that it's a team's inability to overcome its own mistakes that causes it to lose games. He was true to his word and never called to complain about the officials.

Marty Schottenheimer was also typical of the Parcells ilk. He didn't want his teams to think that officiating had anything to do with winning or losing.

I will tell you that kind of behavior is not common among today's NFL coaches. It seems the new breed of coaches is always looking for excuses. Guys like Parcells and Schottenheimer weren't that way.

I remember getting a call in 2001 from Schottenheimer when he was coach of the Redskins, and he told me he had a deal for me. He said that he would never call me when they lost, that he would only call to ask me questions if his team won.

Fair enough, I thought.

We didn't get to talk much that season because the Redskins finished 8–8. But when he would call, technology had developed to a point where he could just tell me to look up a play number.

For example, he'd tell me to call up play No. 32 on offense and we could both pull it up and look at it together. He was trying to learn from an officiating perspective and I was trying to learn from a coaching perspective.

Schottenheimer would tell me that play 32 looked like illegal contact to him. So we would run the play and I'd explain why I didn't think it was illegal contact. On that particular play in question, I told him to look at the quarterback, who had rolled out of the pocket. Even though the contact was six yards downfield, by the time the official looked back, the quarterback was clearly out of the pocket and the restriction was off.

"I got it," he would say. "You win that one. Let's go to the next one."

We'd go back and forth, and it was wonderful. We'd go over several plays, and at the end of the day, sometimes I'd win and sometimes he'd win.

Again, we didn't get to talk much that season, but the following year he went to San Diego and his teams started winning—a lot. Marty was always true to form. He would never call me after his team would lose, only when they won.

Then, it happened. The Chargers suffered a very tough playoff loss to the Jets in overtime in 2004…and the phone rang. Marty was on the line, and I was shocked, not knowing what was going to come next.

"I know what you're thinking," he said. "I said I would never call when we lost. But here's my justification…we covered the spread."

We both laughed for a good minute. Marty was, and still is, a priceless character. He's a friend, a great human being, and one of the guys I really enjoyed in the coaching profession. I always enjoyed our great conversations.

One coach who wasn't the biggest Pereira fan in the world—
and I know many of you are finding that very hard to believe—
was former Buffalo coach Marv Levy.

It was the last game of the 1997 regular season—in my second year—and I had a Bills game at Green Bay. Buffalo great
Steve Tasker, one of the best special teamers to play the game,
announced that he would be retiring after that game.

I was the side judge and we were only 1:37 into the game
when Tasker attempted to field a punt. The ball, though, hit
the ground, then a Bills player, and then bounced into the end
zone. Green Bay's Tyrone Davis recovered it and I ruled it a
touchdown.

Tasker didn't realize what I called and while he was leaving the field, suddenly concluded I said it was a Packers touchdown. He turned around and charged into the end zone to yell
at back judge Tom Sifferman, claiming he never touched the
ball. He bumped into Sifferman, and I know he never intended
to, but he was flagged for contact with a game official and was
ejected from the game. Here I am, only my second year in the
league, knowing that I'm going into the league office the next
season, and I make a call that leads to an ejection of a seven-
time Pro Bowler less than two minutes into his last game.

Referee Mike Carey was the one who officially ejected
Tasker—who was right, he didn't touch it. The ball actually
grazed off teammate Raymond Jackson's back before going into
the end zone. But nevertheless, because he bumped Sifferman,
Tasker was kicked out.

I was standing on the sideline afterward, and Levy was letting me have it.

"How could you throw a guy out who is in his last game?"

"How could you do that?"

"How could you do it just 1:37 into the game?"

"Do you have no conscience?"

All I could do was stand there quietly with my hands in my pockets and take it. While I had empathy for what Levy was saying, there was not much I could do about it at that point.

I got to know Tasker better when I moved into the league office, because after he retired he became a broadcaster for CBS. To this day, when I see him along with Carey, the three of us still laugh about it.

My relationship with Levy, as I said, wasn't the best. But the thing I did like about Marv was that he was a no-nonsense guy. He wouldn't really argue, but rather just state his belief. If my opinion was different, he'd make his point and move on and we would agree to disagree.

I always looked at Levy as someone who was straight with me. Unlike some of the other coaches, who would try to "work me," I always felt Marv was sincere in what his intentions were.

From one straight shooter to the next, another coach who was one of the straightest of them all was Bill Belichick. What you see, hoodie and all, is definitely what you get.

I'll never forget a wake I attended during the 2005 season for Giants owner Wellington Mara. I saw Belichick across the room, but we really didn't get to talk until we were both leaving.

Belichick told me that he was looking at me from across the room and then told me that I looked like shit. I swear. Those were his exact words. *You look like shit.*

I know how that might look, but he didn't really mean it the way it sounded.

"I was thinking about it," Belichick told me, "and I suddenly realized something. You never win, do you? Because you have to deal with the losers every week."

By losers, he was referring to me getting complaints about the officiating from teams that lost every week. I told him that I hadn't really thought about it like that, but that he was correct on both counts.

"When you're a coach and you win, it's the most euphoric feeling in the world," he continued. "There's nothing better as a head coach than when you win a football game.

"But when you lose it's devastating. It just eats at you. You can't believe how awful it is, and it takes a long time for that feeling to go away. I looked at you and I realized you never get to feel the euphoria."

He told me that he was going to call me someday after a loss, just to tell me that my guys did a good job. I told him I really appreciated that.

I'm still waiting for that call. I never got that call or any others after Spygate, the Patriots videotaping controversy in 2007. Belichick must have thought I had something to do with that. Clearly, as you're about to find out, he wasn't the only one.

When FOX Sports' Jay Glazer broke the story that the Patriots illegally filmed the Jets defensive coaches' signals from their own sideline during their game on September 9, 2007, Glazer also got the accompanying video that aired on FOX to go with his report.

A lot of people, including several NFL bigwigs, thought I had given the video to Glazer. They thought that because the video was first viewed from my office in the NFL Command Center. The NFL's top brass, including Commissioner Goodell, came to see the tape, and they thought I had a hand in sending it to Glazer.

In reality, it simply wasn't true. I didn't give it to Glazer and I don't know how he got it. And quite frankly, I don't give a damn. To this day, I still don't know.

But at the time, the league made me feel like I was the one being investigated for doing something wrong. Over the next month, I got called into the NFL security department several times and interrogated about how FOX got the tape. It felt a little like how I imagine the Nuremberg Trials went.

It finally got to the point where I was fed up, and I told the NFL to give me a lie detector test if they didn't believe me. I told them over and over again that I didn't have anything to do with Glazer getting the video.

Belichick and the Patriots were both disciplined. Belichick was fined $500,000, the largest fine ever imposed on a coach, and the Patriots were fined $250,000 and lost their first-round pick (31st overall) in the 2008 NFL Draft.

Because of Spygate, I think Belichick associated me with that and I've never really talked to him again to this day. Belichick has a tremendous ability to unite his teams by saying that people are out to get them. I think it was true of Spygate then, and I think it was true of Deflategate in 2014 as well.

Everyone knows Belichick is a great coach. He's got the uncanny ability to get a team to play together. You can make fun of his hoody pullovers, you can make fun of his news-conference sound bites like "We're on to Cincinnati" when he doesn't want to answer a question, but you can't make fun of his record or the four Super Bowls he's won.

And then there's former NFL coach and current ESPN broadcaster Jon Gruden. If there's one thing I regret since I've crossed over to the media side, at least to some degree, it is an article I wrote on FOXSports.com about him in 2011, in which I called him a blowhard.

Damn Internet. Unfortunately, I was able to find exactly what I wrote:

> I am not a fan of Gruden's. Not today, not yesterday, not when I worked for the NFL and not when I was working on the field as a side judge. He was a loudmouth as a coach who constantly disrespected officials and he is a blowhard in the broadcast booth that spouts off when he doesn't know what he is talking about.
>
> I respect his knowledge about the Xs and Os when it comes to coaching and playing the game of football, but I have very little respect for him when it comes to officiating and his knowledge of the rules.

Looking back on it now, I was probably too harsh. I shouldn't have written that about a fellow media member, but in reality, I did it out of frustration. Gruden was by far the toughest coach that any official had to deal with.

My issue with him was this: instead of coming to me with a problem, which he never did, he would berate officials on the sideline. It really bothered me because it was a matter of total disrespect. I would get calls from officials who told me that Gruden had crossed the line. During those conversations, I would always ask them why they hadn't penalized him for his behavior, because I knew that would have stopped it.

But officials have a tendency not to throw flags on coaches, and he was one guy it seemed they just wouldn't flag. He was awful.

There's no question, from 1998 to 2008 when he was a head coach, if you asked officials who was the worst coach they had to deal with on the sideline, Gruden would have won in a landslide. It was because of the way he would go after them. He consistently disrespected officials during a game.

Then when Gruden got to the broadcasting side, he would bash officials on the air for things they weren't wrong on. It was irritating. And on a late December Monday night, I had finally had enough. So I took out my frustrations and wrote the column.

Look, he's a good announcer. And one could certainly argue he's a heckuva coach. He won a Super Bowl. But the persona of Jon "I love ya, man" Gruden is not the total picture of the man. That was not genuine and not appreciated.

On the other hand, somebody I really came to appreciate quite a bit was former Bills and Colts executive Bill Polian.

My relationship with him is really interesting because I wonder how the hell I can love and hate a guy at the same time. If you've ever had a love/hate relationship with somebody, you know exactly what I mean.

Polian had the fiercest Irish temper I have ever seen *during* a football season. But in the offseason, he was a totally different guy.

He's a wonderfully warm man, whom I enjoyed playing golf, talking to, and learning from. He's just a terrific guy, and my wife and I really enjoyed being around him and his wife Eileen.

But during the season, forget it. Some of my fiercest battles, when I was in the league office, were with Polian.

Intense doesn't begin to describe him. Think Herm Edwards "You Play to Win the Game" intense and double it. He would argue with me on everything when it came to officiating. Teams could call in or send in reports when they had complaints involving officials.

When he didn't like what officials did on the field, he would definitely let me know about it. And many times he didn't like the answers I would give when I explained their actions.

"The fact that you wouldn't agree with me when I thought I was 100 percent right would drive me crazy," Polian laughed when I asked him to recall our battles.

"You would give me, 'Well, we could support that call.' To this day, I don't know what *support* means. Then we had such a great time at the Competition Committee meetings that I would forget. Then I wouldn't get mad again until we got some bad calls."

We had some pretty extraordinary clashes. I didn't want to take his phone calls because they were so difficult. It was like being yelled at constantly by your worst enemy.

I don't know if I'd say the calls were demeaning, because I don't think it was really about me, but rather about Polian's frustrations.

And it didn't matter if it was calling the league office or going after our supervisors at game sites, he would never hesitate if he felt something was called incorrectly. But now being out of the game for a few years has changed his perspective a little.

"I look back now on my competitive days and say, <u>probably 80 percent of the calls that I complained about I shouldn't have complained about.</u> I know you're going to write that and underline," he laughed.

But I will say that he knew officiating because he worked in the league office and in game operations and was involved with the disciplining of players. However, I think his temper got the best of him.

The reason I say that is because I got to see a different side of him during the offseason.

Just like the seasons change, so did Polian's personality when it came to *football* season. Let's just say I knew I'd always need an umbrella from September to January because the forecast was always stormy when dealing with him.

There's no arguing, however, when it comes to discussing how successful Polian was.

He worked for three very successful franchises, the first in Buffalo from 1986 to '92, where the Bills went to four consecutive Super Bowls. Yes, they lost them all, but to this day, no franchise has ever gone to four straight Super Bowls.

He moved on to become GM of the newly formed Carolina team in 1995 and the Panthers went to the NFC Championship Game in only their second season, which led Polian to another great opportunity.

In 1998, Polian became president and GM of the Indianapolis Colts. The Colts selected Peyton Manning with the No. 1 pick that draft, and the rest, as they say, is history.

You see Polian today as a mild-mannered analyst for ESPN, but he was one tough cookie to deal with.

I still consider him a good friend. It's crazy, but that's the way I feel about that man who, deservedly so, was inducted into the Hall of Fame prior to the 2015 season.

Another guy that I became friends with over the years was coach Mike Shanahan, but my first introduction to him was not such a good one.

It was January 4, 1998, and I was a second-year official, while Shanahan was coach of the Denver Broncos. Picture this: it was my first—and last—playoff game as an on-field official, because as you already know, I moved into the league office the next season. As I mentioned in the last chapter, I was assigned to be the side judge in the AFC divisional round game between the Broncos and the Chiefs in Kansas City.

The pressure was enormous. The jump from the regular season to the playoffs is like going from kindergarten straight to junior high. The pressure that bears down on you is incredible.

Butterflies the size of vultures were swirling around in my stomach as the game began, and in the first quarter, Broncos quarterback John Elway attempted a pass to Willie Green, who was running an out and up route. I totally missed making the most blatant, illegal contact call you've ever seen.

The very technical term for it: chocking. Yep, I admit it. I gagged in front of millions of viewers and I didn't need to see a replay to know I missed it. I knew it right after the play ended. I'll never forget it. I'll take the inability to make that call in a big game to my grave.

It was right in front of Shanahan, and he was not happy

with me.

"I do remember that," Shanahan laughed when I asked him recently to recall that play. "When I look back now, what I realized as a coach is that we know what is supposed to happen on a specific play — and the officials don't. And if you take your eye off it for a second, you could miss it.

"I get it. After I was in the league for awhile, if there was a unique play or we were doing something different, I started alerting the officials as to what was going to happen so they'd be aware of it. So even though I was kind of upset at the time, I figured out to tell the officials on a play like that to watch the possible out and up contact prior to the play."

Interestingly, if you ask an official what his best call was, many would probably have a hard time remembering. Ask them what their worst call was and they'll relive it like it was yesterday. It's kind of like arthritis — once you get it, it never goes away.

"I'm just glad you didn't miss the *big* call in that game," Shanahan reminded me.

That was the call I mentioned in the last chapter, the Tony Gonzalez force-out play, where I ruled he wasn't forced out by a Denver defender but rather out of bounds, voiding what would have been a winning touchdown for the Chiefs.

"That was the best call," Shanahan said. "I couldn't even see it from the sideline. Then they had to replay it a couple times and, of course, at that time we didn't have replay. I got a chance to see it in slow motion later on, and it was the right call. It was a 14–10 game at the time; that's why every play, every call is so critical. If you don't make the right call on that play, we don't win the Super Bowl that year."

Denver held on to beat the Chiefs, then went on to beat Pittsburgh in the AFC Championship Game and Green Bay in the Super Bowl.

But I wasn't done with Shanahan, even when I was done with the NFL. I had already begun working at FOX and a funny thing happened on my way to the third hole at the Ancil Hoffman Golf Course on a Monday early in the NFL season in 2010.

My phone rang; it was Shanahan calling. He was in his first season as the Redskins coach and he wanted me to look at a play from his team's game from the previous day, which happened to be a 27–24 loss to the Colts.

I remember laughing while asking him if he got the memo that I had retired. He knew that, but he wanted my opinion on a play because he was interested to hear my take on things since we had worked together for such a long time.

When you're dealing with a class act like Mike Shanahan, some things never get old.

While I've discussed several characters from my past, none were, perhaps, funnier or crazier than Dean Look.

Let me start out by saying Look was a great official. I'm sure many of you will remember one of the most famous plays in NFL history, the Catch, by San Francisco's Dwight Clark in the 1982 NFC Championship Game against Dallas. He's the guy that can be seen in photos and video extending his hands signaling touchdown to give the 49ers a 28–27 win over the Cowboys. Like I said, Look was a great official.

But there are a couple stories of Look dealing with two

coaches, Tom Coughlin and Mike Ditka, who will either make you laugh or sigh. I haven't decided which yet.

Let's start with Coughlin. It was 1999 and my second year as supervisor of officials. There's really no special reason why I was there, but I happened to go to a preseason game in Jacksonville.

Ninety minutes prior to a game, the officials meet with both coaches. I decided to go with the officials to the Coughlin meeting because I had gotten to know him a little bit. We got to his office and I saw Tom, so I shook his hand. The other official shook his hand as well, followed by Dean Look, who also shook his hand.

Coughlin had a strange reaction when we got done shaking hands, but nothing really registered with me at the time. Anyway, the officials went through their normal routine with him and then left.

I stuck around Coughlin's office because I wanted to see how things had been going for him, and as the officials were leaving, he got agitated.

"Did you see what Dean Look did?" he barked at me afterward.

I told him I hadn't, and he followed with this gem:

"He picked his nose and then stuck his hand out to shake my hand," he said. *"He picked his nose!"*

The more Coughlin said it, the angrier he got.

"He picked his nose and then stuck his hand out to directly shake my hand."

I was astonished, and if looks could kill, Dean Look would have been deader than a zebra at a lion convention. I asked Coughlin if he shook Look's hand.

"What am I supposed to do?" he shouted. "I was looking right at him and saw him pick his nose."

I couldn't believe it. I didn't want to believe it. I made my way back into the officials' locker room, where I found Look, and then ask him if he picked his nose and then shook Coughlin's hand. He looked back at me and had a big, ear-to-ear smile on his face. That's the only comment I needed.

There's only one Dean Look, folks....

There was also only one Mike Ditka. The feisty former Chicago coach could have been the logo for the Bears, he snarled so much. But by the time of this next story, Ditka had become coach of the New Orleans Saints, who were visiting Denver for a preseason game in 1998. A person might assume that things were a little bit looser in the preseason, right? Wasn't it our parents who said "Never assume?"

It was Friday, August 14, and Look was working the game. I was there as the supervisor. Late in the fourth quarter, Look called a pass incomplete in front of the New Orleans bench. Did I mention it was a preseason game?

"It was in the last two minutes of the game, and Ditka's quarterback threw the ball and the receiver was going across the middle and the ball was behind him," Look remembered when I asked him to recall the story. "The receiver stopped and came back, and when he tried to make the catch, he hit the ground and so did the ball. The ball bounced up in his hands and then he raised it in the air like he had caught it. I got a good look at it and called it incomplete."

Ditka went nuts on Look. He thought it was a completed pass and he was running down the sideline, ranting and raving.

"He was yelling at me, indicating to me that I didn't have parents and things like that. I just pointed at him and told him that the ball hit the ground," Look said.

After the game, I asked Look what Ditka said to him.

"Ditka yelled that he'd bet me $1,000 that the ball didn't hit the ground."

I might have been almost as astonished as when Coughlin told me Look had picked his nose before shaking his hand.

I asked what his response was, and my voice must have sounded incredulous. "I told him I'd take that bet," Look laughed.

After the game, as we were leaving the stadium, we walked past the Saints' team buses, and out popped Ditka. He got right in Look's face.

As I was wondering if I needed to call in the cavalry, Da Coach asked Look: "Where do I send the check?"

The three of us cracked up laughing. Look told him he could make it out to the Dean Look Foundation and that he'd take care of it from there.

Needless to say, Look never got the check, but check out this story:

"So recently, I take my son-in-law down to a Hall of Fame banquet in Detroit and who should be there, but Ditka," Look told me. "I took my son-in-law over and introduced him, and Mike told him some stories from back in the day."

I asked Look if Ditka told his son-in-law "the bet" story.

"He did. He told him that he almost had to pay his father-in-law $1,000 one time. That was a classic."

Who said the NFL is the No Fun League?

14 THE LOCKOUTS AND IMPACT OF 9/11

There really are some fun and amazing things about being part of the NFL; however, some things are no laughing matter.

There's a word in the English language, one word that I can't stand when it's mentioned in conjunction with the NFL: *lockout.*

It's just one word, but it's a Beast Mode of a word, as difficult a word to get my arms around as it would be to try and tackle Seattle running back Marshawn Lynch on a full head of steam. And unfortunately, that word, *lockout,* has been all too prevalent in my life. I've been directly or indirectly involved with two lockouts and nearly a third. I'm not talking about player lockouts but rather officials' lockouts.

Many of you probably didn't even know there were two, let alone nearly a third lockout of officials in the NFL. In 1994, when I was a WAC official, I had aspirations of becoming an NFL official, as you know. The NFL officials were attempting to organize a Referees' Association and get their first collective bargaining agreement.

It wasn't necessarily a contentious negotiation, but the league knew the negotiations could reach an impasse, which would have required them to find replacement officials.

So what did the league do prior to that season? They set out to put a group of officials together that would call the games if they didn't get the negotiation resolved before the season began. Whom do you think the league targeted? Guys like me, who were already on their list of future officials or guys that had applied to be an NFL official—guys they knew were hungry to be in the NFL.

I'll admit that after you receive a registered letter from the NFL, you do a double take and just stare at the envelope for a few moments almost in disbelief. And if an official thought it might be his best shot at getting into the league, why wouldn't he take a shot for a few games until the dispute was resolved?

In the end, I couldn't do it. I didn't do it because I didn't want to, but rather, I couldn't do it because I had friends that were already officiating in the league. That meant I'd have to cross a picket line and take their job just for some personal fulfillment of getting on the field for a measly couple games if the lockout happened.

While I fully believed in what I did, sending back all the information with a "no thanks" response began to resonate with me that I was turning down the NFL. But luckily, that lockout didn't happen.

The two sides reached a settlement and the officials got a collective bargaining agreement and retirement benefits. It's interesting; when I talked to people who were involved with the negotiations in 1994, some of them were unaware the league even sent out letters anticipating the possibility of a lockout. But the NFL leaves nothing to chance.

In 2001 I wouldn't be so fortunate. By then, I was knee-deep in my quandary with the lockout. I would rather have been locked out of my New York apartment for a month than to go through that.

The first lockout nearly happened because of the forming of the Referees' Association. The second, in 2001, was really over fees. And the third, in 2012, was over pension benefits.

But the lockout of 2001 was definitely one of those *why, me?* moments. After all, it was my first year as director of officiating. What a way to start. Trust me, there's nothing pretty about a lockout.

Commissioner Paul Tagliabue walked in my office one day in July and told me to find 135 officials who could work in the preseason that was only a month from starting. *Sure*, I thought, *I'll just walk over to Saks Fifth Avenue and pick up a few of them in the men's department. No problem.*

I had to organize getting 135 officials ready to replace my friends, and in many cases, my best friends. It was the most difficult thing that I had to do in my entire career in the NFL. Every day the management group and I would meet and I would be asked how many replacement officials I had found.

We had our supervisory staff and our scouts, at least those who would agree to help, find these officials. We first had them scour the bushes to identify current college officials, like the ones who were willing to work in 1994. Another option was to try and find retired college officials that had worked in any of the major conferences around the country.

We even went into bars looking for officials. Because, heaven knows, you would definitely need a stiff drink if you were planning to cross a picket line.

The stress was overwhelming. I remember, in particular, a great woman named Belinda Lerner, who was a member of the NFL's legal counsel. I could tell when I looked at her during these daily meetings that she felt compassion for me. She recognized I was trying to pull this off against insurmountable odds.

Much to my relief—and chagrin—we did pull it off. And much of the credit for that should go to one of my supervisors, Ronnie Baynes, who was in charge of our recruiting program and had numerous contacts across the country. I really don't think we could have done it without him.

We had an amazing number of college officials who actually agreed to work. One of the reasons for that was because certain members of the Referees' Association put together a campaign and sent out letters to college officials who were prospective replacements. The letters said they shouldn't cross the picket line because they'd be "branded" forever. All the things you would expect a union to say.

In many cases, though, it had the reverse effect. A lot of college officials resented the tone of the letters and decided to work to spite the perceived arrogance of some of these NFL officials.

My bosses came to me and asked me, along with the supervisors in my department—Larry Upson, Jim Daopoulos, Neely Dunn, Al Hynes, and Baynes—to "go back on the field" to help these replacement officials get through this period.

"We had some cooperation of some good officials. It was

amazing that we were able to round up that whole thing," Upson remembered. "I recall meeting at various cities across the country with groups of officials trying to teach them very quickly and then having to get out there and work ourselves."

If irony were a one-way street, I clearly would be going in the wrong direction. Think about that for a minute. In 1994 I refused to get involved because I was respectful of my friends that were already in the league. Then, in 2001, I was the one that had to hire people to replace my friends. Also, I was one of the office people that were forced to participate with the replacement officials.

Everything was normal before the lockout, or at least as normal as it could be given the circumstances, prior to the start of that season. We went through our officiating clinics and even completed two preseason games with our regular officials. But the tension was running so high you could have climbed to the top of the Empire State Building and not gotten over it.

Then it happened...the dreaded lockout actually materialized. We had two preseason games to get the replacement guys ready before the season would start for real.

It was a madhouse trying to get everything organized. We had to get uniforms to the replacements and get them physicals, and had to have training camps to get these guys up to speed on the NFL rules, which was hardly enough time to expect them to be able to learn the differences between the college game and the NFL.

I went to Dallas with a replacement crew during Week 3 of the preseason, and I actually hopped on the field and participated for a half. After blowing a down-by-contact call, I remember thinking that I would be better served to be standing on the sideline on headsets giving the replacements instructions on how to enforce penalties, which is ultimately what I did.

After two weeks of preseason, we got everybody in place for Week 1 of the regular season. And while I still find it hard to believe, we survived the first Sunday of games. It wasn't pretty, but we had a fairly decent group that did a pretty good job. Mind you, we had a lot of active college officials that were working their games on Saturday, then coming over to work NFL games on Sunday.

"With what we had going on, I'm not sure given today's travel climate that we would have been able to do now what we did back then," Upson said.

I went to the Monday night game in Denver that week and I brought Dunn and Daopoulos with me. We got through that game, too, although there were some mistakes. But there are always mistakes in a game, even by the regular officials.

As soon as the game ended, I knew we had the following week to deal with. We had to decide who was going to work in Week 2 and get them assigned. So as I headed back to the hotel that night, I knew Tuesday would be a big day.

That would turn out to be an understatement of epic proportions. Tuesday was September 11, 2001...9/11. One of the worst days this country has ever seen.

I was at the Denver airport getting ready to head back to New York. I had just gone through the security line when my phone rang. It was Larry Upson at the league office asking me if I had gotten on the plane yet. I told him I was on the way to my gate and he told me to forget it.

Forget it? I asked if the weather was bad, because I had seen the Yankees had gotten rained out Monday night.

Larry told me it had nothing to do with weather and that I should go find a TV. He said that would explain everything. Unfortunately, he was right.

"That was really a very scary phone call I had to make to you," Upson said when I asked him to recall that day. "But what was happening back in New York was even more traumatic for all of us.

"It was so frightening. It's just one of those experiences I remember so vividly. I was sitting in my office in a meeting with someone when Dean Blandino stuck his head in and told me to turn on my television because a plane had just hit the World Trade Center.

"I turned on my television, and by that time, the second plane was going into the second tower. I knew right away that this wasn't just some plane crash, that it was deliberate. I remember security rounding us all up, telling us to remain calm.

"We're standing there on one of the floors in the NFL offices and there are a lot of TV monitors on the walls and we're all just mesmerized by what we are seeing. Security was talking to us, but all any of us could focus on was what was on TV. One of the towers started to fall and everybody just broke down and started crying."

Helpless. Webster's defines the word as "being deprived of strength or power, to be weak or dependent."

It doesn't do the feeling I felt that day justice. Throw in *paralyzed*, *powerless*, and *forlorn*.

There were several people from the NFL with me, as I said,

and it was extremely upsetting for everybody. As you know, the skies were shut down. There were no flights for a period of four days. We were stranded.

After all of us checked in with our loved ones, we were then left grounded in Denver without any realization as to what, or when, for that matter, would come next.

Though I could think of nothing but those poor people in the Twin Towers at the World Trade Center, I knew I had to try and figure out how we were going to pull off staffing the next weekend's games with the replacement officials. Were we going to be able to get them to the sites to work their games? At that point, the NFL had not yet made the decision to postpone the following Sunday's games.

Ultimately, the league decided to suspend that week's games. It was definitely the right decision and really the only choice we could make.

Those four days felt like four months in Denver, and when we were able to fly again, I refused to go back to New York. I was so distraught that I flew home to California so I could re-connect with everything that was important to me...with Gail, with my mom and dad, and with my sister, Linda.

I wanted to go to the grocery store and walk the aisles with my family so I could have some semblance of normalcy before heading back to New York, which I knew would be anything but normal. In fact, I knew it would never be the same again.

When I finally flew back into Newark, as we approached, I was suddenly overwhelmed with emotion. We were getting ready to land and I remember looking toward the southern tip of Manhattan—a routine of mine—to glance for a peek at the

Twin Towers, but they weren't there anymore. There were only puffs of smoke.

It was such a surreal feeling. It made it very personal for me and it affected everybody that lived in the New York area. Two of the people who worked at the NFL lost their spouses. It was a unifying experience unlike any other—a sad feeling, because it seemed like everyone you knew had a connection to someone who lost their life—as well as a bonding that brought all of us that not only lived in New York, but our country, together.

On that day, I heard stories of people walking from Ground Zero all the way to Midtown, where the NFL offices are located on Park Avenue, covered in ash. It was an incredibly difficult experience for everyone and even more personal for those of us who lived there.

I think besides the bonding, it also brought people back down to earth because you had officials locked out over what was really a minimal amount of money. It seemed everybody, including the league, came to their senses and the lockout was quickly resolved. By the time the season restarted for Week 3, the regular officials were back in place.

But the scars don't go away after a lockout. Memories are long, especially when you're dealing with people who have very strong egos like most officials have, and by the way, have to do the job they do.

The anger from the officials that was directed at the league and the officiating department was prevalent for a long time. The trust factor was definitely harmed, and it was hard for them to understand how we, as supervisors, could do what we did even though we were part of the management team. If they were in a similar situation at their own jobs, they would have done the same thing we did.

However, officiating is a unique avocation, and the lockout caused many friendships to be irreparably harmed, all because of the labor stoppage. I was glad that I never had to directly deal with a lockout again. But I couldn't avoid being involved on the periphery in 2012.

The 2012 lockout of officials was not over a union being formed or over a salary. This time, and you'll never convince me otherwise, it was over pension benefits.

As I've stated earlier, it's not a bad gig working as an official in the NFL. They have a great retirement program with a defined benefit that could give a 20-year official up to $5,500 a month for the rest of his life beginning at age 62.

The league was tired of the defined benefits, as were most companies in America. Why? Because the defined benefits demanded a certain return on money that's in retirement accounts. If you don't get that return on the investment, then a company has to make up the difference and add money into these retirement accounts.

Because the economy went into the tank in 2007, the money that was going into these retirement accounts not only didn't make money but lost money. That required the league to make up a lot of money and, as I've detailed in the chapter on the CBA, the NFL wanted to do what other major businesses and corporations were doing—going to a 401(k) and leaving it for the officials to invest their money.

The officials didn't want to do that, and I can certainly understand why. But that is what led to the lockout in 2012. Luckily for me, I wasn't directly involved, this time only watching the whole thing with replacement officials happen from the sideline, or from my "new" sideline, Stage A at the FOX Network Center in Los Angeles.

I started off being "fair and balanced" every time I spoke or wrote on the subject. I would say that both sides needed to give in and make an adjustment.

That all changed after I received a phone call from NFL executive vice president, Ray Anderson, who proceeded to rip into me for what he said I wrote in an article that I had done about the replacement officials.

He insinuated that I made the statement that all the replacement officials had only high school experience. In truth, if he had read the article I wrote, he would have seen that wasn't the case. I wrote that there were some officials with only high school experience. But I never said that they all fell in that category.

In reality, he read an article picked up by the *Chicago Sun-Times* that had misquoted my article. Anderson's accusation, along with the dumb comments he made about the officials not staying in shape and not giving 100 percent on the field, were the impetus for changing my view.

If that was reflective of the attitude of the league, it was enough to sway me completely to the officials' side. It proved to me that officials are generally disrespected by the league office as I described in an earlier chapter. Not the officiating department, mind you, but I'm talking about the NFL as a whole.

The way I looked at it was this: the lockout could have been avoided if each team put in $100,000 per year for the length of the contact. Instead, the league maintained that the integrity of the game would not be harmed with replacement officials. The league also said that players' safety would not be jeopardized. Really?

That wasn't the case in either lockout if you ask me. I spoke out in favor of the lockout in 2001, saying that things would be okay and the integrity of the game would be fine. Because I worked for the league, what did everyone think I was going to say?

In fact, integrity would definitely come into play in 2012, especially with that group of replacements, who weren't nearly as strong as the group we brought in during the lockout of 2001.

Hell, there were basically no major college officials even working with this group, because half the major college conferences, then and now, are run by current or former NFL officials, so nobody was going to cross the line.

As I stated before, in the 2012 group of replacements, you had some officials that were working only at the high school level, for God's sake. And now, all of a sudden, they're working NFL games!

Remember, this is a league that brings in $10 *billion*—that's with a *B*—a year, and that is expected to increase to $25 billion by 2027.

With a business worth that much money, I feel that more significance should be given to officiating. There is no game without the officials. The NFL has to do everything in its power to make sure that the officials are the best they can be and that they are compensated fairly.

What would have been fair? What could have prevented the lockout? The NFL could have continued to contribute to the defined pension benefit for the current officials in 2011 for the rest of their careers. Then, the NFL could have started the 401(k)-contribution plan for any official hired in or after 2012.

I'm no lawyer, but that seems pretty simple to me. For the cost of only about $100,000 per club, per year, the 2012 lockout could have been avoided. It was a disaster waiting to happen.

It was Monday, September 24, and I had decided to take off after the Sunday games of Week 3 to go fishing. I had promised my wife that I would take her and our friends from Sacramento, Victor Hough and Peggy Bettcher, fishing, so we drove up to the Eastern Sierras in Bishop, California. While driving up to the 9,260-foot level, I was listening to the Monday night game between the Packers and Seahawks.

Besides fishing, the purpose of the trip was just to get away for a few days, and I knew once I stepped out of the car, I might have been like the *Last Man on Earth* because there were no telephones, television, or cell reception in the rooms at the little place we were staying at, the Parchers Resort.

I sat in the car listening until the two-minute warning and Green Bay got the ball and was leading 12–7. So I turned off the ignition and went to the room, not thinking any more about it.

Two words summed up what would happen next: Fail Mary.

Seattle got the ball back with 46 seconds to go at the Green Bay 46-yard line. On fourth down from the Packers' 24-yard line with just eight seconds remaining, Seahawks quarterback Russell Wilson threw a Hail Mary pass toward the end zone. It appeared Seattle receiver Golden Tate committed an offensive pass interference penalty by pushing Green Bay's Sam Shields to the ground. Both Tate and the Packers' M.D. Jennings jumped for the ball, and both appeared to possess the ball equally as they hit the ground.

Two of the replacement officials near the play talked it over and then simultaneously made separate signals, if you can believe that. Side judge Lance Easley raised his arms to signal touchdown while back judge Derrick Rhone-Dunn signaled timeout to stop the game clock, which had already expired.

If you think that's confusing, just wait, because it was about to become downright baffling.

Rhone-Dunn indicated from the signal he gave that he wasn't sure what happened. Easley, from his angle, said it was a simultaneous catch and he decided it was a Seattle touchdown. Referee Wayne Elliott got involved because it was a scoring play and determined, in replay, there was not enough evidence to overturn the call.

Incredibly, it was ruled a 14–12 victory for Seattle. No pass interference and no replay reversal.

The next morning I woke up, and before I went fishing, I walked into the office of the resort and I asked Kristina Karady, the receptionist at the front desk, if I could use the computer for a minute. She told me that she wasn't allowed to let guests do that.

The kind, young woman, however, did ask why I needed it. I told her I was the rules analyst for FOX Sports and I just needed to see who won the Monday night game.

She stared at me for a moment with her dark eyes and 16 rings on each ear and then started to scream: "That was the worst call in the history of football and it cost me my pool. It was unbelievable!"

Obviously, I didn't know anything about the play, but when I saw it two days later, Kristina had actually described it perfectly.

By that time, I figured everyone in the world would be looking for me to get my reaction. I had to make a decision to drive back down the mountain to get reception or go fishing. I went fishing instead and stayed away until the next night.

I think the league was actually happy that I wasn't around, because I had been very vocal in my opposition of the lockout and the NFL was none too pleased. Guys in the front office had even expressed their concern to me about how negative I was and wondered how I could have been so supportive in 2001 and so not in 2012.

Really? Did I actually need to explain that?

The next night, we all went down the mountain for dinner and when I got within cell phone range, my phone blew up. Even more than it did for the Tuck Rule play in 2001. It was wild.

I did a few interviews but really couldn't say a lot because I hadn't seen the play at that point. When I got back to Los Angeles and saw it, I discovered why everyone was referring to the play as the Fail Mary.

For one, it was clearly offensive pass interference on Seattle wide receiver Golden Tate. For those who argued, including the replacement official Lance Easley, that officials should be lenient in those types of situations, they are absolutely right. That's what officials are told to do on those types of plays. But not so lenient to allow a receiver to push an opponent to the ground, which is what Tate did.

Secondly, no matter what the league said, it wasn't a simultaneous catch. The NFL rule is different than the college rule. If one person controls the ball first and then a second person establishes control, it's not a simultaneous catch. That's exactly what happened on that play. Jennings got control of the ball first, then Tate got control with him.

The NFL would eventually breathe a sigh of relief that season, because the Packers, even though they were robbed on that game, would still make the playoffs. But one could argue that they lost home-field advantage because of that call.

While the lockout negotiation had been going on forever, it was quickly resolved after the Fail Mary play, as the league and the Referees' Association came to an agreement just two days after the Monday night game. So the regular officials were back on the field for the Thursday night game, less than 24 hours after the agreement was reached.

That was funny to me, because prior to the settlement, league office personnel told us at our FOX football seminar prior to the season starting that once a deal was reached, it would take up to 10 days to get the regular officials ready.

The league said they wanted the officials to get physicals and to get them to a rules clinic. And by the way, they'd also need new uniforms because we all know how critical that would be.

That 24 hours was the quickest 10 days I've ever seen. Guess you can accomplish anything quickly when you need, or have, to.

The crowd cheered when the regular officials returned to the field for the Thursday, Sunday, and Monday games. The officials doffed their caps and waved to the crowd.

But the cheering lasted about as long as hang time does on a good punt, which is about four seconds. Those same fans were yelling that they wanted the replacement officials back when a call went against their team. Such is the life of an official.

I hope that as long as I stay involved in this game, on any level, I never see a lockout again. However, I can't say with all sincerity that will be the case.

15 PRESSURES OF THE NFL AND WHY I ALMOST LEFT...TWICE

Come to think of it, the word *lockout* may have been a metaphor for my time in the NFL officiating department, at least from 2001 on, because I never really felt secure about keeping my job. There always seemed to be something hanging over my head.

I came into the league office in 1998, one year behind Larry Upson, who was hired as a supervisor of officials after the 1997 season. We all knew that Jerry Seeman was going to retire after the 2000 season, so the question was, who would be in charge? Was it going to be Upson or me?

I'm not sure who ultimately made the decision, but the league made us co-directors of officiating. That would be like having co-starting quarterbacks. When something goes wrong, fans yell for the other quarterback. For that matter, I don't really think co-anythings work. And this one didn't either.

When you oversee a program of that many officials (119 then), replay officials, scouts, and your office staff, it's just not practical, especially in the officiating world. Because there's always conflict between officials and their superiors, and then the issue becomes if an official gets mad at one supervisor, he's going to run to the other—kind of like kids and their parents.

There was never any clear delineation in terms of who was in charge, and it made it very difficult for both Larry and me. We weren't comfortable and neither were the officials, because there was no continuity in the leadership of the department.

And talk about going from dumb to dumber, the league brought in Art Shell as senior vice president of football operations in 2004 and he further upset the apple, orange, and lemon carts because Upson and I reported to him.

Shell was not a good administrator and tried to motivate us by intimidation and fear. He treated Upson and I like we were players and he was the coach. His directives were more like threats, rather than a boss working with his right-hand men, and both Upson and I thought we were going to get fired.

"It seemed like he was just so down on both of us," recalled Upson. I think it had so much to do with the officials' union complaining about us.

"I hadn't been treated that way before, but it seems like he was trying to intimidate us. I couldn't figure it out because I thought we were doing a pretty good job."

Our jobs were tough enough, the pressure was extreme, and the last thing either one of us needed was to be bullied. To have to work in that environment—where you worried about being fired from one day to the next—wasn't healthy.

The officials knew it, too. They all felt that either Upson or I wasn't going to be around that much longer, making it that much more difficult to manage them. It was a horrible environment. So horrible, I decided to look for another job.

It was the first time I thought about leaving the NFL, but it wouldn't be the last.

I remember going home one night to my apartment and talking to my wife and sister, who happened to be visiting. I told them both that they shouldn't be surprised if I came home the next day and didn't have a job.

Talk about frustrating. Luckily for me, Southeastern Conference commissioner Mike Slive reached out to me. Slive's a really good man, and I knew the SEC was ready to make a change with their officiating coordinator and I explained to him the difficult situation I was in with the NFL.

For the three people who don't know this, the SEC in the South is big—dare I say bigger than the NFL. For those of you screaming blasphemy right now, I'd say the SEC in the South is like church and the NFL is Sunday school. Either way, football is a religion in the South, and Slive started courting me to come work with him as an associate or assistant commissioner.

We'd talk every time he came to New York, and I even made a visit to the SEC offices in Birmingham, Alabama. The more we talked, the more interested I was in taking the job. I figured, why not? Why put up with the crap I was dealing with internally at the NFL?

I decided I was going to take it, so I went to NFL commissioner Roger Goodell and told him I was going to accept the SEC's position. I don't think he knew what to say at first, and I'm not sure he thought I was serious, but he quickly got to the point.

He told me if I was taking the job for the right reasons, then

I had his blessing. But if I was leaving for the wrong reasons, he was going to kick my ass.

"The wrong reason," Goodell said, "would be if you're leaving because of Art Shell."

I explained to him that Shell and the NFL had weakened the position of the director of officiating to such a degree that the officials had lost any respect they might have had for the position.

"I remember Shell didn't want to hear our side on anything," Upson said. "He heard everybody else's side, but he didn't want to take into consideration what we were doing."

Goodell and I continued our conversation over dinner, and to his credit, he realized there was an issue. He also told me that regardless of whether I left or not, he wanted me to write a description of what it would take to get the position back to where it needed to be.

So I met with a young woman, Andrea Yelin, who worked in the human resources department of Citibank at the time, and she helped me formulate my thoughts to present to Goodell.

Yelin was a friend of Nancy Behar, who worked in the NFL's broadcasting department. The same Nancy Behar who helped me adjust to life in New York City.

When I pitched my ideas to Goodell, they included such things as making the position of the director of officiating a Vice President and giving the person a multiyear contract so the officials wouldn't second-guess whether or not the boss would be back next season.

Andrea and I worked on the document for a few days and the one thing she stressed to me was that if I submitted the proposal to Goodell—and he accepted it—then I needed to take the job. I really couldn't argue with that. So, accepting that fact, we drafted the proposal and I gave it to Goodell.

After a couple days, I still hadn't heard anything and I knew the SEC was waiting for an answer from me. I also knew that Slive thought I was going to take the job. On the third day, I decided if I didn't hear anything from the NFL by the end of the day, then I was going to accept the SEC's job.

Let me tell you, that third day was crawling. I must have looked at my watch 150 times. The day was moving so slowly I think they could have made the sequel to the movie *Boyhood*.

Just as I was about to declare that I was going to the SEC, Nancy Gill, the head of the NFL's human resources department, came running into my office with a contract—get this—with all of the things that were in the proposal. Everything!

I agreed to stay as the NFL's vice president of officiating in 2004, but to this day, I still regret how things turned out with the SEC. I felt like I gave Slive and the SEC the shaft because they thought I was taking the job as their coordinator of officiating. It was not my finest moment, and neither was the next time that I almost jumped to the NCAA, right after the 2008 NFL season.

As I think back about it now, my original plan was to leave the NFL after the 2009 season—and once again I had been in contact with the NCAA, which was looking to hire a national coordinator of college football officiating for the 2008 season. I even helped them draw up a job description so they could post the job and ask for applicants.

After the position was posted, there were a few people who

applied and they were invited to interview in Dallas. But the NCAA also asked me to interview, because they knew my intent was to leave the NFL after the 2009 season, and they were considering the possibility of waiting a year in order to hire me.

I told Ray Anderson, who was the NFL's VP of Football Operations, that the NCAA had asked me to interview for its position, and if I got the job, I was thinking about taking it after retiring from the NFL following the 2009 season. Anderson said he was happy for me and that he thought it would be a great move for me—and for the NFL—so he told me to go do the interview.

Why did he think it would be great for me to leave the NFL?

Because college football is where the NFL draws its officials from, and if I was going to oversee all officiating for the NCAA, he felt I would make their future officials better.

So off I went to Dallas to interview. I was the last person interviewed and then went back to my room and waited there for a couple hours.

Then the phone rang. They offered me the job and I essentially accepted it and I was to start after the 2009 season. From Dallas, I went to Tampa Bay to catch a preseason game. I was on the sideline before the game when my phone rang. It was Ray Anderson.

Now imagine your worst nightmare coming to life...again!

I told Anderson I had gotten the NCAA job offer and accepted it and he actually sounded enthused, but I could tell something was wrong.

"We have a problem," Anderson said.

Those four words have followed me around like a little,

lost puppy dog seemingly my whole life. *Here we go again*, I thought. *What now?*

Anderson said he told Goodell that I was leaving for the NCAA after one more year in the NFL and he was totally against it. He said Goodell wasn't going to allow it to happen.

Wasn't going to allow it to happen? Damn it.

The *it* in this case was that Goodell was not going to let me stay at the NFL for a "lame duck" year, as he called it. I wasn't ready to leave the NFL yet, so I flew back to New York to meet with him.

Goodell told me that he wasn't going to have a guy that was a lame duck running one of the most important departments in the NFL. He told me that if I wanted to take the NCAA's job that was fine, but I needed to leave the NFL immediately, not after another year.

Here's why I wasn't ready to leave the NFL. We were already in the 2008 preseason and I wasn't going to leave the officiating program high and dry. I also needed to make some financial decisions that were predicated on spending one more year in the NFL.

So I had to go back to some really significant people like Jim Delany of the Big Ten conference, Tom Hansen from the Pac-10, Britton Banowsky of Conference USA, and Tom Jernstedt of the NCAA, and tell them I wasn't going to be taking their job after all. It was Ray Anderson, my boss, who set up me up to fail this time, much like he misplayed the league's position in the 2012 lockouts.

It was a very unpleasant experience, kind of like passing kidney stones.

For whatever reason, these guys thought they had pulled off a coup in getting me from the NFL. Not only would it have been a great job for me, but it also fit into my agenda, being able to work from home in Sacramento. I guess it just was not meant to be.

Ironically, I ended up being a lame duck anyway because five months later it was announced that I would be retiring after the 2009 season.

As I look back on it now, it's interesting that as much as I enjoyed the job at the NFL and all the great things that came with it, I was amazingly insecure. Why? The pressure.

Some of you may think I'm off my rocker with what I'm about to say, but I think the vice president of officiating's job is the second toughest job in the NFL.

Yes, the commissioner has a very tough job putting up with the 32 owners, who obviously have strong egos to deal with as well as a lot of tough issues. But the VP of officiating's job is no walk in Central Park. I dealt with it, as did Jerry Seeman and Art McNally before me, and it was no different for Carl Johnson and now Dean Blandino after me. I say it's the second-hardest job in the league because you are always dealing with people who are upset.

You remember what Bill Belichick told me about me never winning? Think about it; 16 teams become losers every week, not counting the bye weeks, and in today's world, everybody is looking to place blame somewhere other than on themselves and their teams.

The losers always have complaints with the officiating. But quite frankly, even when teams would win, they'd have complaints. It was a hard job to deal with week in and week out. I knew at some point I had to make a decision about when to leave the NFL.

To me, the telltale signs started as early as 2007, because I felt like by then I had mastered the rules. I got so good at knowing the rules that it dominated my life. The rule book was the only thing I read. If somebody called me during the course of a game, for example, like a network dialing in to ask me specifics about a certain rule, I could quote the rule off the top of my head, including the page number and the section. I could do it with 100 percent confidence.

But that was until 2007, when I could tell that portion of "my game" started to slip. People would call to ask me what the rule was on something, and instead of knowing the answer immediately, I would say what I thought it was, but told them I'd have to look it up to be sure.

In a job as important as the VP of officiating, you can't start second-guessing yourself about the rules. And while it took a couple more years, I knew it was time for me to go.

16 THE MOVE TO TV: LIGHTS, CAMERA, SATISFACTION

TIM DAVEY.

The name won't mean much to many of you, but besides not knowing the rules off the top of my head like I used to, what happened to Tim Davey was another reason that validated my decision to retire from the NFL after the 2009 season.

Davey was the assistant director of football operations and was promoted to director when Peter Hadhazy passed away in 2006, but Davey himself died in January 2010. He worked his ass off and never got to enjoy the fruits of his hard work. Davey was one of the hardest-working guys I'd ever seen—and he was only 58 years old.

I could feel the stress building inside me, and I didn't want to end up that way. I knew what I needed to do and knew that my career at the NFL was coming to an end. On top of that, my parents were really struggling and my dad, who had been such a focal point in my life, was nearing the end of his life, and I wanted to spend some I'll-never-forget-you time with him. That was another reason why I decided to move on.

But I needed an awesome plan, so I came up with an extraordinary strategy to help me execute my idea.

It was 2007 and I was 57 years old, and I decided I wanted to work until I was 60, then go back home to California. But I didn't want to totally retire, so I needed a transition. My very thoughtful, yet uncultivated idea, involved the number six.

See, I told you my plan was amazing. The idea was to work my butt off for six months out of the year then take the next six months off. And I wanted to do it for six years and then fully retire.

Wait a minute, that's 6-6-6. What the devil was I thinking? That might explain a few things. But, luckily for me, I didn't get burned.

However, it was a little bizarre how it all played out.

Everything was going according to plan, and the goal was to retire from the NFL after the 2009 season. But here's where it gets interesting.

It was the morning of January 18, 2009, and the Philadelphia Eagles were about to take on the Arizona Cardinals in the NFC Championship Game. On the *NFL on FOX*'s No. 1–rated pregame show, NFL insider Jay Glazer announced I was going to retire as the vice president of officiating after the following season.

I sat there watching from the NFL Command Center in New York thinking to myself: *Is that really news? Does anybody really care?* Hearing someone talk about your own retirement on TV is kind of like walking through a graveyard, and the hair on the back of your neck stands up. It was a bit eerie.

Nevertheless, the pregame show ended and I was just five

minutes into watching the NFC Championship Game when the phone rang. I looked down and saw it was a 310 number, a Southern California area code. I knew it was FOX calling; that wasn't unusual. Frequently, on Sundays during an NFL season, Bill Brown, one of FOX's senior producers, would call for a rules interpretation on a specific play.

At that moment, however, it wasn't Brown calling to see what I could do for him. It was David Hill.

Hill, a television industry icon and the chairman and executive producer of Fox Sports, was on the line. One thing you must know about Hill is that the word *small* does not exist in his vocabulary.

The man has a larger-than-life presence with a ton of charisma and a booming Australian voice. He's so inspiring and persuasive he could probably convince you that black is the new orange.

"Pereira," Hill shouted at me, "you are not retiring. We are going to develop something at FOX that will be totally dynamic, and you're going to be a part of it. I'm not going to let you retire. I'm not going to let you do that to your wife. She doesn't want you home on weekends."

How about that? I had basically just heard my "obituary" from the NFL being announced and then I got resurrected by the head of FOX Sports, saying he was going to figure out something cool for me to do during the football season. It was unbelievable.

The guys at FOX and I had become pretty chummy over the years because of the offseason seminars I used to do with the network. As each new season would approach, part of my job with the NFL was to help educate, so I would do seminars with all the networks that televised the sport—CBS, NBC, ESPN, and FOX. I started doing this in 2001 when I took over as the director of officiating.

At these seminars, I'd talk about the rule changes and go over points-of-emphasis for the upcoming season with the broadcasters, analysts, and producers. I wasn't sure how it was all going to play out when I started these seminars, because I didn't know if the networks wanted to be educated with that many details. I can ramble on with the best of them.

Another reason I did this was because I didn't like the fact that announcers would criticize the officials when they had never officiated before and had no basis of knowledge to condemn them.

But I wound up being pleasantly surprised. They wanted the knowledge. They wanted to be enlightened. The announcers wanted to be right when they went on the air trying to explain the rules. They wanted to know the rules, yet they didn't want to read the rule book. But I can't blame them for that. Who's sick enough to read the rulebook? Only people like me and other officials who have dedicated themselves to the game would do something that silly.

In most cases, the seminars at CBS and ESPN came with time limits. I had a certain amount of time to give my message and then move on. Sometimes, it was as little as 30 minutes, but it was something I felt I had to do, even though some weren't totally enthused about listening to me clamor on about the rules.

That wasn't the case with NBC or FOX. David Hill said the

surveys that the network had done showed viewers expected the announcers to be knowledgeable about the rules. He felt it was extremely important for the announcers to be informed, and I was to take as much time as I needed.

The producers and talent would sit in a square and I would go to the middle of the square and hold court. I'd get badgered with questions about the rules and we'd go back and forth on many things. It was by far the most productive of all the seminars. I grew to have a great amount of respect for the guys at FOX because they would take these seminars so seriously.

So when Hill called, how could I not listen? I wasn't nervous about the possibility of being on television because I had done it before. I did a show called *Official Review* for the NFL Network with Rich Eisen in 2003. We had a weekly banter session, and usually there were controversial plays and I would explain why calls were made or not made.

It was fun. I did it for a year and then it got canceled because teams complained that they weren't allowed to discuss the officiating, yet someone from the league office could go on television and talk about it. My nickname around the league office became "Canceled," but their fun at my expense would be short-lived since I was back on the air a year later.

So what was it that made Hill think of hiring me?

Start with the fact he's got a very creative mind. He was the first to introduce America to the box on your television screen that includes the score, time, down, distance, and quarter information. It's known as the FOX Box in the L.A. headquarters of the network, but it's something that all networks that televise football eventually adopted.

Another of his brilliant ideas was the yellow-line first-down marker, something that the other networks also use today.

For better or worse, I was the next Hill innovation. I had come a long way from the fields of Lodi, California, and the American Legion game where my dad told me I wasn't worth the quarter it took to buy a Coke. FOX would become the first network to hire a former official to help with the education of replays and rules.

"It had been something that had been going backward and forward through my head ever since I first met you at the seminars," Hill said when I asked him the *Why me?* question. "What I realized was that production is very much like teaching and that there should always be an educational process, especially in sports.

"The best piece of advice I ever got was from a boss of mine, Ronald Patrick Casey. He was the general manager of a channel that I worked for in Australia when I was growing up. Even though he was a great television executive, he was also a fan. He loved sports. He was a great play-by-play announcer as well. He took me out of news and put me into sports, something that, as it turned out, I would end up doing the rest of my career.

"Casey created a show called *World of Sport*, which ran in Australia on Sundays. It had such an impact on the public that all church services would eventually be moved forward an hour so people could watch the show."

Hill was just warming up. The man can tell a story.

"Casey asked me why I thought the show was so popular.

I told him it was the personalities. He said no, that wasn't it. Then I guessed that it was the results. He told me again that wasn't it, that people could get that from the paper or radio. I went through everything I thought made sports popular."

As I was talking to Hill, I was now racking my brain, too, trying to come up with it. But Casey would provide us both with the answer.

"Casey told me when a man is born, he believes that God touches him in the center of the heart and that he knows everything there is to know about sports," Hill explained.

"They don't, of course, but they think if they admit that to their friends, they won't fit in. Because it's a very important thing for a male to understand everything there is to know about sports. So he told me that people watched that show because of 'nuggets.'

"I had no I idea what he was talking about, but he explained to me that we gave the viewers nuggets of information they could make their own, so when they were talking to their friends the next day, they could sound knowledgeable. It was the most important piece of advice I ever got from anyone."

I got it. I'm a nugget. Hill looked at me as someone who could provide FOX's viewers with bits of information so they could sound smarter on Monday mornings when talking about the big calls from Sunday.

"I firmly believe that one of the reasons why football is so popular today is because people understand it more now," Hill said.

However, before I could begin cooking up my nuggets, I still had the 2009 NFL season to go through before retiring. I didn't really hear from FOX again until after the next season.

When I was finally ready for my close-up, I sat down with Hill and Ed Goren—Hill's sidekick, vice chairman at FOX Sports, and another brilliant mind. We met with a bunch of producers about how we could mold my basis of knowledge and what I could bring to the table.

I think they initially believed that my reports would be more Internet-based than on-air, but nobody knew for sure as the 2010 season approached. It became obvious that we were going to try and do something on TV that allowed me to present my opinion on plays from an officiating perspective.

Think about it. When it comes to analysts, who do the networks usually hire? They hire ex-players and ex-coaches to discuss the nuances of the game from their standpoint. But nobody had ever hired an ex-official to explain what the referee might be looking at in a particular situation, be it a replay or a rules interpretation.

So for the 2010 season, Fox built out a little studio inside one of the control rooms for me that had a camera and monitors where we could see every NFL game—not just on FOX but CBS as well. The camera was positioned to where I could be brought into any FOX broadcast live and talk to the announcers about any play in question.

I then hired a bunch of local college and high school officials in Southern California, quite a mix of people, who would each be assigned a game and a TiVo system so they could track every play and penalty called and alert me to something unusual or controversial.

The NFL season arrived on Sunday, September 12, 2010. It

was Week 1, and none of us were exactly sure what to expect or how things would play out.

If there was a question about the officiating, or a controversy, I would jump on the air and give my opinion quickly on what was going on. Talking in quick, short sound bites is something I had to adjust to because I like to talk.

What happened next, Scorsese couldn't have scripted any better.

Detroit and Chicago were nearing the end of an exciting game, with the Lions trailing the Bears 19–14. The Lions had the ball second-and-10 at the Bears' 25-yard line, with just 31 seconds left in the game. Quarterback Matthew Stafford launched a pass to the end zone and Calvin Johnson leaped for the ball and made what appeared to be a great catch and a touchdown that could have won it for the Lions.

One official signaled a touchdown and another signaled an incomplete pass. On a quick glance, Johnson appeared to have gotten both feet down inbounds and rolled over before letting the ball go. It would eventually be ruled an incomplete pass on the field, but then it went to a replay review.

It certainly looked like a catch, and the announcers in the FOX booth, Thom Brennaman and Brian Billick, the former Baltimore Ravens coach, were saying as much. It was time to bring in the new kid on the block...me. Butterflies the size of seagulls began flying around in my stomach as they asked me what I thought. It was live television, folks. No pressure.

I told them—and the rest of America—that the rule states that if you're going to the ground you must hold on to the ball when you hit the ground, not yet taking a stance.

They countered that Johnson wasn't going to the ground and I said that he was. We were almost arguing on the air whether it was a catch or not. The review was taking an eternity when one of them finally asked me what the ruling was going to be.

Wow. Really? I guess there's nothing like making an impression in your first week. So there I am, expected to make a decision on a game-deciding play on national television, which could quickly turn into either a career-defining or career-ending moment.

If I was right, I was supposed to be. If I was wrong, on what would turn out to be the biggest call of the day, I might have been walking down Pico Boulevard outside the FOX Network Center with a cup in my hand.

I finally got the words out of my mouth and said that the rule states you have to hold on to the ball when you hit the ground. I told them I thought that they would stay with the call of an incomplete pass. I remember hearing Billick in the background yelling, "No way! That's a catch!"

We all watched as referee Gene Steratore came out from under the hood and headed back onto the field to make the announcement. Somebody could have put a bucket under me, I was sweating so much.

"After reviewing the play," Steratore started, "the ruling on the field stands. The receiver did not maintain control of the ball when he hit the ground."

When I heard the announcement, I let out a huge sigh of relief but also felt my knees about to buckle. Good thing my chair was close by.

But that was just the beginning. The Brennaman–Billick argument with me would be a tremor for the volcano that was about to erupt. Fans were going crazy on social media, especially Lions fans, saying the decision didn't make sense.

It really did look like a catch to most people, but it's a very complex rule. However, what I had done—going on television to explain to viewers what the referee was looking at and clarifying why he was going to rule the way he did before he did it—was a significant moment for me...and for FOX.

David Hill had taken a chance on me, doing something no other network had done before, and it was paying off the very first week.

FOX NFL insider Jay Glazer flung open the door to our little control room and shouted, in typical Glazer fashion, "Pereira, you just hit a grand slam on your first day!" As you might already know, despite his small stature, Glazer's personality makes him about 6'9".

"What you did that day and continue to do is a vital service, not only to fans but to the National Football League," Hill recalled of my fateful first week.

He was right. Again. What I did actually deflected some of the criticism away from the officials and placed it on the rule. The league would certainly rather have the judgment placed on the rule rather than on officials. The officials were just going by the rule, so they got the call right. It's the rule that's screwed up.

How about that for a first day?

When I look back on it now, there were no rules analysts on television prior to 2010. But thanks to David Hill, I not only became a "nugget," but a trendsetter.

Rules analysts began to spread on TV faster than some viruses, and I'm not sure there's a cure. But many of the networks have jumped on the bandwagon and added former officials to help interpret the rules.

And it's not just the NFL. Let's take a look at a breakdown of rules analysts by network.

- ABC/ESPN has added Jim Daopoulos and Gerald Austin on the NFL; Dave Cutaia, Bill Lemonnier, and Doug Rhoads on college football; and Steve Javie on the NBA.

- CBS has added Mike Carey on the NFL.

- FOX has added David Fay on golf, Andy Petree on NASCAR, and Dr. Joe Machnik on soccer.

- NBCSN has added John Adams on college basketball.

I think it's great; the more the merrier. Because the more fans know about the rules, the better off everyone will be.

Every network uses them in different ways, but since 2010, I've mostly been at the FOX studios in Los Angeles on Saturdays and Sundays during the college and NFL seasons. I also go to playoff games if there is only one game on FOX on a given day. Then I'm in the booth on site and can give my feedback on calls immediately.

When I'm in L.A., I'm in constant communication with the producers, directors, and announcers of all the FOX games. I'm watching the games, and sometimes it can get pretty crazy with five or six games going on at once. But on particular plays, I can get information to the different broadcast teams on certain rulings or my opinion on how something will go, even if I don't go on the air.

Many times on a play in question or a review, when the game goes to commercial break, I will be watching the replays with a particular broadcast team and giving them my thoughts on what replays are being used to make the decision by the referee. I also tell them how I think it will be ruled.

I'm very proud of the announcers at FOX. They are going to make mistakes because things happen quickly, but they seldom do, and even when they do, they are quick to correct themselves. I also send each crew "training tapes" each week, and I think they've all become very knowledgeable about the rules.

And then there's Twitter.

Hell, I didn't even know what Twitter was when the social media folks at FOX asked me to sign up during my second season.

Here's a funny aside. I was at the yearly FOX football seminar, just prior to the season starting in 2011, where they bring in all the broadcasters and producers. So the new social media team asked Jimmy Johnson and me to sign up for Twitter. So we briefly left the meetings to sign up, and then we headed back to the seminar.

About two hours later, we returned to the Twitter sign-up area to see how many people decided to follow us.

Final score: Johnson, 1,500; Pereira, 2.

Initially, I didn't have much interest in Twitter. I didn't think people really cared if I was sitting down with a glass of Tito's vodka, but they actually do. But I made up my mind that I was going to use those 140 characters to try and teach people the rules and explain what might be going on during a replay review, or just answer questions they might have during the games on both Saturdays and Sundays.

Believe it or not, I get a lot of questions during the course of a day's games, and now I'm up to nearly 300,000 followers. Not bad for a guy who only had two after his first day on Twitter.

When it comes to Twitter, as with most things, with the good comes the bad.

While I know the majority of people really appreciate my responses, there are some twits on Twitter who feel like they can insult you and say vulgar things. I find that fascinating, considering most of them doing that don't really have much knowledge of what they're talking about. They hide behind their anonymity and I just try to keep it in perspective by imagining them sitting in a basement in their underwear with no education, no job…and no teeth.

But hey, when I'm really offended I've come up with the perfect response: the block button. Problem solved.

Getting to be on television for FOX has really worked to perfection with my "number six" plan—work for six months, do nothing for six months, and retire when I'm 66.

Except for one thing. I'm not sure I'm ready to give it up, because I'm having so much stinking fun. I might have to change my number to seven, eight, or nine.

So much for me scripting things out the way I thought they should go.

17   THE FUTURE OF OFFICIATING

WHILE THINGS MIGHT NOT BE SO CLEAR ON WHAT LIES AHEAD IN my future, I definitely have some thoughts on the future of officiating, and I don't even need a crystal ball.

I don't have an answer for global warming; I don't know if we'll have flying cars some day; and I'm certainly not clear if we'll have chips embedded in our brains to watch TV at some point. However, I definitely have some ideas that could make officiating better for the next generation.

But before I give you the answers, you must first know what the key questions are.

- Is the officiating in the NFL as good as it could be? It's a very simple answer. No.

- Is officiating as consistent as it should be? That would also be a no.

Want proof? Just take a look back at the 2015 playoffs. Hell, the first two rounds of those playoffs could have been a case study all by themselves. Let's start with the NFC wild card game between the Lions and Cowboys in Dallas.

With a little less than nine minutes to play and the Lions leading 20–17, the Lions had the ball on third-and-1 from the Cowboys' 46-yard line. Detroit quarterback Matt Stafford attempted a pass to Brandon Pettigrew, but a pass interference penalty was called on Dallas linebacker Anthony Hitchens. Moments later, the flag was picked up by the officials with no good explanation. The penalty flag should not have been picked up, because it was pass interference.

The only people happy with the final call were fans of the Cowboys. That flag being picked up went over in Detroit as well as an announcement that BMW was about to build a new factory there would.

In fact, there could have been at least two other fouls called on that one play. Hitchens grabbed Pettigrew's jersey and could have been called for holding. Then Dallas receiver Dez Bryant ran onto the field without a helmet on to dispute the call. He could have been called for unsportsmanlike conduct, but wasn't. The original call of pass interference would have given the Lions a first down deep in Cowboys territory. Instead, the Lions punted and the Cowboys kicked it into gear and rallied for a 24–20 win.

Need more? Just a week later in the NFC divisional round game between Dallas and Green Bay, a controversial reversal took place with a little less than five minutes to play. Green Bay led 26–21, but Dallas had the ball on fourth-and-2 at the Green Bay 32-yard line.

Cowboys quarterback Tony Romo lofted a pass to Dez

Bryant, who leapt up and appeared to make an unbelievable catch at the Green Bay 1-yard line. The ruling on the field was a catch and down by contact at the 1-yard line. While it appeared to everybody that it was the correct ruling, after a replay review, the call was reversed because Bryant did not complete the process of the catch. The Packers took over and then held on to win. While the decision in instant replay was correct, the rule is ambiguous and difficult to grasp.

Thank heavens for the NFC Championship Game that same season. After two consecutive weeks of controversy on the sport's biggest stage, the NFC title game between Seattle and Green Bay would prove to be the saving grace.

In one of the greatest miracle finishes that many of us had ever seen, the Seahawks rallied from a 19–7 deficit with barely more than three minutes left in the game and then went on to defeat the Packers 28–22 in overtime.

Then two weeks later came Super Bowl XLIX between New England and Seattle, which turned out to be one of the best Super Bowls in a long time. The Patriots rallied late to overtake the Seahawks, then needed a game-saving interception from Malcolm Butler on the goal line to preserve their 28–24 victory.

If not for the latter two games, the 2015 playoffs would have been more about the officiating than the game, and nobody wants that, whether it be the league, the coaches, the players, the fans, or even the officials.

Is the dissatisfaction with the officiating a new thing, or has it been pretty much the sentiment every year?

I think it's probably the latter and, in my mind, it has become more prevalent with the advent of social media and the epidemic of rules analysts on television that I wrote about in the last chapter.

So you ask, what can be done to significantly improve officiating?

I've actually had the answers for a while now, but seemingly nobody wanted to listen. In fact, before I left the NFL in 2009, I put together a plan because I thought it was time to entertain change, even though I felt that the training and evaluation methods had become fairly established.

I asked those questions in 2009 and I would ask the same ones today, because I feel the overall performance of officiating needs to be improved.

When I was still with the league, I remember Commissioner Goodell telling me we had to get better. He said we had to get better as officials and keep pace with how players were getting better. At Goodell's "State of the League" address prior to Super Bowl XLIX, he said that the NFL would look at ways to improve the officiating for the 2015 season.

"We are looking at the other ways to enhance replay and officiating. That includes potentially expanding replay to penalties if it can be done without more disruption to the pace of the game," Goodell said then.

"And we are discussing rotating members of the officiating crews during the season as a way to improve consistency throughout our regular season and in the postseason. In officiating, consistency is our number-one objective."

That's true, but it depends on what your definition of *consistency* is. The commissioner and I might not be on the same page on this one. Hell, maybe not even in the same book.

I think Goodell believes consistency is calling 14.5 fouls per game each week. In my opinion, that's not what clubs want. If you ask any of the 32 coaches in the NFL what their biggest complaint about officiating is, I'm pretty sure their response would be consistency. What's their definition of *consistency?* They want consistency from one crew to the next, from one week to the next, and from one play to the next, meaning whatever foul is called in the first quarter, it should be called the same way in the fourth quarter. That way they know what to expect.

"That's the most important thing," former NFL executive and Hall of Fame executive Bill Polian told me. "Because you can't teach your players the appropriate techniques if in one game, they follow the standard that's been established by the officiating department and the competition committee, and then in another they simply ignore it. What we're talking about, by the way, are 'the big five' — offensive and defensive holding, defensive pass interference, offensive pass interference, and illegal contact. Those are the calls that change games."

I think you let the teams dictate the number of fouls per game, not the officials. Matchups, more than anything, determine the number of fouls per game.

Goodell had suggested rotating the officiating crews to me even before I left. But I felt that was ridiculous. I'm not sure what you would gain by doing that. If anything, it might add more inconsistency to the mix. I didn't like the idea then...and I still don't.

But listen; I get it. The majority of you seem unsatisfied with the officiating, so how can we improve it?

It needs to start with change, dramatic change. The NFL should make the 17 referees full-time as a way to take officiating to the next level. I was never one who thought that was necessary, but I also thought I'd never be on television every week of the football season, either.

But it's time. Those 17 referees carry the weight of their crews' performance on their shoulders every week. No matter what some other officials might say, the referees are the most important of all the officials. If you have confidence in the referee, you have confidence in his crew.

For example, you may have no idea who Gene Steratore's field judge is, but if you have confidence in Steratore and his swagger, then you're going to have confidence in his field judge and feel strong about the remainder of his crew.

Make the referee 100 percent of the focus. While I might not be able to predict the future, I'm definitely sure of this. I've finally seen the light about the men in the white hats. And with this change, I think it's very reasonable to expect perfection when it comes to rules knowledge, announcements, and signals.

From a coaching perspective, Mike Shanahan sees a lot of merit in the idea.

"I really don't think people realize the importance of everybody getting on the same page with officiating," Shanahan said recently. "I think it's impossible to expect somebody to do this on a part-time basis. You're asking a guy to come into a situation when he's not looking at it every day. I don't know how you could get really good at something when you don't do it all the time."

So what now for these full-time referees? Hold on to your white hats for this one, but you develop an officiating institute. The location should be in an NFL city in the central part of the country. My pick: Dallas.

After the games on Sunday during the season, these full-time referees wouldn't go home; they'd go back to the institute in Dallas. There, they would work together all week with the other referees and either the vice president of officiating or the director of officiating. Then on Friday, they would head to their games.

That means they would evaluate games together. They would follow the rule book and the mandate of the Competition Committee and determine which penalties need to be called or not called. They would look at all the calls and then evaluate them together. It needs to be a total buy-in by all 17 referees. Most importantly, they would take consistent messages back to their crews. During the season, they would work on every aspect of the officiating program, including looking at coaches concerns, developing rules tests and making training videos, etc.

Then they sing "Kumbaya." Okay, I'm only partly kidding.

I would want them to develop a procedure to spend less time looking backward and more time looking forward. Much of their time should be spent watching video of the two teams their crew would be working that next weekend. Take a look at the formations that each team presents. Take a look at motions that may end up shifting responsibilities of each official. Have them do some role-playing as a group—no, not that kind, you dirty-minded people—game-situational role-playing.

If you've got a flag picked up, develop a procedure to get the proper information from your crew so you can communicate it properly. Stand in front of the other referees and simulate the announcement that needs to be made so they know the right way to inform fans, announcers, and everybody else for that matter. Give them the proper information instead of leaving them in the dark to figure out why the flag was picked up.

There's so much that could be accomplished with this institute, like having the referees taking management and leadership classes. And how about taking public speaking courses to improve microphone use and preparing them to deal with the media? Then, there should be a conditioning program in which the referees can stay in shape.

And all this should start in the preseason, where the referees would go to multiple games. They could actually go to another referee's game and watch from the replay booth or even the sideline. Referees would be training other referees. What a novel idea.

Like I said, during the season, it would be a full-time job. The league would provide housing at the institute during the season. If they want to move their families there for the season, so be it. They could go to their real homes when the season is over. By the way, every referee gets two weeks off during the season, so if their families don't come, they could go home during those weeks.

They are no longer lawyers, high school presidents, or even accountants, for example. They truly are full-time referees. And they need to be paid accordingly, which means the NFL would have to step up to the line of scrimmage and pay them. The NFL needs to compare what full-time umpires get in baseball and what full-time referees get in the NBA. That's your starting point.

Now that we have the season of the future in place, let's take a look at what the offseason could look like.

We've established that there are 17 referees. There are 32 teams. In my plan, you assign 15 of the referees two teams each. The other two, most likely the newest referees, have only one. These referees would then work with their teams on a year-round basis, but more specifically, in the offseason.

Why? Because I feel like there has always been a big disconnect between how the game is officiated and how the game is coached. Players and coaches don't understand officiating. And officials, for the most part, don't understand the game, because very few have ever played at that level. So much about officiating is about advantage and disadvantage.

Here's what I mean by that. If you don't understand techniques and schemes, then how do you know what action creates an advantage or disadvantage? If you're a coach, how do you know what to expect to be called when you don't know the philosophy that is used to determine whether a call should be made or not.

So how do we connect that disconnect?

Start by having the referees attend their team's mini-camps, OTAs (organized training activities), and training camp. While they are there, they need to work with the players and coaches and then, most importantly, they would need to sit in on their team's meetings. For example, hang out with the offensive line coach and learn the techniques that are being taught to the players.

What it comes down to is this: the referees need to learn how the game is being coached.

The referees should make multiple presentations to the coaching staff that would be position-specific. Another example: meet with the defensive backs coach, a wide receivers coach, and a tight ends coach, and explain to them what officials are looking for in regard to the passing game. They need to let them know what an official's trigger point is when it comes to making a decision to either call or not call a foul. The key is to develop a better relationship between the clubs and officials.

By doing this plan, is there a potential for a conflict of interest? Yes, of course. Let me alleviate the concerns for all those questioning this part of the plan. That referee would not be assigned to the team he is working with. Referees would also rotate teams every two years.

And here are some other things the referees could do during the offseason:

- They could go to the Competition Committee meetings.

- They could work in another league, a developmental league, or the Arena League.

- They could make instructional videos or be a part of the NFL officiating clinic as well as other local clinics in an attempt to develop and recruit other officials.

- They could also make and take rules exams together, talking about the rules and making sure everybody understands the enforcements.

Have I mentioned that it's time to take the 17 referees and make them full-time? Are you listening, Roger?

What if some of the referees might not want to do it? Maybe a guy's already got a successful job and he doesn't want to give that up. Then you get somebody else.

If a referee doesn't want to do it, put him back in his original position before he became a referee. I guarantee you if you make a new referee full-time, and if you have an institute like this, the referee will improve at a rate five times faster than he does now.

All it would take to accomplish this is one thing: money.

But the NFL doesn't like to spend money on officials. Remember what I wrote about the lockouts of 2001 and 2012? However, if the NFL truly wants the officiating to improve, as Goodell said, then he and the league should consider my all-encompassing proposal.

So how much money are we talking?

Once this institute is built out, I'd guesstimate it would cost $300,000 per year, per club. That's approximately $10 million. The NFL takes in somewhere in the neighborhood of $10 billion a year and it has already gone on record as saying it wanted to increase revenue to $25 billion by the year 2027. That's $25 billion. All we're talking about is $300,000 per team. That's chump change in the big picture.

Is it worth it? Yes, if your goal is to have better officiating. And this is coming from the same guy who was never an advocate of full-time officiating.

Could the league finally be ready to listen? Could we really be inching toward major progress?

Bill Polian thinks so.

"As a matter of fact, the past chair [of the Competition Committee] put together a group a few years ago, a working group about the future of officiating, and that was the conclusion we reached. There has to be a unified message, and if there is going to be a future for full-time officials, it is going to have to be 17 who would translate the word directly to the crews."

But there's more that needs to change, specifically, the culture of competition.

Here's what I mean by that: officials compete against each other for playoff assignments and, ultimately, the plum assignment of the year, the Super Bowl. Since it is no longer a crew-based system that moves officials into the playoffs, officials compete against one another and the league office for grades that will positively or negatively affect their rankings.

It's an outdated system. Listen, I'm not saying I shouldn't have my wrists slapped a bit because I helped perpetuate it while I was in the league office.

As a result, officials often don't share their wisdom. In fact, many of them have learned how to officiate for grades versus just for the good of the game. At one point after getting a downgrade when I was still on the field, I was told that I needed to make 10 calls that were graded correctly to keep myself in playoff contention.

How do you do that?

When other officials called obvious fouls, I was advised to throw my flag on top of theirs so I would be given a correct call. I was young and gullible and followed the suggestion that I was given. However, once I got into the league office, I changed the grading procedure to where only the responsible officials would get credit for making the call if there was more than one flag thrown. Nevertheless, that's an example of the competition and trying to beat the system.

I'm not against competition, but I'm a believer in teams competing against each other. However, I don't think the same holds true for the officiating crews. To me, officiating is one crew, not 17 crews. They have to collaborate with each other to make things better. There has to be a common goal that all 122 officials strive to reach. Not just one person who is happy because he or she got a playoff assignment.

So the question becomes how do you get all 122 officials on board together? How do you teach them to buy into a new concept together, from 1 to 122?

I know you might be a little shocked, but I also have some thoughts on this, and they involve grades and playoff assignments.

Eliminate the word *grade* from the officiating vocabulary. It's a negative word. Use performance to teach, not to categorize. Develop a system to advance officials to the playoffs that takes into account their overall performance, not just the times they throw a flag. Maybe even predetermine which officials would be in the playoffs at the end of the season based on past performance and seniority, so officials don't have to work their way into the playoffs. However, they could still work their way out based on their overall performance.

This, unlike making the referees full-time and building that officiating institute, is not an easy fix.

Speaking of playoffs, let's fix that, too. Since the officials' collective bargaining agreement does not allow for playoff assignments to be crew-based, the NFL should limit the number of officials who advance to its best 28. Everyone would work in the wild-card round and division games. Fourteen would advance to the championship games and, ultimately, seven would advance to the Super Bowl.

Under the current system, 70 officials move into the playoffs. That means you have officials who are ranked in the bottom half of the staff making the postseason, while one of your best officials may end up working only one playoff game. If you want All-Star crews, then truly make them All-Star crews.

That's not really an issue of money, since all officials who qualify for the playoffs participate in the playoff money pool.

I made this very proposal to Ray Anderson, who was the executive vice president of football operations, and a few members of his staff before I left the league after the 2009 season.

The reaction? It fell on deaf ears. Nobody wanted to support it. Of course, the first complaint was that it would cost too much money. The second thing was that there would be referees who wouldn't want to give up their regular jobs as I've discussed.

Seven years later, I think my plan for the future of officiating is still relevant and the league has begun to recognize it, although not in the same context as my plan.

In the current collective bargaining agreement with the officials, the league is allowed to hire up to 17 officials full-time. The hold up has been caused by the union's concerns of making full-time officials at-will employees. I get that. You can't ask a guy to give up his regular, full-time job without some sense of security that he won't be dropped in a year.

However, the NFL doesn't necessarily think hiring the 17 referees is the way to go. The league is looking at their staff of full-time officials to be made up of a roster from the seven different positions on the field.

In the end, it's all about money and job security. The money is there, and the job security can also be there if the NFL offers their referees something like five-year contracts. After all, players are offered multi-year contacts, so why can't the 17 referees be, too? They are so vital to officiating and the game, they should get the same treatment.

If you want to address the complaints from the clubs, coaches, owners, players, fans, and the media—I believe I included everybody but the ushers—then take the next step. Think outside the box for a change. Try to make it better. It can't hurt. They just have to finally move forward with it.

William Shakespeare once wrote, "It is not in the stars to hold our destiny but in ourselves."

The NFL has the power and the ability to make officiating better.

18 THE BROTHERHOOD AND THE BATTLE WITH MY OLD NEMESIS

CANCER'S A SCARY THING. I DIDN'T NEED A SHAKESPEARIAN QUOTE to let me know that. I got to live it when I had it—and beat it—at age 25. I can't begin to describe the exhilaration I felt.

But you never get over the fear of cancer coming back. It's always in the back of your mind that one day it'll be back, kind of like that annoying, crazy uncle everybody's got. Besides the job insecurity I had working in the NFL offices, I always had that anxiety that I'd be facing my old nemesis again.

And that nightmare became a reality in the spring of 2007 when a routine colonoscopy would make my life difficult and challenging yet again. I'm now resigned to the fact I'll have to deal with this the rest of my days.

After a routine checkup, it was discovered that I had polyps, which a lot of people have. But unlike most people, my polyps were in the folds of the colon and couldn't be removed by a normal colonoscopy. I didn't even know there were folds in your colon or why they are there in the first place. Lucky me.

My doctors in New York told me that I would need surgery

to have a portion of my colon removed to prevent the precancerous growths from turning into cancer that I would have to deal with later on.

So back under the knife I went.

Bruce Yaffe was the doctor who detected the polyps and I'm so thankful for that. Then the NFL's doctor, Dr. Elliot Pellman, directed me to doctors who would perform the surgery.

The surgery was successful, but like any surgery, it was painful. However, just like my dad's friends who rallied around me when I had testicular cancer in 1975, I was humbled and inspired by the fraternity of football officials that supported me.

Now this just might be me blabbing, but I don't think there is another group of people that care about each other the way officials do. I know I'm biased, but officials can totally relate to one another's frustrations, and that forges a special bond.

Well, maybe it's not just me.

"It's because you get so close. You're assigned a crew and you get together every week for almost half a year. You find out all the intricacies of everybody's life," legendary referee Jerry Markbreit said in describing the fraternity of officials.

"You hear about their family and social problems that we would discuss in our meetings. We would become mentors to one another and support each other. You develop this closeness with your crew because you are out there fighting a battle together. You really start to love one another."

That's exactly right. I felt it. Guys are sympathetic when something happens to another official. They feel for one another when they make a mistake on the field, and that's the fraternity. I imagine that most officials who make it to the college or NFL level would tell you that most of their best friends are officials. That's certainly the case for me.

After all, I joined this fraternity when I began officiating in the PCAA in 1982. I made friends for life, such as Tony Corrente, who, if you've forgotten, was my best man at my wedding to Gail in 1997.

When I went for my surgery, this group rallied around me like you wouldn't believe. The cards were nonstop, as were the phone calls, and random fruit baskets just showed up at my apartment. I got so many cards I could have started my own Hallmark store.

"Officiating becomes a brotherhood, an extension of the family," Corrente said when I asked him to describe the fraternity.

"It becomes a respectful thing, because you find out who is willing to do what's best for the game and what's in the best interest of the entire...maybe conference or crew, versus the selfishness of the 'I'm-in-it-for-me' guys and we've all met those people.

"Football is different from other sports. Since there are not as many games to a season, every time there's a game, it's an event. And they become an event for the officials, too. It's a bonding."

And it didn't stop there. I belonged to another group called the Officiating Development Alliance, which is supported by the National Association of Sports Officials based in Wisconsin.

The group met twice a year and was made up of officiating leaders of multiple sports, including football, basketball, baseball, hockey, men and women's college basketball, volleyball, softball, and soccer.

Twice a year, you'd go behind closed doors with no media, no computers, and no BS, just you and your soul. It was almost like a cleansing.

Nothing you said ever left that room, and I was never afraid to bare my soul to these people because they all understood. It was kind of like those "what happens in Vegas, stays in Vegas" commercials.

I even remember crying in front of this group. Okay, I know what you're all thinking—there's no crying in football. But I can't explain to you the pressure that came with being the NFL's VP of Officiating.

I cried out of fear—the fear of getting fired, the fear of failure, and the fear of losing my job.

This group listened, sympathized, and was wonderfully warm. We shared anything and everything. I shared my cancer with them. It was deeply emotional for me. And the support I got was beyond amazing.

And even though I might have downgraded some of the NFL officials from time to time, and might not have been their favorite person, all of them got behind me in my time of need. Talking about it became therapeutic for me.

Marcia Alterman, the executive director of the Professional Association of Volleyball Officials, invited me to come speak at her clinic in Seattle. I started to feel more comfortable talking to groups about my cancer with the purpose of helping others.

I would tell them that they had to take care of themselves and that they should get checked regularly, because the type of colon cancer I had was preventable as long as you get checked and attack it early.

Like I said, I survived the first surgery in 2007—the removal of a foot of my colon—but my old nemesis and the polyps came back again in 2014.

And unfortunately for me, I'm producing the kind of polyps that are difficult to treat. The layman's term is *flat polyps*, which unlike normal polyps can't be snipped out. Instead, they have to be scraped off.

I know, too much information.

It's a very delicate procedure, and my doctor in Sacramento, Dr. David Arenson, who initially discovered these flat polyps in a routing colonoscopy, said I'm a prodigious polyp producer. Isn't that special? I'm sure if there were a Hall of Fame for polyp producers, a bust of me would very likely be front and center.

It's an ongoing battle that I just have to live with. You know, I've had so many colonoscopies that doctors may start assigning roman numerals to them, in honor of the 50th Super Bowl that was played in February. The only difference is, there's no Lombardi Trophy waiting for me when I get done. I've almost gotten to the point where I like them.

Well, let me clarify that. I like that second-and-a-half feeling you get before you get knocked so silly that they can do what they have to do.

In all seriousness, I'll always be at risk going forward because flat polyps are difficult to remove. I've got some doctors telling me that they want to completely remove my colon, and I have a specialist, Dr. Kenneth Binmoeller, in San Francisco telling me it's not time yet. That alone makes him a brilliant doctor in my mind. He says with a strong maintenance program I can stay on top of it.

While my stomach might be twisted up, the doctor won't have to twist my arm to hold off on that surgery.

I've had a lot of help and support. And my buddy Corrente knows exactly what I'm talking about. He developed throat cancer in 2010 and he discovered it after doing a Steelers–Ravens game that season. He got knocked down during the game and started spitting up blood the next day. He went and got it checked out, and it was detected that he had esophageal cancer with a tumor in his throat.

With the help of former great referee Red ("First Down") Cashion, Corrente got to MD Anderson Cancer Center in Houston. The news was not good, but they treated it with radiation and chemotherapy.

"It was the day after Christmas and I moved to Houston in order to go through the daily, five-day-a-week radiation treatments along with once-a-week five- or six-hour chemo treatments," Corrente remembered.

"I moved into a Residence Inn by myself and immediately started to receive cards through the mail that were being directed to me. I started to receive emails and phone calls. It was wonderful, but it was really interesting, the actual cards became extremely important to me."

You're about to find out just how important those cards would become for Corrente.

"My throat got to the point where I just literally couldn't swallow and I started to lose a lot of weight. The doctors were planning on putting a feeding tube into me and I said no,"

Corrente said.

"I was on a liquid diet, drinking these Ensure Plus protein shakes, but even that became so painful that I couldn't get them down. It hurt so bad that I had a very hard time dealing with the pain.

"I remember one day I was about to give up and pack it in. I was going to leave, and I got to the front door and as I turned the handle and opened the door, I looked over to the mantel above the fireplace, where I must have had 100 cards that officials had sent me. Every single one of them said that I could persevere. They said I had strength of character and that I had led them through all of these years. I looked at those cards and I slammed the door shut."

"I said to myself, 'Okay, you bastards,' and I walked over to the refrigerator door and popped open an Ensure. I drank it in about five seconds and it hurt so freaking bad that I fell to my knees with tears in my eyes. Then I drank another. And another. Three times a day, three bottles at once because those cards kept telling me how strong I could be, and I found out.

"I didn't know how strong I could be. But it was my friends that encouraged me, who pushed me, and I think it was because I had to prove to them they were right."

Once again, the fraternity came to the rescue. I know first-hand how important that support is, and so does Corrente.

But there's one more story I need to share with you. However, first I need the orchestra to cue up Phil Collins' "Against All Odds."

Okay, now that you have that soundtrack playing in your head, get ready for the mother of all comeback stories, which involved referee Bill Vinovich.

Vinovich, for a point of reference, was the referee in Super Bowl XLIX in February 2015 between Seattle and New England.

But there was a point in time back in 2007 when Vinovich wasn't sure if he was ever going to referee again, let alone referee the Super Bowl. Hell, he didn't even know if he was going to live.

Vinovich was working out near his Southern California home in April 2007 when he suddenly felt like "two knives were stabbing him in the back."

He went to the hospital, and doctors discovered that he suffered an aortic dissection, which is a tear inside the wall of the major artery that carries blood out of the heart. The doctors told Vinovich that it was inoperable and that the next 48 hours would determine whether he would live or die.

The survival rate, Vinovich was told, for those who suffered the same kind of dangerous tear that he did was...*2 percent*. That's a 2 percent chance to live!

After those 48 hours, he spent 11 more days in the intensive care unit and weeks of rest at home. Vinovich was actually told that he'd never officiate again by the NFL's officiating doctor, Jeffrey Borer.

I asked Vinovich to recall the painful conversation he had with Borer.

"It started with shock then, obviously, it turned to sadness. I had an empty feeling," he said. "You work so hard to get to that point and then something like that happens. Then a good part of your life is not necessarily taken away, but a good part of your life is gone."

In fact, the league even sent him a big severance check. But he didn't cash it. Because cashing it would have meant he was giving up. And that's just not who Bill Vinovich is.

Part of the reason might be that the CPA by day is a third generation official. His grandfather officiated for 40 years in Pittsburgh and his dad another 40 years in Southern California.

As you know, I was in charge of the officiating department during that time, and I told him that I was not going to let him go. I would find something for him to do.

"I remember your call," Vinovich said. "You told me you wanted me around the league for the next 15 years and asked me what I wanted to do."

He chose to be a replay official for Ed Hochuli's crew, and he proved to be so talented that the following season I hired him to be a regional supervisor, watching, grading, and training officials.

"I liked being able to go to the games, still being able to be around the guys and staying close to the rules," Vinovich said. "But I didn't really enjoy grading. I enjoyed watching the young officials and helping out the guys along the way."

When I retired after the 2009 season, Vinovich applied for my job, but Carl Johnson got it.

Frankly, I thought Vinovich should have gotten my job because he had done it all. He had officiated in college football, the Canadian Football League, the Arena Football League, and the NFL. He had also been a regional supervisor. He had done just about everything that could be done in terms of officiating to run the NFL's officiating program.

However, he still had that burning desire to get back onto the field. With the league still skeptical, Vinovich asked four different doctors to write to the NFL in 2010 to say that he was healthy enough to referee a football game.

Unfortunately, he got turned down again. I asked him if he ever lost hope.

"It wasn't losing hope as much as it was that I needed to take a different route. When I didn't get your job, that's when I started seeking advice from thoracic surgeons throughout the country.

"It was interesting, the older thoracic surgeons wouldn't sign off on me officiating again, but the younger ones said everything was fine. I had several clearances, but Borer kept saying no.

He tried again in 2011. He asked Borer what he could do to get back on the field. The NFL's officiating doctor told him he'd have to get cleared by Yale's cardiac surgeon, Dr. John Elefteriades.

Before he would be cleared, however, Elefteriades would have to do yet another surgery on Vinovich.

Having been through hell and back, the doctors and Borer finally gave Vinovich a clean bill of health, and in May 2012, he got an email from the NFL saying he was cleared to return to the field as an NFL referee.

"I just couldn't believe it," Vinovich said. "I just sat there reading the email trying to absorb the feelings. It was just really surreal."

That was probably the greatest story of perseverance that I came across during my time in the league office. I had guys get really sick before, but I always tried to be supportive, leaving the door open for them to get back on the field when they overcame their illnesses.

But Vinovich was special. His return to the field may have meant as much to me as it did to him, because I didn't want him to leave. I wanted a career path for him to stay involved with the league.

And what about that fraternity that helped Corrente and me? How big a difference did it make for Vinovich?

"I don't think I could have gotten through it without that support," Vinovich said. "The emails, texts, cards, and phone calls when the news first got out was amazing.

"Everybody was so supportive. When I started saying I wanted to get back on the field, the Referees' Association and Mike Arnold were saying they'd do anything they could to help. Everybody's support meant so much to me."

As you can see, the bond is strong, and that helped all of us to get through some very difficult times. To this day, I know if I need them to be with me during this polyp ordeal, they'd be there.

It took my specialist in San Francisco three times, but he finally got those flat polyps scraped off. Now we're back at maintenance, and that includes getting a colonoscopy every six to eight months. I hope when the flat polyps return—and I know they'll be back, kind of like Arnold Schwarzenegger in the *Terminator* movies—we will be able to get them removed successfully.

But I know in the end, pun intended, I'm going to lose my colon. So on every trip to San Francisco I have that fear of having my life permanently altered. Each time I leave there and I know I'm clean, it buys me an extra 8 to 10 months of freedom.

When you go through a health scare like this, I can't tell you how important family is. And it wasn't just my immediate family, but my officiating family that stepped up as well. It's one of the reasons I wanted to write this book. I hope it gives you a better perspective of the type of men, and now women, who do this job.

Officiating is a noble profession. I know some of you look at officials a certain way when you see them out on the field, but if you are lucky enough to know them the way I've known them, you'd also realize just how great these people are. And even if a few of you look at them a little differently now, I've accomplished part of my goal.

I've had a wonderful life, testicular cancer, polyps, and all. I think I might even be worth 50 cents now. Unfortunately, a Coke costs a lot more than it used to.